to Elisabetta

Business & law on the Internet

To obtain further information on this subject, connect to
http://www.legalsupport.com

Business & law on the Internet

Olivier Hance

Translated from French by Suzanne Dionne Balz

Under the direction

of

Olivier HANCE

BY

Olivier HANCE and Suzan DIONNE BALZ

IN COLLABORATION WITH:

Elisa AMEDEO   Fidel NDESHYO NGARUYE   Xavier PIETRA,

and

Caroline DE COCK, Frédéric DECHAMPS, Alexandre de STREEL,
André GRENACS, Tristan KRSTIC, Philippe MEULDERS,
Jean-Philippe MIKUS, Géraldine BALTHAZAR,
Bruno NOWAK, Wim SABLON, Christophe STENMANS,
Anna ZUBRZYCKA.

assisted in specific areas by:

Benoit LIPS and Emmanuel WILLEMS

Administrative management:

Philippe MEULDERS

This book is sold without any guarantee whatsoever regarding the content of the book. This work does not constitute a legal opinion. Neither the authors and col-laborators, nor Best Of Editions and the distributors have any liability vis-à-vis the purchaser of this book or any other person or institution for any direct or indirect damage which may occur further to reading this book.

D-1996-7452-3   ISBN 2-930150-05-X

Preface

There can be no single factor which has had such a profound effect on business practices in the last 30 years than the impact of Information Technology. In that period, there have been innumerable developments in the way that businesses have harnessed the changes in technology to improve their competitive position. During that time, technology has moved on from the large computers run in bunkers underneath major institutional buildings manned by boffins in white coats, which characterised the 1960's and 1970's, to the PC used by professionals which has characterised the 1980's and early 1990's. Now we are entering the next generation of technological development characterised by cheap, pervasive networking which is personified by the Internet and will take information services for all into the home.

Businesses will need to understand this profound effect and the associated issues to compete effectively. However, they will need to approach this business opportunity with both enthusiasm and care. Data Security, Fraud and Intellectual Property Rights are significant issues which must be addressed in any Internet strategy in order to minimise the risks. This timely book tackles these and other important topics highlighting the key factors which business people need to consider to best avoid the pitfalls. I believe the Internet offers us all an exciting chance to exploit new concepts and market opportunities and to push forward the boundaries of existing business relationships.

John Davison

Board Director - ICL

The Internet, the Information superhighways, the Information Society: much has been written on the potential of new interactive on-line communications and the transition to an information-rich multimedia world. Similarly, there are many surfers' guides explaining how to navigate this increasingly rich gateway to the world's information and how to use such a novel and potentially powerful international communications channel. However, in order to achieve the Information Society with its promised wealth of on-line access to arts and cultural information, electronic commerce, interactive medical, legal and/or financial and interactive multimedia information and entertainment services, there is still much to be done.

Even the novice surfer cannot fail to notice that the Internet is beginning to suffer from congestion as thousands struggle to reach their most popular World Wide Web sites. This congestion aptly signals how some of the networks that we are navigating will require extensive and costly upgrading. These Internet traffic jams not only reflect the phenomenal growth in demand that the Internet is experiencing but also demonstrate how the public purse will not be contributing to reach the political objective of the Information Society. Although world leaders seem to have a variety of different opinions as to what form this promised Information Society should ideally take, they have managed to reach the consensus that public money will not fund its development. In other words, whether we like it or not, unless the Internet carries a dynamic and indeed significant flow of commercial traffic it will not generate the returns required for its extension and upgrading which the Information Society objective calls for. Without these commercial services the use of, and benefits from, the Internet will be limited to a few selected institutions and privileged homes rather than be diffused to the public at large.

The present book, therefore, represents a welcome addition to the expanding literature about the Internet since in addition to the surfers seeking commercial applications, it is primarily aimed at the existing and future service providers whose commercial activities will attract private capital to the extension and upgrading of the network itself. It seeks to address the first fundamental issue that any budding entrepreneur is faced with when considering developing and /or launching a commercial service on the Internet: what, if any, are his/her trading rights? The existence and nature of legal protection underlying the distance contracts between the ser-

vice provider and his/her sub-contractors/suppliers and/or con-
sumers/clients are the keys to his/her confidence to invest in such
services. If the service provider cannot trust that his/her rights will
be protected or the consumer cannot trust the supplier's offers of
remunerated services then the Information Society will be nothing
more than a pipe-dream.

Mr. Hance has considered how well covered and protected such
contracts are. The current situation is clearly explained in general
terms and the questions that remain to be considered are exposed.
The key issues are raised without going into exhaustive detail. For
those wishing to trade in Internet services, some of the key areas
of national and international law are introduced. As the book is not
a publication of the European Commission, the description and
views of this regulatory framework, are of course, those of the
author and not those of the Institution that I work for..
Nevertheless, this book represents a useful contribution to the current, developing debate concerning the legal framework for services which will use the Internet. Indeed, I hope that it will encourage readers to approach their relevant regulatory bodies (including
the European Commission) for information and/or for its views on
these issues.

In addition to this key role of helping widen the important debate
on the regulatory framework of the Internet, in my opinion, the
book has three key messages.

First, it destroys the myth that the Internet represents a regulatory
void. It confirms that a regulatory framework exists albeit with
national variations in certain areas.

Secondly, through a clear exposition of each of the key issues, it
demonstrates that trading on the Internet is not that difficult. Thus
it provides the basic guidelines that the business professional or
consumer on the network requires to understand what his/her
legal rights are and the extent to which they are protected. The
authors have done their utmost to be comprehensive. All the relevant legal issues are touched upon: from the right to freedom of
expression, through authorisation, copyright protection, protection of privacy, electronic commerce and marketing regulations,
the legality of encryption and protection against piracy to responsibility and proof.

Thirdly, it demonstrates that the regulatory environment to date is out of step with one key characteristic of the Internet, namely its cross-frontier dimension. This is an issue of key concern given my responsibility of heading the Directorate General in the Commission responsible for the Internal Market. The fact that certain regulations, as explained in the differing sections of this book, have already been harmonised does not imply that there exists a uniform European framework. Indeed, the authors identify some areas where, in their opinion, differences in the national regulations persist within Europe. This would not be a problem if one were to limit one's service provision to national borders but this could detract from the main benefits of using the Internet in the first place.

A number of factors suggest that the commercial services offered over the Internet will have to be of a transborder nature; the most apparent is the technical inevitability of promotional messages on the Internet being consulted from various parts of the world. The supplier could, of course, limit contracts to national orders but there are three key economic reasons for suggesting that this would not be a viable business proposition. The first is that, in order to be viable, a service offered over the Internet will need to be greatly differentiated (either by being supplied at a distance, unlike before, or because it is totally new) from the «traditional» services that, as consumers, we currently use. Consumers are unlikely to invest in the hardware, in the form of PCs or PC/TV sets, for marginal improvements in service provision. They will be seeking significant improvements in terms of the range of services that they could benefit from as well as new innovative on-line multimedia service concepts that they cannot currently have access to. In effect, the Information Society represents a situation where access to a wealth of differentiated niche services allows the individual to benefit from that ideal mix of services that are best matched to his/her personal tastes. This contrasts with the present situation where the average consumer finds it difficult to have access to, or indeed be aware of, the full range of services he/she would prefer. The transition from this current situation of restricted choice to one where we can meet our personal preferences will be determined by the diversity of services offered over the Internet. Without a very broad range of niche distance services the possibility of making this transition will not be realised. Therefore the potential demand seems likely to be for a very broad range of strongly differentiated niche services.

The second condition for encouraging the public at large to make the necessary investment in the hardware representing the «on-ramps» to the Internet seems likely to be that the commercial services are priced at an affordable level to stimulate mass market demand.

These two conditions imply a third. Niche markets cannot be supplied at mass market cost unless the niche can be exploited across a very wide geographic area. This can, of course, be achieved via the Internet where the development of a global «niche» market that surpasses certain national «mass» markets could be feasible. The commercial service provision over the Internet will therefore typically be of a transborder nature.

In this respect, this book's demonstration of the differences in national regulations signals the potential threat of legal uncertainty. In particular, the notion that services should be able to circulate across borders once they conform to the national regulations of the country from which they originate (a principle enshrined at the European level in Internal market law) would seem to be the ideal approach to apply. However, all surveys conclude that new legislation will be needed to adapt existing rules to new Information Society services. Yet in certain cases it may be possible for countries to lawfully restrict the free movement of services and thus not mutually to recognise the legal regimes of other states. In such instances harmonisation may be necessary. But first the issues need to be fully explored to be sure that the fundamental needs of the regulations and the most appropriate form they could take are understood.

As the Director General responsible for the services of the Commission that monitor the integration and efficient operation of the Internal Market, I recognise the role of the European Commission in this respect and the introductory references to the existing European legal framework in this book identify how we have already begun our important task. The challenges facing us remain. Our objective of achieving an Information Society can only be met if we can provide Internet users (both service suppliers and consumers) with an international regulatory framework that will provide the necessary reassurance to allow them to invest and to purchase new Internet services.

In my view an approach based on well tested Single Market principles offers the legal clarity and certainty to the cross-border service provider since the regulations of his/her country of establishment are the only ones on which he/she would need focus. Equally importantly, the Internet consumer would be offered protection and the right of redress wherever he/she ordered his/her preferred service.

All this is for the future. For the present I hope that this useful and well-researched book will encourage its readers to become commercial users (either as suppliers or consumers) of the Internet and thus discover and develop the exciting and challenging market place it promises to be. I have no doubt that the book will give rise to as many questions as it answers but that will, in my opinion, be a measure of its usefulness. The questions it raises will help launch the essential international policy debate on the development of the regulatory framework for services using the Internet which has been somewhat neglected in the policy debates on the Information Society to date.

John F. Mogg

Director-General
DG XV - Internal Market
and Financial Services
European Commission

Foreword

The future of electronic communications is anticipated with a certain precision by the Internet, the network of networks founded on the use of a common computing language or more precisely on the use of the same family of protocols, and which enables millions of computers to «communicate with one another».

There can be no doubt that the appearance and particularly the development of global electronic communications, which is sometimes allegorically described as a «global village» or «cyberspace», will substantially alter the conditions, methods and other characteristics of much of our future communications. Without radically changing our relationship with the Other, or with knowledge, these technological upheavals - which we carefully and rapidly named the information «society», and no longer the information «market», rather quickly losing sight, after this initial step forward, of the fact that a «communication» society would have been more promising than an «information» society - should not be underrated or underestimated.

The Internet already offers the possibility of accessing an amazing quantity of information, but it does not offer Knowledge, Ethics or «pre-programmed» answers to the human, moral or scientific questions of Man, our questions. Between information and decision-making, knowledge or the choice of life, a certain human space must be occupied by our analysis, our value judgments, our intuition. Happily the most amazing of networks cannot deprive us of these functions which distinguish us, to a certain extent, from the animal kingdom, and which probably confer to us a certain mission in relation to our environment, to other people and to ourselves.

From a pragmatic point of view, each of us is already certain to have access to far too much information which we have to sort out, understand, analyze and interpret. More necessary than ever, then, is our capacity for analysis and reflection, in order to process and «use» this information in most of our spheres of activity.

The professional sphere has a vital need for people who are capable of reflecting upon and interpreting information, as instruments of action and of the building of an economic destiny. In the social sphere, information remains the raw material of collective knowledge, whose elaboration requires that men, now as in the past, show proof not only of intelligence but also of intuition and ethics. The educational sphere also reflects this reality - now more than ever, it is necessary to teach young people to learn, to «process» information and above all to maintain a certain degree of objectivity with regard to information which is often fed to them without any analysis or via biased analysis, if it is not altogether curtailed.

In other words, interpreting information is and will remain more important than finding it, a fact which is all the more reassuring in that it guarantees our dignity as beings with the capacity for thought.

So that the Internet may fulfill its role, it has been restricted to the status of a vehicle, a purveyor of information in the three spheres referred to above. Of course, the network must be able to offer a structured system of access to information, thus confirming the worth of the various experiments in the area of the structuring and arrangement of information on the Internet (indexes, sites highly developed in terms of hypertext links), but in addition to this, Society and the Law must, through their intervention, be able to ensure that the system is reliable, both for those who publish on it and for those who use the network passively, for private and commercial purposes.

Until now, the situation may have seemed alarming to the uninitiated. In fact, the majority of legal and media circles have tended to claim that there are no rules of law applicable to the Internet. This work, which it is my pleasure to promote, demonstrates the opposite and, without wishing to anticipate the author's introduction, this message, which is also mine and that of my colleagues, is not only true but also welcome.

I must, however, agree with the author that the legal framework is not explicit as regards all Internet activities. There are still shadowy areas on which some light needs to be thrown. The problem is that the Law is never more than the reflection, a priori, of deliberations and hypotheses - we would hope ethical ones - and a posteriori of the often contradictory conduct which we are attempting to legitimate. Tied to men, to their conduct and to their value judgments, the Law is the reflection of Society. And this Society is not monolithic in its approach to the Internet. Some wish to strictly monitor and regulate all activity on the network, others want everything to be unrestricted. Such is the difficult balance of democracy.

But the areas of shadow should not make us forget the numerous spaces of light, the clarity and the certainty offered by the legal beacons highlighted in this work. How can we not applaud upon reading this work, which brings together the certainties of the legal team which it has been my pleasure to lead at ITEL Consulting. The law on the Internet - or at least the law applicable to the Internet - contains stable reference points which, when approached with logic and rigour, offer solutions to the day-to-day problems encountered on the network of networks. Let us say it loud and clear-there are very few legal lacunae in the law on the Internet, but there is a huge jurisprudential vacuum, which can be attributed to the relatively recent explosion of the network, at least in Europe. Let us never lose sight of the fact that we live in a world which is constantly changing. Nothing is frozen... and especially not the law, fortunately. The law governing the Internet exists. It is in full development, and it will confirm itself.

In this book you will find a comprehensive presentation of that which may today be called the law on the Internet, and covering trends in North America and Europe. Maître Olivier HANCE has produced an authoritative work, which will furnish jurists with accurate bases of analysis and action. Businessmen, private individuals, users or simply those who are interested will find in this work a simple explanation of the legal principles which govern the Internet. All are sure to appreciate the clarity of the texts, which is due to the author's considerable pedagogical skills.

Thanks to Olivier HANCE's work, everyone will have the opportunity to be well informed.

Edmond DE MOOR

Managing Director ITEL Consulting
edemoor@itelconsulting.be

Acknowledgements

It is the privilege of the main author and scientific director of a work to be able to thank those who have assisted him, those without whom this book would never have been possible. Before going any further, I would like to say that this book is the work of a team which I was fortunate enough to direct. Even though I wrote every line, my position was that of the conductor of an orchestra: the sound comes from his baton but the baton itself does not make a sound.

First of all, I would like to thank Suzan DIONNE BALZ, who agreed to follow me in this crazy adventure, with her marvellously artistic temperament and her love of discovery. Counting neither days nor nights, she has brilliantly co-written this work, taking responsibility in particular for the sections on American and Canadian law. This book owes her a great deal.

I would then like to thank Philippe MEULDERS who, in addition to his enthusiastic and interesting cooperation on the first part of this work, which is due to his qualities as a jurist, an economist and a connoisseur of the world and the sites of the Internet, agreed to take on a thankless task-that of the administrative management of this work, of relations with the members of the team, scattered over several continents, of relations with translators, with the publisher, and so on.

It is difficult to disassociate the work of Elisa AMEDEO, Fidel NDESHYO NGARUYE and Xavier PIETRA. They were all at my side during the four months that it took to produce the final draft of the book, each providing their own brilliant contribution in their own field. Elisa and Xavier concentrated in particular on the evidence law, contract law and liability law. Fidel focused on issues concerning licensing regimes, advertising and marketing and, to a lesser extent, the protection of privacy. As my main collaborators, they each helped with this creation in their own way, Elisa through her dynamic approach, Xavier through his good humour, Fidel through his quiet strength. And all three by their outstanding sense of responsibility and by their boundless courage.

All the collaborators have helped to give this work its form and its content. Some of them have provided not only specialised, but also general assistance. Jean-Philippe MIKUS made a notable contribution to the third part of this work on standard contracts, but also to the study of American criminal law. Christophe STENMANS brought the full force of his competence to bear on the chapter on crime, but also on the understanding of the general legal issues highlighted by the work. Géraldine BALTHAZAR also offered not only her knowledge of liability law, but in particular her spirit of innovation and her willingness to help in whatever way she could. This is also true of the assistance given by Caroline DECOCK and Tristan KRSTIC who, in addition to their general availability, researched questions of payment via the Internet and English law of evidence respectively.

Others agreed to deal with certain particular issues in depth. Thus Alexandre de STREEL brought his genius to bear on the subject of intellectual property, André GRENACS his lucidity on issues of cryptography, Wim SABLON his perspicacity on the area of privacy and freedom of expression in Europe. Bruno NOWAK and Frédéric DECHAMPS assisted Elisa and Xavier with their deliberations on the law on liability. Anna ZUBRZYCKA assisted Suzan in her research, particularly as regards licensing regimes in American and Canadian law.

It was, of course, extremely important for all the members of the team to understand the technical reality of the Internet. We were able to rely on the unstinting assistance of Benoit LIPS and Emmanuel WILLEMS, whose contribution went as far as to draft certain paragraphs in Part One and in the chapter in Part Two on electronic money (electronic commerce).

I would like to thank Alain LÉONARD, Gérard and Michèle PIETRA, and Leo VAN DER WEES for their outstanding rereading. Alain also offered us his patience and his perseverance, qualities which proved indispensable to the completion of this work.

Jean BERGEVIN and Emmanuel CRABIT of Directorate General XV of the European Union were very kind in submitting to the «legal assaults» of my colleagues and in answering my own questions. Any errors or shortcomings in this work cannot be attributed to them, whilst much of the wealth of the book, as regards European law, is due to them.

Faithful translation has never been an easy task. I would like to thank Matthijs van MILTENBURG, Gerienne LAMERS, Gabriele PUCCI, Anna GARBAGNI, Patrick CLERENS, and Stephan KRAUTRÄMER who undertook this task with so much patience, and especially Suzan

DIONNE BALZ, Léo VAN DER WEES, Mr and Mrs Hermann SCHMITZ-WENZEL, Elmar KRINGS, Elisa AMEDEO and Carla GIULANI who intelligently supervised the translations.

Thanks are also due to the founder of ITEL Consulting, Edmond DE MOOR, for having given me the courage to believe that the law on the Internet existed, and to my publisher, Jean de GHELDERE, for having continued to believe this...

Finally, as we all know, acknowledgements can sometimes take the form of apologies, such as those which I would like to offer to my parents, my family and especially my wife, Elisabetta, for having virtually disappeared from view for four months. Dedicating this work to her is scant recompense for the effort which was made not by myself but by two of us.

Thank you.

Olivier HANCE

Introduction

Internet: the word itself is provocative. We all have an opinion about the Internet. For some of us, it's a dream. For others, a nightmare. The former emphasize the revolution in electronic communications which enables tens of millions of people to communicate with one another and to exchange ideas and information, a new commercial and advertising tool on a world scale, an obstacle to the setting up or maintaining of social, administrative or financial barriers, the end of pointless hierarchies. The latter point to the lack of any real human dimension to this mediatized form of communication, asserting that the Internet is built more on promises than on success stories, more on appearance than on reality.

The purpose of this work is not to settle this debate which, moreover, in many respects is a false debate. The Internet, as a tool, is offered to man. It cannot and will not be worth more than man decides to make of it. However, in the torrent of a society which - as the third millennium approaches - is turning more and more towards intangible and information-based activities, it seems necessary to recall certain rights, certain forms of protection which are the fruit of historical evolution, of reflection, of a certain formalization of ethics but also of compromise. These beacons provided by the law on the Internet are not permanent or absolute truths. They do, however, provide preliminary reference points for the reflection which is sometimes in danger of foundering in the gloom-mongering so dear to those who know how to gain from it.

So there is a law on the Internet. The message is «*shocking*», but propitious.

It is «*shocking*» for at least two reasons. First of all, because the pervading reports in the press and even sometimes in legal circles tend to suggest the opposite. We appear to have been caught short by the «newness» of the Internet. We are in an area of non-law or worse yet, of radical uncertainty. Secondly, because it makes us realize, upon reflection, that if the law on the Internet exists, ultimately this is because behind the machines, there are people whose conduct, and in particular whose relations with things and with other people, but also with information, must comply with the law and, as far as possible, with a code of ethics.

But the message is also propitious for people, businesses and politicians. The message is a welcome one for individuals, because on the network they are accorded basic rights and freedoms, which they must ensure that they retain and which they must thus exercise. It is also welcome for companies, for which it provides the beacons guiding their action on the network of networks, so that they can dare to throw themselves fully into the adventure of worldwide electronic commerce. Finally, the message is welcome to politicians, who are asked to continue to play their role as the guardians of the general interest in the electronic world of today, just as they did in the real world of yesterday and will in the virtual world of tomorrow.

This work is divided into three parts.

Part One, *The Internet in practice and in business* is devoted to a brief examination of some technical aspects of the Internet and of its importance for the business world.

Part Two, *Internet Law*, describes the content of American and European law in areas considered to be of greatest interest to the reader.

Part Three, *Twenty business contracts for the Internet* provides a description - through key elements - of twenty model contracts which are increasingly being concluded in the *«Internet world»*. For the reader's convenience, these are given in the language of the work and in English, which is the dominant language of business and of the Internet.

This work has been conceived and written with a view to providing those who are not jurists (users, businessmen, the self-employed, etc.) with an understandable look at Internet law, and to providing jurists with indispensable references which will nourish further reflection.

Its structure has also been devised to permit a quick read: each chapter of Part Two is preceded by a description of the relevance of the chapter *(Why should you ask yourself questions?)* and of the basic issues covered in the chapter *(What questions should you ask?)*. Each chapter is followed by a summary of the answers that it provides *(To summarize...)*.

Part one

The Internet in practice and in business

Introduction

The Internet, the precursor of the information superhighway, is a new computing and communication tool, as well as a tremendous vehicle of economic growth. The aim of this work is to facilitate access to and the development of activities for everyone, and in particular for business, on the network. It is intended to provide businesses with «safety beacons» for their activities, and to explain to private individuals the legal limits of their freedoms and their rights.

In order to do this, it is important to understand - from the point of view of the jurist and of the businessman, and not of the computer scientist - what the Internet is, where it comes from, what applications and communications it permits, and how it can be used by various business departments.

A. *Where does the Internet come from?*

The ARPA (Advanced Research Project Agency) was set up at the end of the 1960s by the American Defense Department, with the intention of accomplishing the simple yet strategic objective of ensuring the dispatch of orders to fire from the control centre to the ballistic missile bases even after, and in fact especially if communication networks were partially destroyed by an attack. This mission was quickly extended to include access to and the sharing of all the computing resources of the United States. The new network was called the ARPAnet.

By establishing a chain network linking major computing sites and by using information divided up into «autonomous» batches, it was possible to set up a flexible structure, irrespective of the types of computer used. The use of TCP/IP protocols, which were very quickly adopted by the military on a separate network (MILnet) and by the universities, was strengthened in 1984 when they were selected by the *National Science Foundation (NSF)* when it was establishing five major calculation centres equipped with super-calculators intended to allow the entire scientific community access to the information stored. Every major university centre then established a connection with the network set up by the NSF, which acted as the backbone for all of the traffic on these sub-networks. Henceforth, it was possible to access any point on the network from any connected university site.

In order to manage and increase the capacities of the NSF network, a contract was granted to *MERIT NETWORK INC., IBM and NCI* in 1987. Since 1992, the *NSF* has withdrawn its investments, thereby leaving the door open for other types of financing and therefore other uses.

The Internet is a federation of networks which is constantly developing and which can now be accessed by everyone. After the university researchers and the employees of public institutions, private companies and individuals have now seen the benefits which can be gained from surfing on the networks. Once forbidden, commercial use has been developing steadily over the past few years, contrary to the initial spirit of the Internet inspired by its pioneers. The Internet is now experiencing exponential growth. It brings together over 25,000 networks throughout the world and the number of users is estimated at around 40 million.

B. *Some technical details*

Put in the briefest possible terms, the Internet is made up of a shared infrastructure («the Internet network», network of networks), set up by all of the parties «speaking the same language» (the TCP/IP protocols) and linking computers scattered throughout the world, thus enabling these computers to communicate in different ways (different applications).

The infrastructure established brings together several means of telecommunications (from telephone cable to satellite communication), each party (university, government body, access provider, individual user, etc.) being responsible for setting up his or her network and bearing the costs of interconnection with other networks. Private individuals or businesses thus connect to the Internet via an access provider and themselves bear the costs of the telephone line when connecting to this provider, as well as the costs of the subscription to the provider, who is connected to the network and whose job it is to provide others with access to it. A distinction should be made between *access providers* who provide a telecommunications service and certain computing services, and the various *servers* on the Internet, whether professional or otherwise, who disseminate information on the Internet.

The Internet being, by its very nature, open to everyone and using unprotected communication protocols, certain applications such as the development of commercial transactions or the provision of private information services pose problems as regards the confidentiality of exchanges and access monitoring. Although the general problem can be technically resolved by the use of tools for encrypting the data exchanged, it is far from negligible, since in terms of security and risk analysis, it will never be possible to achieve a «no-risk» situation.

Accessible services range from the simple consultation or transfer of documents (F.T.P., Gopher, Web, etc.) to the use of tools permitting mediate or immediate interactivity between individuals (e-mail, chat, etc.). We will analyze these under point C of this section.

Regardless of the type of connection used, the Internet is always accessed via a connection to one of the numerous networks making up the Internet. For individual users or for businesses this means, as we have indicated, access via an Internet access provider who, in return for a subscription, provides access to his or her network, which is in turn interconnected to other networks, all of which make up the Internet.

In practical terms, this connection to the access provider can be established by a dial-up line via the conventional telephone network (analogue or digital), via special connections more suitable for data transmission (X.25) or, in the event of greater and more permanent requirements, via permanent connections (leased telephone lines).

Once he or she is connected to a branch of the network, the user has access to the various services and applications available on the Internet. Moreover, Internet users can access private telematic systems, some of which cost, and some of which do not. These are known as *Bulletin Board Systems*. They often comprise a computer and a number of modems. The B.B.S. or electronic message bases are used both by private individuals wishing to disseminate specific information and by major commercial systems, such as *CompuServe*[1].

C. The Internet in practice:
eight communications applications...

1. Electronic mail or e-mail

Electronic mail allows users with an electronic address to communicate with one another in the same way as does conventional correspondence by post. In practical terms, the e-mail writer's message is sent to his or her e-mail server (for a private individual or a small company, this will usually be the Internet access provider), who sends it to the addressee's mail server via the network. The addressee of the mail opens his or her mail server, consults his or her mail box, and receives the message.

As with the conventional postal service, this is a private communication forwarded from one geographical point to another within a certain period of time, the difference being that an e-mail reaches the addressee's server about fifteen minutes after being dispatched (even for an e-mail sent from Paris to New-York), and users can open their mail box several times a day if they wish.

Wrongly addressed mail could get lost, but it usually returns automatically to the sender's server, who recovers it when opening his or her mail box.

Around 4,000 messages are sent via the Internet every second[2].

2. *The World Wide Web (WWW or Web)*

The World Wide Web or the Web is one of the most user-friendly tools for seeking and disseminating information on the Internet. It was created by the C.E.R.N. five years ago and allows simple consultation of resources thanks to «hypertext» links inserted into the text by the author. The hypertext link, which is usually indicated by a word which is underlined, framed or appears in a different colour, points to a different zone in the server or to a different server, sometimes ten thousand kilometers away. In the body of a text on intellectual property under French law, for example, the underlined word «copyright» can «project» the surfer who «clicks» on this word to an American server dealing with the same issue. The Web is thus a particularly user-friendly application which enables users to «surf» on the Internet by «jumping» from one server to another in a couple of seconds. The user can navigate from server to server with maximum flexibility, viewing texts, images, sounds, even animated sequences. In addition, he or she can use search engines made up of hypertext links or key words which refer to other Web servers.

From the server's point of view, use of this method of disclosing information is very similar to editing a trade magazine with a large circulation, the difference being that all users can easily create their own Web servers and these can be updated constantly.

There are several hundred thousand Web sites on the Internet, and this number is growing exponentially.

3. *Telnet*

Telnet, which is less user-friendly but more «powerful», enables «terminal emulation» via the network-it enables a computer to take full or partial control of a distant computer. A computer set up in Tokyo can, for example, be «controlled» from Berlin. Although frequently used for long-distance work in the early days of the Internet, this method is now rarely used, except by information services wishing to make available on the Internet information systems which operate on the basis of other search systems (e.g. the American Library of Congress, travel agencies, banks, etc.).

In most cases, use of Telnet is confined to consulting textual information.

4. F.T.P. (File Transfer Protocol)

F.T.P. is a reduced version of Telnet, and can be used to transfer files, such as files containing texts or software programs for example, between distant computers. If he or she has the necessary authorization, a user can connect to an F.T.P. server in order to «retrieve» files from it (*downloading*), but also in order to place files in it *(uploading)*. A European user connected to an American F.T.P. server can therefore easily take any file whatsoever from this server (a work by Shakespeare or an Internet navigation software package for example), or place any file on it (subject to server authorization), which other users can then retrieve in turn. Thanks to user-friendly F.T.P. applications, these operations are almost as easy to execute as are the transfer of a file from hard drive to disk. F.T.P.servers often include a section accessible to everyone (*«public domain»*) and sometimes a «private» section, to which access is limited by a password requirement.

5. Gopher

Caught between F.T.P. servers (from which they evolved, in part) and Web servers, *Gopher* servers constituted the first attempt to integrate the various network resources. We will not consider them here, however, since they were soon swept away by the Web storm. Telnet, F.T.P. and Gopher, the first tools enabling the constitution of «electronic libraries» accessible to the largest possible group of people, are gradually giving way to the Web, which integrates and extends the consultation facilities of each of these tools.

6. Mailing lists

A mailing list is a list of users wishing to exchange information or ideas on a given subject. Any user can create such a list. By analogy, the mailing list is a forum for the collection and dissemination of information sent by people from their homes, «without moving».
In practical terms, the user must subscribe to the list of his or her choice by sending a standard e-mail to the list manager, in which

the user indicates his or her wish to subscribe. The principle behind these lists is very simple - each message sent by electronic mail to the list is automatically redistributed to the electronic address of all of the subscribers. This is thus mail intended for a large audience. The user is of course free to initiate private correspondence by ordinary e-mail (see above) with a user that he or she meets via the list.

7. Discussion groups

The purpose of discussion groups, also known as forums or *Newsgroups* is the same as that of a mailing list, to exchange information and ideas on a particular subject. Any user can create such a group. By analogy, a discussion group is a meeting place, like a tea room where people go to talk. The discussions do not, however, take place in real time nor do they occur between the players directly. Thus we can picture users as coming to and going from the same place, posting their messages on the wall and reading the messages left by other users. Unlike mailing lists, then, discussion groups do not involve the use of e-mail to send or receive public information.

That which Internet users tend to refer to by the term *Newsgroups* goes far beyond the context of the Internet, and constitutes a huge information network, parallel to but interconnected with most telematic services, including those of the Internet.

There is no central *News* server, but rather several thousand computers which each keep a copy of the *News* and exchange their respective contributions using very complex processes. These servers are synchronized several times a day on the basis of information flow diagrams which are governed by site administrators.

Whatever the software used, discussion group consultation is based on simple principles. From the list of all of the discussion groups, the user selects the groups of interest to him or her and «subscribes» to them. This subscription enables the software to keep a record of the user's consultations. With each of his or her connections, the user therefore simply has to consult new messages from within his or her selection. Consequently, the user can read messages, «post» replies via the News or reply directly by e-mailing their authors, directly, or formulate his or her own questions[3.]

8. The chat function or IRC (Internet Relay Chat)

Unlike a discussion group, «chat» communications take place directly between interconnected computers and are therefore only accessible to those who are connected during the session.

D. The Internet and business

At global level, the advent of the information superhighway, of which the Internet is the precursor, is fundamentally altering economic data, and is leading towards the internationalization of markets and increased competition. From a business point of view, the Internet constitutes a new economic weapon and a sophisticated tool for expanding the reputation of a company and of their products and services, for analyzing markets and for client prospection, for carrying out commercial transactions, for research and development or for recruiting staff.

The 10 million American commercial references (*US Business Listings*) in the *Central Source Yellow Pages* bear witness to business interest in the Internet[4].

1. The Internet for commercial transactions

a. The Internet for advertising and marketing

Above all, the Internet is a marvellous way for businesses to enhance their reputation (advertising, «disguised» advertising, lobbying) and to study the market they wish to prospect by using its various applications, such as posting messages (not necessarily commercial messages) to forums, dissemination on the Web, or e-mail. «An electronic address and well targeted online advertising brought in around 3 million dollars for the *Ceram Corporation* in San Diego, California, in 1994»[5].

Marketing and advertising methods are, however, fundamentally different on the Internet. Originally, the scientific vocation of the network excluded the pursuit of lucrative aims. Commerce has developed on the Internet today, but advertising remains subject, in addition to the application of the law, to self-regulation and good cybermanners (netiquette). For example, it is highly inadvisable to disseminate advertising within most mailing lists and discussion groups[6]. Companies would consequently be well advised to create their own lists or groups of consumers and experts for the purposes of encouraging discussion about their products and services[7]. By using these applications - the Web, mailing lists and discussion groups - it is possible, within the limits prescribed by the law, by self-regulation and by good cybermanners, to precisely target and define a group of consumers, and to establish certain consumer profiles.

Interactivity enables Internet users to select company sites as they navigate through the network. It is not easy to create an attractive Web page containing interesting advertisements, given the wide range of potential clients. This is not a new problem, but it is a problem which has now taken on an international dimension (conventional advertising campaigns «operate» at a national level). The Internet has the advantage, however, of enabling the constant dissemination, at a low cost, of an almost unlimited quantity of information about the products and services on offer, in particular in the form of *FAQs (Frequently Asked Questions)*. The success can be spectacular, as can be seen from the case of the company *Flowers Stop* which, having launched its Web site in June 1995, recorded around 10 to 20,000 visitors a month, 1.5% of whom made purchases[8].

Retroaction can be automatic on the Internet. Thus from among the thousands of commercial Web sites, 100 and then 25 sites were selected by the *editors at Interactive Age,* on the basis of criteria such as wealth of content, ease of use, the use of hypertexts links, the quality of the *design,* but also on the basis of having accomplished «with the Web application, something which they would never have been able to accomplish using another media»[9]. In addition, some methods enable companies to personally measure personally the profitability of their Web site[10] (to track the number of visits, for example).

b. The Internet for commerce

Internet access providers and certain consultancy firms naturally exploit the commerce linked to the use of the network by users (such as access, training, Web page creation, or information searches). Many SMEs and multinationals (including *Siemens Nixdorf* [11] or *McKinsey & Company* [12], etc.), however, have also integrated the Internet into their commercial strategy for selling their products and services. All consumer goods and services are marketed on the Internet, on the site of a company or trader, or in huge virtual markets such as the *European Business Center*[13], the *London Mall*[14], the *Holland ExPo*[15], the *Italian Business Institute*[16], the *CommerceNet*[17], or the *IndustryNet Online Marketplace*[18]. This latter site, created in 1991, presents 250,000 industrial companies and 10,000 new products every month. Over 40,000 users, 18% of whom are non-Americans, from 26 countries throughout the world visit the cybermarket every month, and the estimated total traffic of cyberconsumers is expected to exceed one million in 1996[19]. International business relations are facilitated by the presence on the network of hundreds of chambers of commerce, including the *CyberNet Chamber of Commerce*[20] and the *International Chamber of Commerce*[21], of embassies such as the *Electronic Embassy*[22], and of international bodies such as the *World Trade Organization*[23], etc.

c. The Internet for making and receiving payments

The future of business on the Internet is linked in particular to the development of electronic money (*E-money*) and the appearance of new commercial intermediaries whose tasks will include making transactions and particularly payments on the Internet secure. Justified or not, the security and confidentiality of payments by credit card are matters of concern for consumers purchasing products or services. Some banking organizations such as the *Mark Twain Bank* [24] use E-money (on the basis of the software developed by the company *Digicash* [25]). Other non-banking institutions already act as commercial intermediaries to guarantee the security of transactions effected via the Internet such as, for example, *First Virtual Holding* [26]. The various methods have advantages and disadvantages relating to security, confidentiality, the anonymity of transactions, ease of use for the purchaser and of operation for the seller, and to the cost and speed of the transaction.

Furthermore, numerous financial and banking institutions (banks, stock exchanges[27], intermediaries[28]) offer financial information consultancy services[29] (e.g.: *FinanceNet* [30], which is supported by the *National Science Foundation* or *CorpFinet*[31]) on the Internet, as well as certain *home banking* or *electronic banking*[32] services. Finally, international organizations such as the World Bank[33] or the International Monetary Fund[34] are also present on the Internet.

2. The Internet and communication (internal and external)

E-mail is the most widely used Internet application. It is easy to integrate into the corporate culture and it is useful both within the company (parent company and subsidiaries, etc.) and externally, to communicate with partners, sales representatives, and customers, for example. Thus in 1994 the *Digital Equipment Corporation*, which had 40,000 computers connected to the Internet, already dealt with over 2 million messages a month and had about 125 internal Web servers[35].

This application can be used for regional, national and international communication, at a cost which is very low compared with conventional methods of communication such as the telephone or fax machine. Apart from the cost of subscription to an Internet access provider, the cost is in fact only that of a local communication, even to send international mail or to connect to a server which is ten thousand kilometers away. File transfer by attachment, without any restriction as to the number of pages, enables the recipient to reprocess the data received. Costs for envelopes, paper and stamps are reduced. The reduction in costs can also be seen in terms of time saved by obviating the need to handle envelopes and stamps.

The automatic mail server (a sub-application of e-mail) also enables companies to distribute brochures or documents on its products and services automatically upon request, particularly to users who only have e-mail facilities and who therefore do not have access to Web sites.

To this should be added the recent developments in telephony and videoconferencing via the Internet. These revolutionary new applications, which still need improvement and which are still, in our view, contrary to European law, will no doubt have serious economic implications.

3. The Internet for research, development, and the exchange of professional information

The Internet, the largest data base in the world, offers several thousand servers[36] containing data and information relating to every possible subject: political, economic, social, cultural, scientific, and so on. The Web, F.T.P. and Gopher applications can be used to access these data, often free of charge, while discussion groups and mailing lists provide forums for debates and meetings between international experts on specific subjects. Thus the «*Civil Engineering and Related Internet Resources*»[37] Web site, as its name indicates, encompasses press releases, publications, conferences, ongoing studies, and reports concerning on civil engineering.

Furthermore, some international organizations disseminate their work on the Internet. The «*International Organization for Standardization (ISO)*»[38], a vast worldwide federation (2,700 committees) whose aim is to promote and develop standardization (in the fields of textiles, agriculture, the cinema, iron and steel, chemicals, telecommunications, information technology, etc.) in order to facilitate the liberalization of international trade, is present on the Internet.

Information is also provided by industrial or multinational groups such as *Matsushita Electric Works - LTD.RD Laboratory*[39] or *N.T.T.*[40] which disseminates the results of research and development programs, or gives access to various internal research laboratories via hypertext links. The Web server of the *Fortis* group[41] illustrates the type of information which can be obtained from major industrial groups regarding their activities, their objectives, their structures, their annual reports and other economic information which they decide to disseminate.

4. The Internet for personnel management and recruitment

The Internet facilitates the decentralization of work within a company, in particular thanks to telework, and the resultant benefits in terms of productivity and economy. According to a survey conducted by *Dataquest*, over 60% of the bosses of American SMEs and large-scale companies have access to the Internet network and have granted access to employees for whom they are responsible[42].

A large number of companies recruit via the Internet. Multinationals such as *Procter & Gamble*[43] and *Philips*[44], as well as SMEs disseminate job advertisements internationally and at a low cost, within specialist sites or simply on their company's home page. For example, the *Electronic Embassy*[45], a virtual embassy on the network, receives and transfers job opportunity information to the American *Employment Office*. A search via *Infoseek*, an Internet search engine, reveals job offers disseminated internationally[46]. Some professional organizations such as trade union associations are also present[47].

The Law on the Internet

Introduction

Before commencing the second part of this work describing the law on the Internet, it may be useful to explain the standards which we have taken into consideration during the drafting this book.

Self-regulation and good cybermanners

This book is primarily a law book. Since we will also be referring to self-regulation and good cybermanners (netiquette) on occasion, however, we feel that it is important to define these terms and their value in the world of the Internet and as regards the law from the outset.

Those taking part in an activity may sometimes decide to themselves determine the rules to which they will be subject. This may involve the spontaneous definition of the rules of a group game, or regulations which apply to a group of companies, for example in the advertising sector. The Internet is also characterized by the development of such voluntary standards. Some major networks, in particular the NSFnet, have drawn up *acceptable use policies* which stipulate the rules of use applicable to the network. Similarly, the founders of a discussion forum often draft rules which Internet users must comply with if they wish to take part. In all of these cases, the rules are not created by the legal system, but rather by a relatively spontaneous process of developing voluntary rules, of self-regulation.

What strength and value does such self-regulation have? First of all, it must be said that for those who participate in the network or in a given activity and who wish, from a social point of view, to continue to do so, these rules have considerable power, since failure to respect them is penalized by the community itself, which may go as far as to exclude the party concerned from the group. A user may be forbidden to take part in a forum, for example. Furthermore, the group can exercise pressure in ways which may be technically and sometimes economically unpleasant, such as by *flaming*, either individually or en masse, the party having contravened the rules. Occasionally pressure is also exerted on the user's access provider. These are all penalties which emanate from the community concerned in itself.

Failure to respect these self-regulations may also be taken into consideration by the law and by the courts. This requires that it be possible to integrate these voluntary standards into the law. These integration possibilities can be illustrated by means of a simple example - a judge who must decide a dispute relating to the Internet could, in order to assess the behaviour of the parties concerned, examine common practices on the network or in a particular forum. An *acceptable use policy* would provide him or her with precise indications which he or she could well take into consideration, despite the fact that the *acceptable use policy* does not constitute a rule of law.

Finally, besides the formalized rules developed by a particular community or microcosm in the interests of self-regulation, good manners have also made their appearance on the Internet, in the form of good cybermanners. They are not officially codified, and they are in constant evolution. Ultimately, these are rules of courtesy - we learn them because we are in the know, or at our own cost. Caution is essential, however, since their disrespect can also be condemned by the community and could, in rare cases, be taken into consideration by a court of law.

In Europe: the law of the European Union, the law of the Council of Europe, and certain national legal systems

It is not the purpose of this work to describe to the reader in detail the contents of the legal systems of each of the various member States of the European Union[1], but rather to indicate the broad outlines of·Internet law within the European Union (which we will refer to as Europe). Standards established by the authorities of the European Union will be taken into consideration, but we will not analyze the specificities of the various national legal systems. Furthermore, the standards of the Council of Europe, which includes the member States of the European Union but also other «European» states[2], in a more geographic sense, are also considered, particularly as regards freedom of expression and privacy. There are two reasons for this. Firstly, all of the European Union States are members of the Council of Europe and, furthermore, as early as 1974[3] the Court of Justice asserted that «*instruments concerning the protection of human rights in which the member States have cooperated or to which they have adhered can also provide indications which should be taken into account*. This assertion by the Court was subsequently confirmed not only by jurisprudence[4] but also by the rules of the *Treaty on European Union*, Title 1, Article F, which stipulates that «*The Union shall respect fundamental rights, as guaranteed by the European Convention for the Protection of Human Rights and Fundamental Freedoms signed in Rome on November 4, 1950 and as they result from the constitutional traditions common to the member states, as general principles of Community law*».

When neither European law nor that of the Council of Europe can offer a response, we will analyze a few of the national legal systems, often French and English law.

In North America: the American and Canadian federal legal systems, the legal systems of certain American states and Canadian provinces, and the standards of the North American Free Trade Agreement

Basically, we will consider the American and Canadian federal legal systems when replying to the questions posed in this work. Where these legal systems are incomplete or do not exist, we have researched the legal systems of certain American states and Canadian provinces. For questions relating to the transborder circulation of services, we have, of course, taken into account the standards of the *North American Free Trade Agreement* (*NAFTA*), applicable to the United States, Canada and Mexico.

chapter 1

Your first steps on the Internet and the law

Why ask questions?

The *user's* first «legal» steps on the Internet often coincide with the signing of a subscription contract with an Internet *access provider*. We would draw the user's attention to his or her contractual relationship with the access provider, which sometimes goes unnoticed because terms and conditions of access and use of the services provided are furnished in very little detail.

An *access provider's* first steps, in certain cases and in certain states, will be to make a declaration to or request authorization to provide telecommunications services from the relevant national authority. From a global point of view, the development of the Internet access services markets has been impressive. In November 1995 there were over 1,400 access providers in the world. This development has occurred in the context of a liberalized market characterized by keen competition. The rates charged for the provision of services have fallen rapidly, while the quality of the services provided varies from one operator to another.

Finally, *telematic service providers* on the Internet must request authorization each time the service so requires (lotteries or financial services, for example), irrespective of the method of provision. It is important for both access providers and telematic service providers on the Internet to find out as soon as possible whether the activity they are planning to undertake on the Internet is subject to authorization, so that they can include the various steps to be taken and the delays necessary to obtain authorization in their *business plan*.

Furthermore, it is extremely important for a company (be it an access provider, a telematic server or a company disseminating information on the Internet) to know to what extent its services benefit from a liberalized licensing regime in other countries. Profitability calculations, budgets for advertising and promotional campaigns, the scope of certain intellectual property licences... all these things are changing. We will see the impact of regimes of the free provision of services under European law and in the context of the North American Free Trade Agreement (NAFTA), which facilitate the circulation of services within the European single market and within the NAFTA free trade zone respectively. These provisions are also essential to the provision of services on the Internet from a macro-economic point of view, since they contribute to the construction of international markets for companies based in the countries concerned, a process which is vital to the development of new telematic services and applications in the context of the information superhighway.

What questions?

What is the basis of the relationship between a private user and his or her access provider?

Are Internet access providers subject to a regime of licensing or declaration in Europe? Is this issue harmonized by European law?

What practical impact does the European Telecommunications Office have on Internet access providers?

Are Internet access providers subject to a regime of licensing or declaration under American and Canadian law?

What impact does the principle of the free provision of services, as embodied in European law, have on the activities of Internet access providers and, more broadly, what impact does it have on the activities of any business using the Internet to provide services? What does it provide for?

What legal regime is implemented by the *North American Free Trade Agreement* as regards the provision of services? What impact does this have on access and service providers, and telematic providers in particular, on the Internet?

I. Users

The entry of a private user into the world of the Internet always begins with the conclusion of a subscription contract (for further details, see Part III, standard contract n°1) between the user and an Internet access provider, unless the user's company or university is already connected.

Generally, this contract is not complicated. In most cases, it is a brief standard form specifying the identity of the user-subscriber, a description of the access desired (communication speed, digital or analog communication channel, dial-up or leased line, access to a news server and to an electronic mailbox, etc.), price and billing method. The Internet access provider may offer additional services, such as a telephone help line or a local discussion area, in which case these are included in the contract.

Ideally, general terms and conditions of sale are given on the reverse side of this form, or are attached to it. These may contain specific indications regarding the user's behaviour on the Internet (*acceptable use policy*, see in particular Part III, contract n°20). The legal issues raised by the user's entry into the world of the Internet are thus conventional contract issues.

Ordinarily, private users have limited bargaining power, and will have little margin of manoeuvre in negotiating the conditions of this contract. Professional users, whose bargaining power may be considerably greater, could attempt to obtain specific undertakings regarding for example the technical quality of the service, the degree of confidentiality that may be expected, or the liability of the access provider (see Part III, contract n°1).

II. Service Providers

Service providers enter the world of the Internet upon start-up of their activities. Two major legal questions arise, namely (a) the question of whether or not the provision of services on the Internet is subject to government licensing, and (b) the question of whether or not a service provider may provide services abroad unhindered (free provision of services).

A. Licensing regimes

1. Internet Access Providers (IAPs)

a. The regime applicable in Europe

No European country has a specific licensing regime regarding Internet access providers (IAPs). Consequently, the start-up conditions of Internet access providers are regulated by national legislations governing telecommunications services (a) and the European attempt at harmonization of licensing regimes (b). In particular, these legislations stipulate the authorizations, declarations and licences required of such providers. Worth noting is the significant practical influence of the *European Telecommunication Office*, and of the One-Stop Shopping procedures for IAPs which are nationals of fifteen states (generally European Union countries) (c).

a.1. National regimes
Among all of the European national legal systems[1], this analysis will focus on the French, Belgian, English and German regulations, first specifying *the category of telecommunications services* in which national law places the provision of access to the Internet, and then *describing the resultant authorization or declaration* required of IAPs. The application of these licensing regimes to other providers in the European Union must, however, comply with the general principle of freedom of establishment[2].

In Belgium, IAP activity is considered a data switching service. Consequently, the only obligation incumbent upon the provider is to declare[3] the start-up of its activities.

In France, the law views IAPs differently according to whether they provide access via a *switched public network* (ordinary telephone network or Minitel), or via a *leased line*. Provision of service via a switched public network is considered a value-added service exploited directly on the public network infrastructure, and is not subject to any authorization or declaration. When access is provided via a leased line, however, the activity is considered a support service[4], and is subject to a licensing regime[5]. In practice, for commercial reasons and in order to increase profits, most IAPs prefer to offer the full range of the various Internet accesses. They would consequently be wise to request the aforementioned authorization as soon as possible, but can begin to provide services on the switched network before having received it.

In the United Kingdom, determining the category of telecommunications service to which the provision of access to the Internet belongs is of minor importance. The *Telecommunication Services Licence* of July 1992 introduced a system of *Class licence,* to which are subject all *telecommunications services*, including the provision of access to the Internet. The only obligation incumbent upon an *access provider* is thus to ensure that it fulfills the conditions stipulated by the *Class licence* before beginning its activities and while conducting them. It is not subject to any authorization or even declaration procedures.

In Germany, the activity of IAPs does not fall into any of the categories of services subject to the Deutsche Bundespost Telekom monopoly (transmission channels, telephony services and radio installations). It therefore falls within the field of liberalized services, and only a simple written declaration to the federal minister of postal services and telecommunications[6] is required of providers when they first begin to provide services, upon any modification in the nature of the services provided, and when they cease activities.

In general, the countries of the European Union are leaning towards a relaxation of formalities and the gradual disappearance of authorizations regarding telecommunications services. As a result, the legal system applicable to IAPs may eventually be simplified.

a.2. The attempt at European harmonization

The authorities of the European Union are attempting[7], by means of a *proposal for a directive dated November 14, 1995*, to introduce a common framework for general authorizations and individual licences in the telecommunications services sector. Its objective is of course to overcome the obstacles standing in the way of the creation of a genuine common market of telecommunications services (restrictive administrative procedures, major differences between the licensing regimes of different countries, etc.). Evidently all telecommunications service providers, and in particular IAPs, will want to follow this European development, since they will benefit from the administrative and normative relaxation that it may offer.

In general, and as regards all telecommunications services, this European initiative notably intends to:
- establish a flexible authorization framework by giving priority to general licences in preference to individual licences;
- prohibit any a priori limitation[8] on the number of authorizations to be accorded
- open up the market. States will be able to make access to their market subject to licensing only when really necessary;
- set up harmonization mechanisms regarding licensing procedures and the conditions to which these licenses are subject.

a.3. The European Telecommunications Office (ETO)

In addition to national legislations and the recent directive proposal, an agreement has been concluded, within the framework of the European Telecommunication Office (ETO) created by the European Committee for the Regulation of Telecommunications on April 30, 1994, concerning authorization and licensing regimes in Europe. This agreement is of great practical interest especially to IAPs who are nationals of the signatory states and who wish to provide services in other signatory states[9] without having to confront different national regimes, administrative procedures and languages. It also enables them to ascertain the precise response time to their application for authorization.

Through the *One-Stop-Shopping* procedure in force in these fifteen states since November 8, 1995, all service providers wishing to use liberalized telecommunications services in one or more of these states can submit applications for authorization or licences, or their declarations, to a single site by using a standard form submitted to the ETO. The ETO is therefore responsible not only for forwarding the various dossiers to the competent administrations of the states regarding which the application for authorization or the declaration was made, but also for replying to applications for authorization within a mandatory delay of nine weeks. Evidently this procedure does not exclude the possibility of contacting the national authorities directly, if the IAP so desires. As this advantage is reserved exclusively for nationals of the States which are party to the agreement, a North American or Asian access provider wishing to benefit from this procedure can only do so via one of its facilities legally established within the territory of one of the participating parties.

b. The system applicable in North America

Under both American and Canadian law, according to the definition found in the *North American Free Trade* agreement (NAFTA), the provision of access to the Internet is considered an enhanced or value-added service, insofar as it involves «those telecommunication services employing computer processing applications that:
  a) act on the format, content, code, protocol or similar aspects of a customer's transmitted information;
  b) provide a customer with additional, different or restructured information; or
  c) involve customer interaction with stored information»[10].

Under American law, a company offering enhanced services, such as an Internet access provider, is not required to obtain authorization before beginning its activities. The *Federal Communications Commission* (FCC), the body responsible for regulating and monitoring telecommunications and broadcasting, has decided that enhanced services are not subject[11] to the licensing regime applicable to common carriers[12] established by the *Federal Communications Act of 1934*[13].

Canadian law differs significantly from American law. The *Telecommunications Act*[14] stipulates that it is not necessary to request or obtain any authorization regarding the provision of an enhanced service, such as providing access to the Internet[15]. Contrary to American law, however, the *Telecommunications Act* makes an exception for telecommunications companies which own or operate their own infrastructures[16]. Hence a company which has its own cables or operates its own telecommunications network must request authorization before commencing operations as an Internet access provider[17].

2. Servers

Besides the provision of technical access to the Internet, there remains the vast majority of services provided on the Internet by diverse telematic servers such as Web, F.T.P. or Telnet servers. The variety of services available is infinite. Any service which can be provided telematically can also be provided by an Internet server. Internet servers could thus potentially deliver banking, travel, pornography or lottery services, to name but a few.

In some countries, certain services may be prohibited or subject to strict regulations obliging the provider to request authorization from a public authority. These national legal systems will normally apply to servers based in the country in question and diffusing information on the Internet. Due to the diversity of national legal systems, a detailed analysis of these restrictions is not possible within the context of this chapter. We would, however, strongly recommend that businesses wishing to provide a service via the Internet check with a local jurist regarding national regulations governing the service in question, and particularly regarding the application of regulations to services provided telematically.

Finally, as regards questions of contract, it should be noted that businesses wishing to provide services via the Internet will either have to purchase a computer capable of undertaking these tasks and conclude a subscription for access to the Internet via a leased line (see Part III, contract n°1), or they will have to conclude a contract with a company already possessing of an Internet server able to undertake this task. The form of this contract may vary. It could, for example, be a contract between a company acting as an information provider and an online server (see Part III, contract n°3), or it could be a contract for the rental of space on the Internet (see Part III, contract n°5).

B. Free provision of services and the Internet

In principle, a service provider (whether it provides access to the Internet or one of the numerous other services available on Internet Web servers) authorized in one country (e.g. in France), and which wishes to provide services in another country (e.g. China or Australia) will have to apply for the authorizations to which the provision of those services are subject in each country, and will have to respect the law of the host country, which may strictly regulate its activities in some cases.

Exceptionally, the countries of the European Union[18] and the member countries of the *North American Free Trade Agreement* (NAFTA)[19] have a system of free provision of services aimed at promoting cross-border trade in services between the parties to the international agreement in question, thus allowing an IAP for example to offer access to a customer established in a state other than its own.

It is important to understand the manner in which these two agreements guarantee the free provision of services, in order to determine exactly what possibilities they offer to IAPs and to telematic service providers. As businesses are well aware, the free provision of services is both a question of law and an economic and financial question of calculating economies of scale.

1. The free provision of services within the European Union

Articles 59 and 60 of the Treaty on European Union constitute the essential legal foundations of the free provision of services within the Union. On the basis of these articles, Community jurisprudence quickly asserted that this free provision of services is guaranteed by the *ban on restrictions*: the regulations and measures adopted in one state in the Union may not hamper or render less attractive the provision of a service by other Community nationals. European law therefore forbids *discriminatory* restrictions (related to the nationality of the provider or to the simple reason that it is established in a member State other than the one in which the service is provided), and *non-discriminatory* restrictions[20] (applicable to any provision of services indifferently) which renders the activity of the Community provider more costly or otherwise discourages it, or which prevents potential customers from using the provider of their choice.

In Community law, it is therefore clear that *a service provider must be able to provide services without hindrance in the other countries of the Union.* As concerns television, the Court of Justice in 1992[21] thus considered that subjecting to authorization upon fulfillment of certain conditions the rebroadcasting, via cable, of televised programs originating in other member states, was contrary to article 59 of the Treaty. This should be applicable *a fortiori* to telematic services provided via the Internet.

These general principles regarding the free cross-border movement of services apply not only to competitive telematic services circulating on the Internet (*professional Web servers or even the user home pages offered by Internet access providers in certain cases*[22]), but also to telecommunications services[23] liberalized by the Directive 90/388/EC, (e.g. the provision of access to the Internet).

Certain exceptions provided in specific cases and under strict conditions, however, authorize non-discriminatory restrictions and sometimes even discriminatory restrictions. It is necessary to examine these, since they will very likely be invoked in the years to come by states wishing to restrict services provided on the Internet. It should be noted that most of the restrictions likely to appear will be non-discriminatory and will consist of subjecting a service originating in another member state to the legislation of the country in which it is provided, but whether discriminatory or non-discriminatory, the restrictions must be proportional to the grounds specified by article 56 (if discrimination is involved) or to general interest objectives (if the restrictions are non-discriminatory). It is precisely the analysis of this criterion of proportionality which is becoming increasingly decisive when assessing the conformity of a restriction with Community law.

Derogations permitting states to stipulate *discriminatory restrictions* are very strict, and come from the wording of article 56 of the Treaty on European Union: the measure must involve state protection of public order, public security or public health.

Furthermore, member states can limit access to the provision of services by other member states via non-discriminatory restrictions, namely restrictions which apply indifferently to both national and foreign providers, only if these restrictions are covered by the concept of general interest[24].

European states could *invoke these derogations a priori to prohibit certain types of services* distributed on the Internet by Web servers, such as services relating to games of chance or servers offering hardcore pornography. In this case, an Internet server would not be able to invoke the principle of the free provision of services as regards legislation regulating sites not protected by a code and therefore easily accessible to minors, and offering hardcore pornography (e.g. pedophilia), or incitations to violence or racial hatred. A site offering gambling could also be strictly regulated or even banned since, in Community law, this is an area subject to the discretion of the states[25].

Similarly, regulations aimed at protecting consumers and workers, intellectual property or professional ethics, could be invoked to limit the provision of a service on the Internet[26].

These derogations cannot, however, be invoked easily by member states, notably because the legality of such derogations by member states must be assessed in light of and in compliance with the general principle of freedom of expression[27] affirmed by article 10 of the *European Convention on Human Rights,* whose importance as concerns the Internet needs no further elaboration.

In addition, the public order exception can be invoked only in the presence of a «real and sufficiently serious threat, affecting a basic interest of society»[28]. Moreover, regardless of whether the derogation concerns public order or the protection of the general interest, it will never be permitted when the restrictive legislation is guided by economic motives.

Finally, the measure adopted must in all cases be proportionate to its objective. The Court has frequently affirmed that the general interest must not be susceptible to protection «by less restrictive rules»[29], or «article 56 of the Treaty must (...) be interpreted such that its effects are limited to that which is necessary to protect the interests it aims to guarantee»[30]. Thus although it is evident that the protection of public morality and of minors is a laudable objective, a prohibition must be proportionate to its objective. The Commission specified in its interpretative communication of December 9, 1993[31] that the Court[32] has introduced practical criteria regarding the proportionality of a restrictive measure. To be examined, then, are *the particular situation of the provider in its country of origin* (for example, if the service in question is a pornographic service, is it regulated in the country of origin and does it respect these regulations?), *the type of activity in question* (in this case a pornographic service), and *the protection of the party for whom the service is intended* (if the country for which the service is intended cannot restrict the activity, how can it protect its minors from this pornographic service?).

2. The free provision of services within the NAFTA

The free provision of services within the NAFTA is guaranteed first of all by the *principle prohibiting discriminatory restrictions.* Pursuant to the NAFTA, American law therefore could not create a discriminatory restriction on the provision of services by a Mexican or Canadian professional Web server operating on the Internet.

Furthermore, by virtue of the NAFTA agreement, a member state is obliged to grant providers from another member state either national treatment (the regime applicable to its own nationals in analogous conditions), or most favoured nation treatment (the most favourable regime applicable by the member state to any other party or country), whichever is most favourable[33].

Consequently, whether IAPs or providers of telematic services via the Internet, all NAFTA nationals benefit from this dual regime of free trade.

To summarize...

 The relationship between the user-subscriber and his or her Internet access provider is governed by an often very summary contract.

 The question of licensing regimes applicable to Internet access providers and telecommunications service providers is governed, within the European Union, by national legal systems. The regimes of the various European states covered in this chapter (Belgium, France, the United Kingdom and Germany) vary considerably. In some cases, no formalities are required (not even a declaration), while in others a declaration is required at various times (start-up of activity, modification of the nature of the services provided, etc.), and in other cases access providers must obtain authorization before providing certain services (access to the Internet via a leased line in France, for example)...

 The one-stop shopping procedure introduced by the European Telecommunications Office (not all of whose signatory states are members of the European Union, while certain members of the Union are not signatories to the Office) is of vital importance for access providers. It allows them, if they wish to provide services in one or more signatory states, to submit their requests for authorization or declarations directly to the European Telecommunications Office, without having to cope with different national procedures and administrative practices, and to predict with greater certainty the length of time needed to obtain a response to their application for authorization.

 No authorization is necessary under American or Canadian law to become an Internet access provider, with the exception, under Canadian law, of companies which have or operate their own infrastructure.

 Under European law, the principle of the free provision of services is unambiguous- a service provider must be able to provide services without hindrance in the other member states of the European Union. These states may, however, stipulate exceptions to this free provision of services in very specific cases and under very stringent conditions, by establishing discriminatory restrictions (for reasons of public order, public safety and public health) and in some cases even non-discriminatory restrictions (if they are in the general interest). The control exercised by European Union authorities in these matters increasingly consists of checking that the measures adopted are proportionate to the objective pursued..

 The *NAFTA* includes a dual provision aimed at guaranteeing a zone of free trade. Firstly, it prohibits discriminatory restrictions. Secondly, it includes national treatment provisions and most favoured nation provisions, whereby a member state is obliged to grant service providers from another member state the most favourable of the two regimes, either the regime applicable by the state to its own nationals in similar conditions, or the most favourable regime applied by the state to other parties or third countries.

chapter two

Copyright on the Internet

Why ask questions?

Many works are distributed or disseminated on the Internet every day. The numbers will give us some idea of this reality: 100,000 articles are published on the Internet daily.

It is vital for the *holder of intellectual property rights,* who is often but not always the author, to be aware of his or her rights regarding work placed, distributed or disseminated on the Internet. He or she must be aware of his or her right to prohibit certain uses of the work, or to be paid for them. *Servers* are also affected by copyright laws-they must know whether or not, and under what conditions, an author's work can be placed on their site. If a server breaks the law, an author could claim sometimes considerable damages from him or her, even if the server was not aware of having infringed the author's rights. The *user* (who may be a company) will also wish to be informed of what he or she may or may not do without the author's authorization. A balance between the rights of authors and the rights of users must therefore systematically be sought. The search for this balance has always formed the backdrop to copyright legislation, but the development of the Internet, giving thousands of people the opportunity to gain immediate access to a perfect copy of a work, has given it an entirely new dimension. It does not suffice, however, to strike a balance in the legal texts. It must also be applied to the real world. Without a doubt, this is the most significant challenge posed by the Internet as regards copyrights. Meeting the challenges of this new technology will be greatly facilitated by the use of other new technology, such as the tattooing of works, for example.

What questions?

 What are copyrights?

 What rules protect copyrights on the Internet?

 Which works are protected by copyright on the Internet?

What are the author's rights as regards a work disseminated on the Internet?

Do Internet users have certain rights vis-à-vis works disseminated on the Internet?

To what extent can a user send, reply to and send to a newsgroup or mailing list a work protected by copyright?

Do Web or F.T.P. servers have to obtain the author's authorization before placing works on their sites?

What rights does the author have as regards surfing on the Web and downloading by Web or F.T.P. servers?

How can the author grant authorization to a user on the Internet? Can authorization be implicit?

What liability is incurred by those who violate copyrights on the Internet?

Introduction

Copyrights are the rights of the author of a work to authorize or forbid certain uses of the work. The term used in the countries of continental Europe is «*droit d'auteur*» or author's rights, while the Anglo-Saxon countries use the expression «copyright». During the period in which the work is protected, certain acts carried out without the authorization of the author may therefore incur the liability of the party committing them.

In principle, intellectual property rights apply to the Internet as elsewhere[1]. Texts, images, graphic works, sound recordings and software are already accessible on the Internet, and audiovisual works will also soon be available. All of these works benefit from the protection afforded by copyright[2].

The Internet's most commendable qualities are precisely those which create certain problems as regards the application of these intellectual property rights to a global network. The Internet is not governed by any central authority, nor is there any body authorized to screen for illegal copies. Furthermore, users of the Internet can copy a work and disseminate it internationally in a matter of seconds. Any work on the network of networks is no more than a sequence of numerical data which can be easily copied, transformed and transferred.

Given the deficiencies of traditional law, Internet users quickly developed codes of conduct (self-regulation) and good network manners (cybermanners). This reaction in Internet circles had as its immediate purpose the ensuring of respect for intellectual property rights, in order to avoid the loss of an author's control over his or her work. This self-regulation and these cybermanners generally oblige users or computer system operators wishing to copy or distribute a work to respect all of the author's rights, both patrimonial and moral. These standards go beyond those of traditional law, since often they stipulate an obligation on the part of the user to request authorization from the author before any copying or distributing of a work, even in cases where it is not certain that this is required by law.

This chapter focuses, however, mainly on an analysis of traditional law. Its objective is to provide companies and users with a clear view of their rights and of the penalties which can be incurred.

I. Which works are protected on the Internet?

A. The general conditions governing the protection of a work

In most national bodies of law, two conditions must normally be met in order for a work to be protected by copyright.

1. *First of all, the work in question must be an original creation.* The way in which this condition is assessed by the courts varies from one country to another and depends on the type of work. Anglo-Saxon countries have a tendency to interpret this criteria broadly, such that the work need only be the result of the work and talents of the author. The countries of continental Europe are generally far more strict, and the work must be imbued with the personality of its author. The application of this criteria is generally tending to become more flexible[3] as a result of the appearance of new types of work where the process of creation involves substantial mechanical intervention.

2. The second condition is different in Anglo-Saxon law (notably in American and Canadian law) and in the legal systems of continental Europe. According to American or Canadian law, the second condition is that *the work be fixed in a tangible medium of expression*[4]. Consequently, an oral work would not be protected. As regards works created at the moment of their distribution via the Internet, such as electronic mail, this condition may be problematic. Certain jurists[5] are of the opinion that, as regards communications made via the Internet, the fixation requirement is met only if the communication is saved on a disk or hard drive. It is our opinion, however, that all types of written communication, including electronic communication, are protected[6].

In the legal systems of continental Europe, the second condition is far less restrictive. Often the author need only have marked the work with his or her own personality in *casting his or her creation into a certain form*. This embodiment does not necessarily require that the work be fixed in a tangible medium. Consequently any work on the Internet could be protected, and questions of fixation need not be raised, as they are in American or Canadian law.

Regardless of the legal system applicable, however, as a consequence of this second condition ideas or concepts are not protected[7].

No other condition need be met in order to benefit from copyright protection. It is not necessary, for example, to deposit the work, as is required for patent protection. This formality may nonetheless prove to be worthwhile in the United States, where it enables the rightholder to obtain compensation and the reimbursement of legal fees in the event of an infringement of rights[8]. Similarly, it is not necessary to affix a copyright symbol (©). We would nonetheless advise fulfilling this formality on the Internet, since it costs nothing and has two advantages. Firstly, it provides other users with an easy way of determining the identity of the copyright owner, and secondly, it guarantees the author that any Internet user who infringes his or her copyrights will not be able to plead good faith at trial[9].

Finally, it is to be noted that certain works which meet originality and fixation requirements are nonetheless not protected. These might include official deeds, titles or short phrases, as well as simple press clippings. The precise enumeration of such works varies from one country to another.

B. The different types of protected work on the Internet

All types of work on the Internet are protected, provided that they fulfil the two conditions mentioned above.

1. Written works

Written works are protected. Consequently *e-mail will be protected*[10], subject to the debate regarding the need for fixation (see above). In any case, when an electronic mail system automatically makes back-up copies, and consequently fixes the work, normally the problem will not arise. Electronic mail attachments are often written texts, which may also be protected.

Articles placed on F.T.P. or Web servers on the Internet are also protected, and this protection continues to apply to articles integrated into a database (like a Web page).

2. *Musical or audiovisual works*

Musical or audiovisual works placed on the Internet (for example a song by the Rolling Stones placed on their Web server) or which circulate on the Internet are protected by copyrights.

3. *Images*

Digitized images circulating on the Internet can be divided into two categories; that of images created by a computer, and that of images produced by the digitization (scanning, for example) of paper documents.

Images created by a computer exist in an original form which may be protected[11], and the electronic reproduction of these images would therefore constitute copyright infringement.

Digitizing protected images into a computer-readable form also constitutes a reproduction which infringes the rights of the original owner of copyright[12], or at least constitutes the illegal creation of a derivative work[13]. If sufficient creativity has been brought to the digitization process, it may be possible for copyrights to accrue to the work in its own right[14].

4. *Software*

Software circulating on the Internet is protected by copyright. While in Canada software constitutes a new category of work[15], in American law software is assimilated into an pre-existing category[16]. In the case of *Lotus Development Corporation v. Borland International Inc.*[17], the Court decided that copyright protection extends to the non-literal aspects of computer programs. The structure of a program's menu, the way it is organized, and the command initials can be protected. There are, however, certain elements of software which may not be protected by copyright. In *Apple Computer Inc. v. Microsoft Corp.*[18], the Court ruled that the overlapping windows used in the Apple system are not themselves protected. Intellectual property rights could thus be infringed only by copies of the particular expression used by Apple's graphical user interface, and even then Apple is only protected against reproductions which are virtually identical.

In Europe, the Directive of May 14, 1991[19] stipulates that computer programs are protected as literary works. The Directive does not define computer programs, but the Commission states in its comments[20] that this term encompasses any form, language, notation or coded set of instructions aimed at causing the computer to execute a particular task or function. As the Directive stipulates, the preparatory design work is included in the term «program». As for algorithms, they are protected but the ideas behind them are not.

Software on the Internet is therefore protected under American, Canadian and European law. This protection is furthermore broad enough to substantially restrict certain uses of software on the Internet.

5. Databases

a. The principles of protection

The Internet contains a large number of databases. These are mostly conventional online databases often available via Telnet or online databases made up of Web pages and of the elements which they incorporate.

In all of these cases, it is necessary to distinguish between three elements within a database: the software which operates the database, the data (the content), and the database itself (the container).

The software is subject to specific protection as a computer program, which we have already mentioned. The content will be protected in its own right, independently of the database, insofar as it constitutes a work protected by copyright. Consequently the creator of a database must obtain the authorization of the author of the data in order to be able to use them[21]. If the content is not protected, however, the database creator can use it as he or she wishes. Furthermore, according to the common position[22] of the European Council with a view to adopting a database directive, the creator will hold rights on the contents. He or she will be able to prohibit the substantial extraction or re-use of these data by a third party. But what is the status of the container, of the selection and the choices involved in the presentation of the database? Is the work of creating a database itself protected?

In the United States, databases are protected provided that they are original in their presentation or arrangement. In the *Feist* case[23], the Supreme Court opted for an interpretation of originality more strict than the customary «sweat of the brow» standard. In particular, the database must comprise a minimum of creativity. In this case, a telephone directory was not considered to be sufficiently original in its compilation.

In Europe, the preparatory text of the database directive[24] provides for the protection of databases defined as compilations of works, data or other independent elements systematically or methodically arranged and individually accessible by electronic or other means[25]. The originality requirement[26], such as it is, which must be met in order to benefit from protection is more or less the same as that developed by the American Supreme Court.

Consequently, most professional databases will not be protected by intellectual property rights, since they will not be original either in their selection or in their arrangement[27]. This does not mean, however, that the creator of such a database will be deprived of all legal claims. In certain cases, he or she could claim copyright protection on the content, and will shortly benefit under European law from the right to prevent the unfair extraction of the contents of the database[28].

b. Web pages

The legal status of Web pages is complex. A Web page comprises numerous «hypertext» links which refer either to works or documents, or to an arborescence of other hypertext links. It will be necessary to consider separately the legal status of a hypertext link and of a Web page.

A hypertext link is a URL or universal resource locator, which is a fact and consequently is not eligible for protection either by copyright or by the *droit d'auteur* of continental Europe[29].

As for Web pages, they refer to documents either on the same site or on another site, and in our opinion they constitute an information access structure which is often original and which should be protected like a database.

II. The rights of the author and of the user regarding protected works in circulation on the Internet

A. The author's rights

1. Who owns copyrights on the Internet?

In principle, the person who created the work will own the copyrights. If the work was created by several people, the rights to the entire work belong to each of them. Given that a large number of works on the Internet are created by dozens, if not hundreds of network users whose identity is not always known, the application of this principle to the Internet will prove to be difficult.

As regards creation within an employment context, under American law the employer or the person who ordered the work shall be considered its author, even if they played no creative role. No such provision having been made in some of the legal systems of continental Europe, the principles of copyright law are strictly applied. Unless the employee assigns his or her rights to the employer, the employee holds the rights on works that he or she creates. The software directive[30] nonetheless stipulates that if a computer program is created within the context of an employment contract, unless otherwise provided by contract all copyrights shall be presumed to have been assigned to the employer. Similarly, as regards audiovisual works, national legislations[31] often stipulate a presumption to the effect that the various authors have assigned their rights to the producer. These rules are particularly important when undertaking contractual negotiations with the employee of a company operating on the Internet.

2. The different types of rights

There are two major categories of copyrights - moral rights and patrimonial rights. Patrimonial rights are related to the author's right to profit from his or her creation, and they endure after the death of the author for a period of 50 years in the United States and Canada and for a period of 70 years in Europe[32].

a. The author's moral rights

Where they are recognized by national legislation, moral rights include: the *right of publication* (the author may choose when to disclose his or her work to the public), the *right of attribution or association* (the author has the right to be associated with the work as its author) and the *right to the integrity of the work* (the author has the right to oppose any modification of his or her work).

These rights may vary greatly in their formulation from one country to another. The American *Copyright Act* does not include any specific acknowledgement of these rights but its provisions concerning derivative works have been interpreted by the courts so as to offer similar protection[33].
All of the countries of the European Union as well as Canada[34] expressly recognize moral rights, but to different degrees. France adopts what is certainly the most dogmatic approach to these rights, while German or English jurisprudence is much more flexible.

On the Internet works are constantly modified and then resent or redistributed, either by their original author or by other users, and this complicates the application of moral rights on the Internet, and particularly the application of the right to the integrity of a work. In consequence, some jurists[35] argue in favour of a genuine relaxation of these rights.

b. The author's patrimonial rights

The classification of these rights varies from one country to another. Anglo-Saxon law, being imbued with pragmatism, does not protect broad categories of rights but rather a list of specific rights. On the other hand, continental legal systems tend more to be organized around broad classifications. This difference in point of view will effect the drafting of assignments of rights contracts; while in countries which apply the concept of copyright, such contracts will necessarily contain very long enumerations of rights, in countries which apply the concept of *droit d'auteur,* contracts could be far more concise.

All legislations nonetheless protect four major types of rights. It is important to remember that the author of a work on the Internet (text, Web page, software, database, etc.) must grant his or her authorization as regards each type of right, and will be able to receive payment in return.

b.1. Right of reproduction
This is the right to authorize or to forbid the fixation of a work in a tangible medium. A work accessed via the Internet is considered to have been reproduced when it is printed out, saved on a disk, or stored on a computer's hard drive[36]. Saving into the RAM of a computer (Random Access Memory), however, which is only transitory, is not generally considered to constitute reproduction[37], except possibly as regards software and databases, concerning which this question is the subject of much debate in European law[38].

b.2. Right of transformation
The author has the right to authorize the translation, adaptation, arrangement or any transformation of his or her work. A user who downloads an image available on the Internet in order to modify it is thus infringing the rights of its author on two counts; the user is infringing the author's right of reproduction, but he or she is simultaneously infringing the author's right to prevent modifications of the work.

b.3. Right of distribution
The right of distribution allows the author to control the way in which his or her work is made available to the public, whether by sale, gift, or by leasing and lending. These latter two rights are the subject of a specific European directive[39].

These rights will likely gain in importance as the practice of selling and leasing software and other works on the Internet emerges and develops. This practice must itself be resituated within the more general framework of the development of network intelligence: networks are increasingly concentrating computing intelligence (software, for example) on the network itself, which enables computers to evolve towards operating purely as terminals. Software leasing is a result of this trend to a certain extent. Leasing furthermore offers the economic advantage of relieving the user of the obligation to purchase software which he or she requires only temporarily.

b.4 . Right of public communication

By virtue of his or her right of public communication, the author controls the direct communication, or communication in the absence of any tangible medium, of his or her work to the public. This right notably includes broadcasting by cable or satellite, which is the subject of a specific European directive[40]. Since the communication must be public, private communication within the family, or even within a company in some countries, do not require the author's permission.

This distinction between distribution rights and public communication rights, which dates back to the analog age, is proving extremely difficult to apply in the age of digital data transmission[41]. Some consider such transmission as distribution[42], while for others it constitutes public communication[43].

In any case, the digital transmission of a work via the Internet is subject to copyright protection, and therefore requires contractual authorization. Since the legal qualification of such transmission is the subject of much debate, it would be useful for contract provisions to be extremely specific in their delimitation of what is authorized and what is not.

B. The legal limits (exceptions) to copyrights: the user's rights

1. The user's rights in general

Although copyrights grant certain rights to the author of a work conveyed by the Internet, they also take into account the interests of users. With a view to achieving a balance and in order not to hinder communication and culture, national legislations always stipulate that certain uses of the work, although they constitute acts of reproduction, transformation, distribution or communication to the public, do not require the author's authorization. These special cases, however, must not adversely affect the normal exploitation of the work nor cause unjustifiable harm to the author's legitimate interests. American law is more flexible in this respect than Canadian and European law.

American law is in fact very flexible, since it authorizes all uses which may be considered fair (*fair use doctrine*)[44]. The notion of fair use originally permitted pedagogical and critical uses[45]. Today four factors are taken into account in determining the fairness of a particular act: the aim and character of the use (commercial or nonprofit), the nature of the work in question, the quantity and substance of the part used in relation to the work as a whole, and the effect of the use on the work's potential market or on its value. It is thus clear that while American law will allow a university student using the Internet to make copies of a certain number of works, the same act on the part of a private company systematically exploiting the Internet's documentary resources may be prohibited.

American law also authorizes a certain number of specific uses as regards libraries and education[46]. This exception allows archives to reproduce or distribute original works if the publication in which the work is to be reproduced and distributed has a pedagogic or scientific rather than a commercial purpose, and if the reproduction contains a copyright notice. This exception is particularly important to the Internet's continued ability to fulfil its role as a disseminator of science and culture on an international level.

Canadian and European law are much less flexible in that they do not contain any general exceptions but rather only certain specific provisions authorizing particular uses. These uses vary from one country to another, but they generally include the following:

- authorization of reproduction for the user's private use (private copy): This exception has traditionally been intended to allow a person to copy a work for his or her own personal use. The scope of this exception obviously depends upon which uses are qualified as «private». Some countries[47] consider that a copy of a work within a company is a private copy. Other countries have a less extensive notion of this legal limit on copyrights[48]. Some legislations[49], however, stipulate that a fee be levied in advance on the sale price of the medium to be used to make private copies, such as on the sale of computer discs, for example.
It is nonetheless not clear that this exception will necessarily be of any great help to users subject to European law, for several reasons. Firstly, the software directive[50] and the draft database direc-

tive[51] do not contain this exception regarding private copies. European law therefore does not permit the copying of software or databases found on the Internet, even for private use. Furthermore, and more generally, it is uncertain whether or not the private copy exception regarding analog mediums is applicable to the digital era, since current legislation rarely governs electronic copies. A majority of jurists moreover consider that the private copy exception does not apply to digital communications and is therefore inapplicable to the Internet[52].

- authorization to reproduce, when reproduction is limited to short quotations.

The conditions of application here vary from one country to another. Some countries require that the quotation be reproduced for critical or journalistic purposes. In addition, this exception does not apply to musical or audiovisual works on the Internet.

2. The user's rights as regards software

The European directive on the legal protection of computer programs[53] defines the four cases in which the user need not obtain the author's permission before making a copy: a copy necessary in order to use the software or in order to determine the ideas which underlie it (provided, of course, that the user is authorized to use the software), a back-up copy, or a copy for decompilation purposes (for purposes of interoperability and in accordance with strict conditions established by the directive).

American and Canadian law also stipulate certain cases of legal software copying: a back-up copy, a copy necessary in order to use the software[54] provided that it be destroyed «should the user no longer be in legitimate possession of the software program»[55], and a copy for decompilation have been authorized as applications falling within the *«fair use»* exception[56].

In consequence, there are very few cases in which the author's permission is not required. Yet the volume of traffic in pirated software on the Internet is an indication of the difficulty of enforcing legal protections. The industry has developed certain self-regulatory bodies such as the *Software Publishers Association* (SPA), which monitor electronic newsgroups in search of illegally distributed software. The SPA then asks the offenders to remove the illegal software, purchase legal copies, and pay a fine equal to the price of the software, upon penalty of legal action[57].

3. The user's rights on the Internet

a. The user and electronic mail (e-mail)

Two questions arise regarding e-mail:

a.1. Can a user send a protected work via e-mail?

In principle, a user may not send a protected work via e-mail without the authorization of its author. Sending such mail would in fact imply the reproduction of the work by the sender, or at the very least its communication to the public[58]. The user must therefore obtain the author's permission. Although this solution is not disputed in the context of a newsgroup (dispatch to several persons), the sub-committee of the Canadian Information Highway Advisory Committee[59] as well as various European authors[60] consider that point to point electronic mail between individuals, even if it contains a protected work, does not constitute copyright infringement, since the transmission between two persons is not public.

a.2. Can the addressee of an e-mail copy it and:

1) return it to the original author;
2) send it to a newsgroup or to a discussion list;
3) send it to a specified third party.

Copying and forwarding messages sent by e-mail is a customary and well-known practice on the Internet. In fact, it is a preferred method of communication there. Let us consider the different hypotheses. Can the addressee copy e-mail and...

1) Return it to its original author (reply):

The reply function, which permits the user who has received a message to reply by copying the message received, does not seem to pose any problems. This use is covered by the private use exception and in any case does not harm the author in any way.

2) Send it to a newsgroup or to a discussion list:

In the context of a newsgroup or of a discussion list, users are aware of the practice of copying and forwarding their messages. Certain authors have therefore raised the possibility of an implicit assignment or waiver of copyright[61], but no consensus has yet been reached on the subject.

3) Send it to a specified third party (forward):
Use of the forward function, which enables the addressee of a letter to copy it and retransfer it to one or more third parties of his or her choice, seems to be risky in terms of copyright law in the absence of the author's permission. Such use could also constitute a breach of the sender's privacy rights.

Given these uncertainties, it is advisable either to obtain the author's permission before copying a work, or to retranscribe the information and modify its expression, since the author's right does not protect the ideas but only their expression[62].

b. The user and file transfers (F.T.P.)

As regard file transfers (F.T.P.), a distinction should be made between two actors in the chain of transmission, these being the server and the user.

b.1. Servers
The *server* - understood in its general sense, evidently we refer to the administrator of the server - must first of all copy the file onto his or her computer, thereby reproducing it, and then he or she makes it available to the public, thus committing an act of electronic communication (distribution or communication to the public). The server will thus have to obtain a twofold authorization from the author: permission to reproduce the work and permission to communicate it electronically. An F.T.P. server therefore cannot distribute files (texts, software, etc.), without the authorization of their author, which may be implicit (for example, the author who places files on the server using the *put* function). Of course, in the event that the servers are themselves authors, as is often the case on the Internet, obviously they have no obligation to obtain authorizations regarding their own works.

b.2. Users
The *user* may download the file (*get* function). This act constitutes reproduction and, consequently, the user must obtain the author's permission. If the user acts for private and personal purposes, can he or she benefit from the private use exception? As we have seen, this exception is hotly debated as regards electronic works and its

application is expressly excluded as concerns software and databases under European law. Consequently, it is advisable to obtain the author's permission, even in cases where the author's permission appears to be implicit (see below).

In practical terms, the most frequent cases that arise are the following:
1) the user downloads software distributed as shareware or freeware (see below). Within certain limits, the author is considered to have authorized the user to use the software.
2) the user downloads a file, for example a word processing file, placed on the Internet by its author for widespread communication. In this case, the author does not exercise his or her patrimonial rights, but nonetheless conserves them. The user is here restricted only by the author's moral rights and cannot, for example, modify the work or claim it as his or her own.
3) the user downloads a file containing a notice specifying the limits within which the file may be used. As we will see, this is a case of explicit authorization, in which the conditions of use for the work are specified. The user must therefore verify his or her conformity in all respects with the various conditions stipulated before using the file.

c. The user and surfing on the Web

As regards surfing on the Web, it is necessary to distinguish between two groups of operations carried out successively by the user to the consultation of Web pages in order to locate the address of the server containing the file of interest to the user, and the final operation consisting of downloading the relevant file.

c.1. Consulting Web pages.
Once again, the role of the server is distinct from that of the user. The *server* must first of all copy the Web page onto his or her computer, thereby reproducing it, and then he or she makes it available to the public, thus committing an act of electronic communication (distribution or communication to the public). The server will therefore have to obtain the author's permission on two counts: permission to reproduce the work and permission to communicate it electronically.

As for the *user*, he or she downloads Web pages into the RAM of his or her computer. Depending upon the qualification of this operation (as constituting reproduction or not), the user either does or does not have to obtain the permission of the Web page author. That said, legal discussion serves little purpose here, because this consultation is the very foundation of netsurfing, and thus it will almost always be considered that the author of a Web page implicitly assigns the right of consultation to all users.

c.2. Downloading files from Web pages
Downloading a file from a Web page is treated in copyright law in the same way as is downloading a file from an F.T.P. server.

C. The contractual limits[63] to copyrights: contracts concluded between the author and the user

Servers or users wishing to carry out an act which is regulated by copyright law must obtain the authorization of the rightholder, whether explicitly or implicitly.

1. Explicit authorization

Authorization to distribute a work given by its author to a *server* should ideally take the form of a contract. This is certainly the safest path for the server and we would strongly recommend it. In fact, as regards a subject as fiercely debated as the application of traditional copyright law to the Internet, a clear and precise contract is a far better option than the sometimes unpredictable interpretations offered by jurisprudence. These contracts will always be restrictively interpreted in favour of the author (for example, if the author assigns his or her right of reproduction as regards the printing of a book, this does not mean that he or she has assigned the right of reproduction as regards storing the work in the memory of a computer). Similarly, the assignment of patrimonial rights does not include the assignment of moral rights[64] which, moreover, are inalienable in many countries[65]. Finally, in many European countries, some of these contracts are very specifically regulated.

As regards *the users*, concluding a contract between each of them and the author is hardly feasible in the context of an open, international network like the Internet. Explicit authorization will thus take the form of a notice affixed by the author, usually at the beginning of his or her work, specifying the limits (for example non-commercial use) within which the work may be used[66].

There are two types of software authorization which should be noted in this respect - shareware and freeware[67]. Shareware is a widespread means of publishing computer programs, which enables the creator to save the usual marketing costs by distributing his or her work via a computer network. The author allows network users to download the software and to try it out for a certain period of time. If the user wishes to use the software beyond this period, he or she must send payment to the author, and failure to do so constitutes an infringement of copyright. As concerns freeware, the user is under no legal obligation to pay.

2. Implicit authorization

Authorization may also be implicit. In the context of a newsgroup, as we have seen, it is generally considered that the sender of a letter to the group has implicitly authorized the reproduction of this letter for all the members of the group. Conversely, there is no implicit authorization for this letter to be sent to other newsgroups. The author is considered to have authorized all uses of his or her work which can be expected upon sending email[68].

As regards establishing hypertext links between Web pages, a doctrine is developing whereby the construction of a Web page implies its author's implicit authorization for other Web page creators to establish links to his or her page[69], since life on the Web is based on the possibility of joining pages anywhere on the Web via hypertext links. It is clear that this theory could create problems. A protected work, legally reproduced in a Web page in virtue of the fair use defence, could be joined by a hypertext link established by another author to an entirely different context, such as a commercial context, where this fair use defence would no longer apply[70]. This is probably why netiquette recommends requesting authorization from the author of a Web page before linking to his or her page.

The legal status of this implicit authorization, however, is not the same in North America and in Europe. While American jurisprudence tends to admit the doctrine of implicit authorization fairly easily, particularly as regards the Internet, it seems to us that European jurisprudence will be more reluctant to embrace this theory. In fact, Europe has always adopted a more dogmatic view of intellectual property rights, and is therefore more hesitant to accept the implicit assignment of these rights.

Does this mean that most Internet users, who only rarely have explicit authorization to download a particular file, are liable to be incur penalties? We do not think so, since users could be exonerated from potential liability by the application of certain common law mechanisms regarding obligations, such as good faith, legitimate uncertainties or the implicit waiver of a right. Nevertheless, we cannot repeat often enough that in matters as new and consequently as controversial as this, clear and explicit authorization is always the best solution.

III. Penalties

Infringing copyrights, which is known in law as an *act of forgery*, can lead to two types of reaction on the part of the author:
- an injunction, which consists of preventively prohibiting the committing of an unlawful act. This action will be particularly useful as regards Internet servers.
- an action in civil or criminal liability against the offending party. In this respect, we refer the reader to Chapter 9 (Liability on the Internet).

It is interesting to note, in the context of copyright infringement on the Internet, that under American law the copyright infringement includes no knowledge (scienter) or intent requirement. Consequently, the offending party can be prosecuted even if he or she did not know that the work in question was protected[71]. Intent is only a factor when calculating damages. This severe rule notably facilitates the penalizing of servers which distribute illegal copies of protected works.

To summarize...

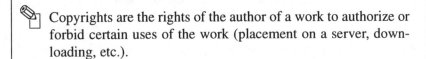

Copyrights are the rights of the author of a work to authorize or forbid certain uses of the work (placement on a server, down-loading, etc.).

Respect for copyrights on the Internet is required by law, by self-regulation and also by good *cybermanners*.

All works (written, musical and audiovisual works, software, databases, Web pages, etc.) are protected insofar as they are orig-inal and, depending on the case, insofar as they are either cast into a certain form or fixed in a tangible medium of expression. Consequently, no copyright registration or symbol is required.

The author has economic rights and, under certain legal sys-tems, moral rights. In particular, the author's permission is required in order to modify the work, reproduce it or commu-nicate it to the public.

Users have rights, too. Consequently, under American law they need not obtain authorization in order to make 'fair use' of the work.

In principle, anyone wishing to send a protected work by elec-tronic mail must request the author's permission. The addressee of an e-mail can return it to the sender (*reply*) and, under cer-tain legal systems, he or she can send it to a newsgroup or to a mailing list, insofar as the original sender could not reasonably have expected his or her message to be private (*Newsgroup*). The addressee of an e-mail cannot, however, forward the e-mail without having obtained the author's permission.

F.T.P. and Web servers must obtain authorization from the authors of works that they wish to include on their sites.

Users can download a file provided that they respect the condi-tions stipulated by the author. They may also consult Web pages.

The author's authorization may be explicit (contracts with a server, notice of rights at the beginning of a document intended for users, *shareware* and *freeware*) or, in some cases and under some legal systems, authorization may be implicit (works sent to a *Newsgroup* or to a mailing list).

 Violations of copyright very often and in most legal systems lead to civil and criminal liability.

chapter 3

Freedom of expression

Why ask questions?

Mailing lists and newsgroups constitute forums for debate between users with different perspectives. As on Web servers or elsewhere on the Internet, here again the balance between freedom of expression and respect for public order, public morality, privacy and the reputations of others is not an easy one to maintain. Pornographic messages and incitations to hate and violence are disseminated over the Internet with increasing frequency. Internet access providers, servers, companies and private individuals have to be aware of the legal limits imposed on the dissemination of information on the Internet in order not to incur liability. This knowledge is all the more vital for companies providing broadcasting (via the Web. for example) and distribution services (via electronic mail, for example), the content of which is at the limits of legality (such as in the case of certain pornographic messages).

What questions?

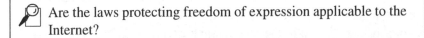 Are the laws protecting freedom of expression applicable to the Internet?

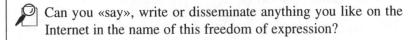 Can you «say», write or disseminate anything you like on the Internet in the name of this freedom of expression?

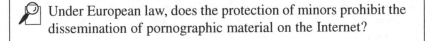 What is the *Decency Communications Act* and what impact does it have in American law?

Under European law, does the protection of minors prohibit the dissemination of pornographic material on the Internet?

Introduction

Freedom of expression, in its simplest form, is the freedom to express oneself and to communicate. This freedom, which is of fundamental importance to all democratic societies, is of a dual nature: on the one hand everyone has the right to *communicate and to circulate* information and ideas to others, and on the other hand everyone has a right of access to the information and ideas disseminated by others. The scope of this freedom is extremely broad, and it covers even offensive, shocking or worrying information[1] as well as commercial information.

The Internet is a medium lauded for its accessibility, and as such freedom of expression is one of its pillars, but the Internet has also augmented the *practical consequences* of exercising this freedom of expression to an international scale. Any citizen with access to a computer and a modem can, with very little difficulty and at very little cost, disseminate his or her own version of the truth to the public at large, or request and receive information.

This justifiable optimism must, however, be tempered. The other side of the coin is that the Internet, like any other medium, can be used for example to criticise others, to distribute pornography, or to threaten other users. American, Canadian and European law is not disempowered in the face of such excesses. They foresee limits on freedom of expression.

I. Internet and freedom of expression in the United States and in Canada

A. The affirmation of freedom of expression

Under American and Canadian law, freedom of expression is protected by the American and Canadian constitutions[2], by *specific laws* which may vary from one jurisdiction to another, and by the *common law* (the law created by judicial precedent)[3]. This freedom fully applies to electronic communications, which include notably the various operations of electronic mail.

B. The limits of freedom of expression

Although American and Canadian law affirm and protect freedom of expression, they nonetheless recognize that it has certain limits.

1. Defamation

In the United States and in Canada, within the frameworks established by the American and Canadian constitutions, defamation is for the most part governed by common law rules[4].

We will successively examine the criteria which must be met under Canadian and American law in order for defamation to occur on the Internet, and the defences which the author of such defamation could plead in order to relieve him or herself of liability.

a. Criteria of defamation

1) For defamation to be established, there must first of all be *a published communication*. Under American law, it is clear that this publication requirement does not foreclose on the possibility of defamation occurring on a computing system. On the Internet, publication will take the form, for example, of messages posted to

a newsgroup, of articles disseminated via an electronic periodical, or of files disseminated by F.T.P. or Web servers[5].

As regards the liability which may be incurred by the author of defamatory remarks, one of the criteria to be considered is the written or verbal nature of the defamation, since written or printed words are considered to be more harmful than spoken words[6]. In this respect, the Internet is a very particular environment. One of its distinguishing features is certainly that it is a rapid means of communication, like the telephone for example, yet it nevertheless remains a means of written and more or less permanent communication. Given the spontaneity of electronic mail communications it is possible, for example, to read a provocative message in a newsgroup and to send a response expressing one's discontent within the space of a few seconds, very much like the swift verbal retort that almost everyone has at some point made and later regretted. Yet this communication is permanent in some sense, and capable of provoking the same degree of damage and liability as any written communication.

2) A «defamatory» communication is further defined as a communication which tends to harm the reputation of another person, «so as to lower him in the estimation of the community or to deter third persons from associating or dealing with him»[7]. It is not necessary, then, to prove actual harm to reputation, nor the actual refusal of third persons to associate with that person, but only that the words in question are likely to have this effect[8].

Furthermore, «community» does not necessarily refer to the community as a whole, but rather to the «relevant» community[9]. In the case of a message posted on an Internet newsgroup, for example, the relevant community could well be only the other users of the forum, which sometimes constitute fairly specific professional communities[10], thus lowering the threshold for a finding of defamation.

As might be expected, defamation on the Internet raises delicate problems of evaluating the lowering of a person in the estimation of the community as a result of defamatory remarks, but it also raises problems as regards determining the community concerned by the message, which will have an impact on the evaluation of harm to the victim[11]. First of all, as regards assessing the actual damage to a person's reputation in the estimation of the community, it seems reasonable to distinguish between professional forums, which are often moderated, and non-professional and unmoderated forums, which are consequently often much more informal and often more inflammatory in tone. A defamatory message posted to a professional newsgroup may seriously lower the victim in the eyes of other users of that forum, and may therefore damage the victim's professional reputation. On the other hand, messages posted to non-professional and unmoderated newsgroups[12] should be less likely to constitute defamation or, at the very least, should be less likely to result in significant damage, since they will often have less considerable impact on the opinion of the community[13].

As regards the community to be considered when determining the existence of defamation or when evaluating damages, the interconnectivity of the Internet means that defamatory remarks can *potentially* reach a very wide audience, and since it will be difficult to determine exactly how many people actually saw the remarks in question, a judge may assess damages on the basis of the number of *potential* readers. Although such an approach is clearly misleading, there is a serious risk that judges will follow it, and awards for damages caused by defamation on the Internet could consequently be high.

b. How can liability for defamation be avoided?

a. At common law in the United States and in Canada, *the truth or justification* of a defamatory remark is a complete defence to an action for defamation[14].

b. Another defence common to both Canadian and American law is that of «privilege»[15]. Under Canadian law *qualified privilege* covers notably statements published in the public's interest while carrying out a recognized duty, protecting a public or otherwise important interest, or reporting on public proceedings[16]. Under American law, qualified privilege applies to any *fair comment* published and relating to issues of public interest, if the statement is made in good faith and with the sincere conviction of its truthfulness[17]. *Fair comment* constitutes an adequate defence under Canadian law; the statement must be made in good faith and must concern an issue of public interest but, contrary to American law, it must be based on facts which are true[18]. This defence of qualified privilege is therefore clearly more limited than the American standard[19]. Apart from these admittedly significant differences, however, this defence should cover, under both legal systems, a considerable number of instances of defamatory remarks made in good faith on public political forums on the Internet.

2. *Other restrictions on freedom of expression*

Other traditional restrictions on freedom of expression also apply to the Internet. Thus an Internet user cannot, on the basis of his or her freedom of expression, disseminate *speech advocating lawless action* or *fighting words*. Similarly, criminal law in North America habitually prohibits *threats* and the use of communications systems to convey them[20]. Finally, traffic in *pornographic and in obscene material* is rarely protected by the principle of freedom of expression[21]. Newsgroup users who had arranged, via computer, to produce «snuff films» (pornographic films in which the person filmed is actually murdered on film), were convicted under American law[22].

One of the difficulties as regards the Internet lies in the fact that American courts have been unwilling to find a national standard for obscenity. The American States are therefore free to legislate and to limit the availability of obscene material differently. To avoid prosecution, those who disseminate obscene material or messages will therefore have to respect the most severe of these different criteria[23]. With the exception of child pornography, which is governed by separate legal criteria[24], this situation therefore implies that system operators must be familiar not with just one obscenity standard, but with fifty standards, or even more if the system is international[25]. In the case of *U.S.* v. *Thomas*[26], for example, further to an order placed by a client in Memphis, Tennessee, the operators of a bulletin board system located in California were convicted in Memphis, under the local community standards applicable in Memphis[27]. It is interesting to note that this decision was appealed, and that one of the appellants' arguments was that the decision established an international obscenity standard, which is unconstitutional, and which is furthermore that of the community of Memphis, Tennessee[28]! The appeal, however, was rejected[29].

The *Telecommunications Regulation Bill,*which was recently adopted by the American government and which includes the *Communications Decency Act*, prohibits the presentation by means of an interactive computer service of indecent material in a way which is accessible to a minor. The indecent nature of the material is determined on the basis of the standards of the local community[30]. Since all material on the Internet can be accessible to minors in every country and in every American state, determining prohibited indecent content on the Internet could imply consideration of the most severe of American local community standards.

These provisions are already being contested on constitutional grounds by the American Civil Liberties Union, and many authors are of the opinion that they will be held to be unconstitutional due to overbreadth, and because the government has not used the least restrictive means possible to achieve its purpose[31].

II. INTERNET AND FREEDOM OF EXPRESSION IN EUROPE

A. The affirmation of freedom of expression

Freedom of expression is one of the foundations of a democratic and pluralist society[32]. As such, it is incorporated into most European constitutions.

Fundamental human rights, and particularly the *Covenant on Civil and Political Rights* and the *European Convention on Human Rights* of the Council of Europe, are furthermore integrated into the jurisprudence of the European Court of Justice as a general principle whose respect it assures[33]. Article 10 of the *Convention*, which guarantees freedom of expression and the right to transborder information flows[34], clearly applies to electronic communications[35] and in particular to all forms of communication on the Internet.

B. The limits of freedom of expression

In Europe, as in North America, freedom of expression is not absolute[36]. Article 10.2 of the *European Convention on Human Rights* in fact stipulates that national legislatures can adopt exceptions to the principle of free expression if three cumulative conditions are fulfilled[37]. The exception must be clearly and precisely prescribed by law, it must meet an imperative social need and it must be proportionate to that need, and finally it must have a legitimate purpose such as national security, crime prevention, the protection of public morality, or the protection of the reputation or the rights of others. Under the supervision of the Commission and of the European Court of Human Rights, national authorities therefore have considerable room to manoeuvre as regards the stipulating of limitations on freedom of expression. These restrictions, which are usually foreseen by European national laws, permit the suppression of most tortious circulation of information on the Internet (defamation, threats, obscene publications, speech advocating lawless action, etc.).

As regards defamation, the European Court of Human Rights makes a distinction[38] between value judgements and objective facts. According to this jurisprudence, no national legislation can oblige Internet users to prove the accuracy of their value judgements in order to escape conviction for defamation. On the other hand, national legislatures can require that Internet users prove the truth of the objective facts (provable facts) which they put forward. This distinction enables Internet users, and in particular newsgroup participants, to assess the limits of their freedom in practical terms. In addition, and in order to assure free political debate, it will be more difficult to qualify as defamation criticisms regarding politicians in the execution of their duties than the same criticisms made regarding private individuals[39].

Similarly, messages circulated on the Internet which advocate lawless action, racist or xenophobic statements, and calls to violence or terrorism are unlikely to be protected by the principle of freedom of expression. It should be remembered that servers advocating violence were recently banned in France (calvacom).

In general, all attacks on public order and on the public morality, and in particular the circulation of obscene messages, are prohibited. However, this assertion could be qualified by the position of the Commission, which considers that freedom of expression encompasses the projection of pornographic films, provided that the protection of minors is guaranteed and that no adult is confronted with the projection of such a film without having intended to see it, or even against his or her wishes[40]. Internet servers circulating pornographic services will therefore benefit from the protection afforded by freedom of expression as long as they provide effective protection for minors, for example by requiring users to enter an access code which is only granted to adults.

Among the countries of the Council of Europe, however, there is no uniform criteria of morality common to all of the European states. That which may seem normal in a country where standards are liberal, such as the Netherlands, may not be in a country of traditionally more puritan standards such as Ireland. The European states nonetheless unanimously prohibit child pornography, as do the countries of North America.

To summarize...

 Freedom of expression is protected in the United States and in Canada by the constitutions, by particular laws and by the *common law*. In Europe, the *European Convention on Human Rights* provides full protection for the freedom of all Internet users to express themselves, communicate, and disseminate and receive information and ideas. The scope of application of this freedom is extremely broad-it covers information which is offensive, shocking or worrying, as well as commercial information.

 The American, Canadian and European legal systems do, however, stipulate certain limits to freedom of expression, such as defamation, the dissemination of incitations to illegal activity and the dissemination of certain pornographic material.

 The *Decency Communications Act*, which is part of the *Telecommunications Regulation Bill* adopted by the United States in February 1996, prohibits the presentation via an interactive computer service of indecent material in a manner accessible to minors. This provision, which carries criminal and civil penalties, applies to most of the pornographic services accessible on the Internet, thereby rendering them illegal under American law. The *American Civil Liberties Union* has already contested the constitutionality of this law.

 The law of the Council of Europe, which is integrated into European law, is more flexible with regard to pornography disseminated on the Internet than American law, since pornographic message servers on the Internet are covered by freedom of expression as long as they provide effective protection for minors, for example, in our view, by asking users for an access code (such as a credit card number) which can only be granted to adults.

chapter 4

Protection of privacy
on the Internet

Why asking questions?

The development of marketing and commerce on the Internet is greatly conditioned by privacy protection laws. On the Internet, it is extremely easy to develop computerized personal data files - customer information, occasional contacts or surfers who have left their details in «guestbooks» are recorded, stored and analyzed. *Consumer profiles* are created. Although the law does not forbid the creation of such files, it does strictly regulate the conditions under which they can be constituted, and it *restricts the export of personal data* to other countries (transfers from the subsidiary of a multinational to the parent company via the Internet, for example). It also stipulates the technical protections which must be provided by those transmitting such data on the network. These laws constitute economic parameters which businesses must take into account.

Furthermore, the protection of employee privacy, particularly under European legal systems, significantly limits *an employer's control over employee activities on the Internet.* Even under American and Canadian law, however, employers wishing to monitor employee communications on the Internet would be well advised to clearly inform employees of the possibility of monitoring and to obtain their consent.

Generally, and in addition to the ethical reasons for respecting the privacy of others, it is financially hazardous (civil liability) for businesses to conduct their commercial activities on the network without regard for the right of each individual to a certain degree of privacy protection.

What questions?

 Is privacy protected on the Internet?

Can government authorities electronically monitor communications on the Internet?

 Does the protection of privacy in respect of electronic monitoring prevent access providers and servers from carrying out their work?

 Can employers monitor employees use of the Internet?

 What impact do regulations on the computerized processing of personal data (computer filing) have on business activities on the Internet?

Introduction

The speed, power and storage capacity of computers constitute a serious threat to privacy. The Internet considerably augments this risk, on the one hand by making communication between computers which may be ten thousand kilometers apart easy and affordable, and on the other hand by rendering wide-scale electronic publication accessible to all.

The *general laws, and the jurisprudence* which has developed as regards privacy, offer protections against these dangers. In most of the states of the European Union and in North America, privacy has rapidly come to be viewed as an essential value which must be protected. The legal means adopted to this end vary from one country to another - in some, a law asserts a general principle of privacy protection while in others jurisprudence has produced the same result. The purpose, in any case, is to acknowledge the right to privacy of every individual: the right to a zone of privacy, to a certain degree of confidentiality, and to a private life which must be permitted to remain private. These basic principles are of a general nature, and are thus applicable to the various new technological developments[1]. They are applicable to all types of networks, whether open or closed, including the Internet and its players, such as access providers, service providers and users. These laws and jurisprudence applicable to the Internet evidently restrict the unauthorized circulation of information representing an invasion of privacy. Consequently users, businesses or Internet operators are strongly recommended to exercise as much caution as possible before disclosing any text or image, for example, which could clearly be detrimental to the privacy of another person and for which breach of privacy they could accordingly be liable.

The threat to privacy represented by the Internet came to light in the media with the «publication» on the Web, in violation of intellectual property rights, of the book by Dr. C. Gubbler and Mr. Gonod on the medical and political history of the former President of the French Republic, François Mitterand. *Le grand secret* was available on the Internet, just a few days after its sale in bookstores had been banned[2]. The scale of the network and its effects, the difficulties of implementing the decisions of national courts in an international context, and especially the media infatuation of this event aside, the problem is classic: the right of privacy limits the freedom of expression of the author which, as regards certain important matters of public interest, is reinforced by the public's «right» to information. The author's freedom of expression and sometimes the «public's right to information» on the one hand confront the privacy of a head of State and his family on the other. Between the two is a delicate balance, assessed on a case by case basis by magistrates called upon to decide, in the particular case before them, which of these freedoms and values will prevail. The Internet adds nothing new to this particular problem, and servers disseminating information which constitutes a breach of privacy may face an action to prohibit diffusion or in civil liability.

We will not, however, analyze the regulations and self-regulations which establish general principles of privacy protection here, not for lack of interest but rather in order to focus on the texts which specifically govern the *monitoring of electronic files and mail,* and *the computerized processing of personal data*, areas whose importance to the Internet is not difficult to grasp.

I. Protection of the confidentiality of files, mail and communications circulating on the Internet

Many users circulate confidential files, dossiers or mail via the Internet, or store them on a computer connected to the Internet. In this interconnected world, the temptation to infringe this confidentiality may be great, both for public authorities and private individuals alike. As regards such behaviour, the law in Europe and in North America distinguishes between «monitoring» by a public authority or by a private individual.

A. Confidentiality and government authorities

1. Under American and Canadian law

In the United States and in Canada, privacy protection in the *public sector* is guaranteed by the constitutional right to privacy, which applies fully to electronic communications[3], and which therefore applies to the Internet. This constitutional protection applies only to government bodies or to «state action».

By virtue of privacy protection laws or dispositions (the *Electronic Communications Privacy Act*[4] in the United States and the *Criminal Code*[5] in Canada), *the interception of electronic communications* by law enforcement agencies requires a search warrant or other authorization[6]. Thus the police cannot intercept the contents of e-mail, or of F.T.P. or Telnet transfers without a warrant. It should be noted, however, that the American *ECPA* authorizes law enforcement authorities to employ technical devices which can be used to record either the numbers dialed from a telephone (pen register), or the telephone numbers of all callers to a given telephone (trap and trace device)[7]. The application of these provisions to the Internet would probably relieve American law enforcement authorities of the need for a search warrant as regards the identification of computers establishing a connection with a computer under surveillance.

It is also worth noting that the American *ECPA* prohibits *access, without a search warrant, to information stored in a computer*[8].

Finally, under American law certain professional telematic Internet servers will probably benefit from the additional protection provided by the 1980 *Privacy Protection Act*[9]. The *Act* notably *protects electronic publishers against the search and seizure of all «material related to the fulfillment of their work»* in the possession of a party disseminating a form of public communication in the context of or affecting interstate commerce[10]. This protection against seizure does not, however, cover cases where there is a valid reason to believe that the person in possession of the data has committed or is committing a crime relating to this material[11], or when immediate seizure is necessary to prevent a human being from being seriously injured or even killed[12].

2. *Under European law*

As regards protection against monitoring by public authorities, the European States are governed by their national legislation and constitutions[13], and by the *European Convention on Human Rights*. The *Convention*, whose scope of application is sufficiently broad to include the Internet[14], is particularly interesting in that it limits[15] the measures adopted by the national legislatures of signatory States permitting the monitoring of communications in general, and of communications on the Internet in particular by government authorities, as well as their power to adopt such measures.

Section 8 of the *Convention*, which guarantees a right of privacy and of the confidentiality of correspondence, has two consequences for public authorities. On the one hand, they must ensure the respect of privacy between private individuals (see below, section B) and, on the other hand, they must themselves refrain from all interference, unless certain cumulative conditions are satisfied (see s. 8 para. 2). The exemption must also be prescribed by law[16], and the interference must be necessary and proportionate by the standards of a democratic society, and finally it must have as its objective either national security, public safety, the economic welfare of the country, public order and crime prevention, the protection of health or morality, or the protection of the rights and freedoms of others. The cases in which a European public authority can breach the confidentiality, secrecy and privacy rights are thus strictly limited.

On September 6, 1978, the European Court of Human Rights declared that, although telephone conversations[17] are not mentioned in section 8 of the *Convention*, they form an integral part of the concepts of «privacy» and «correspondence», and consequently benefit from the same protection[18]. On the basis of this section 8 of the *Convention* and of the jurisprudence of the Court, the member States of the Council of Europe are now obliged to adopt *clear and precise regulations regarding situations in which the interception of telephone or electronic communications is authorized.* In our opinion, the confidentiality of the *various types of interpersonal communication on the Internet (e-mail, Chat, Telnet) also clearly merit this protection.* Circulating a message electronically does nothing to alter the sender's privacy right.

In application of this European jurisprudence, the French law 91-646 of July 10, 1991 on the confidentiality of correspondence transmitted via telecommunications[19] stipulates the cases in which public authorities may record the content of information transmitted, or in which they may trace the numbers calling to a specific device, or dialed from a specific unit (Zoller device). The law limits this violation of the confidentiality right to cases of necessity justified by public interest concerns, and prescribed by law. The law applies to two types of interception: legal interception, which is only possible in the context of a judicial inquiry and will only be authorized in the event of a sufficiently serious offence[20]; and interception for administrative or security reasons[21], which must be based on one of the legal grounds for interception enumerated at section 3 of the law (such as the prevention of terrorism or crime, for example).

Similarly, under English law the Secretary of State may, on the basis of the *Interception of Communications Act* of 1985[22] issue interception warrants for reasons of national security or for reasons of crime prevention and detection in cases of sufficiently serious crime, or to safeguard the economic interests of the country.

B. Confidentiality between private parties

As we have seen, the cases in which a public authority can monitor Internet communications, or the content of mail or files circulating on it, are strictly regulated. The situation is evidently more extreme as regards private individuals, who may incur criminal sanctions if they violate this privacy right.

1. Under American and Canadian law

As regards *unlawful access,* section 2701 of the *ECPA* prohibits unlawful access to communications stored on a computer[23]. Evidently access on the part of computer system administrators to files stored on their own systems does not constitute unlawful access[24].

The American *ECPA* punishes by fine or imprisonment «anyone who intentionally intercepts or attempts to intercept» any interstate electronic communication[25]. This sanction clearly applies to the «misappropriation» and monitoring of communications circulating on the Internet (e-mail, Telnet, etc.). The *intentional disclosure or use of the content* of this communication by a person who has knowledge of its illegal interception, or who could reasonably suppose that this is the case, is also prohibited by the *ECPA*[26]. This clearly applies to the behaviour of the Internet user who disseminates information, for example in newsgroups, which has clearly been obtained in violation of privacy rules. The Canadian *Criminal Code* also prohibits the interception of communications which may reasonably be expected to be confidential[27].

These regulations do not prevent system operators, including IAPs, servers (Web, newsgroups, etc.) and finally anyone who manages an electronic communications service or whose facilities are used in the electronic transmission of communications[28] *on the Internet, from completing their mission, for several reasons.*

Firstly, the scope of the prohibition on interception is currently under debate, and some jurists suggest that it applies only to real-time monitoring by the system operator, and not to the monitoring of a file which has already been transmitted over the Internet and which is now stored on a computer[29]. As regards e-mail systems which operate by storing and retransmitting messages then, this would mean that the same message which is not susceptible to interception during transmission, could legally be monitored once it is stored[30] since, as we have seen, system operators have lawful access to files stored on their own systems.

Secondly, the laws on the confidentiality of communications themselves provide system operators with frequent exceptions to the prohibition on intercepting private communications.

Both section 2 of the *ECPA* and section 184 of the Canadian *Criminal Code* stipulate that system operators and their employees may intercept private communications when such monitoring is necessary to the proper administration of the computer system, in order to protect the rights and ownership of the service provider, or in the case of random monitoring for the purposes of mechanical or quality control checks[31]. These exceptions may also apply to employers, at least where a company has its own internal communications network[32].

System operators also benefit from other exceptions to the prohibition on intercepting private communications. In particular, interception will be condoned:
- where a message is transmitted to a service provider so that it can be forwarded to its final destination (American law)[33];
- when the system operator obtains the message inadvertently and it appears to relate to a crime (American law)[34];
- when the message is disclosed to law enforcement authorities (American law)[35];
- when the message is configured so as to be easily accessible to the general public (American law)[36];
- when the sender of the message consents to the interception (American and Canadian law)[37].

Concerning the application of this last hypothesis (consent of the sender) to Internet users in an employment context, according to American jurisprudence the employee may *implicitly* consent to the monitoring of his or her communications by an employer if the employee has been advised of a company policy of monitoring communications, *or* if the system is reserved exclusively for business purposes (which is usually the case). In this latter case, the jurisprudence finds that such monitoring is not prohibited if the employer can prove that monitoring was undertaken for legitimate business reasons, or that the communication in question concerns a subject which justifies the employer's interest in monitoring it.

Finally, there exists in the United States a common law privacy right which is distinct from the constitutional privacy right[38]. According to this common law tort, «anyone who intentionally intrudes, physically or otherwise, upon the solitude or seclusion of another or his private affairs or concerns, is subject to liability to the other for invasion of his privacy, if the intrusion is highly offensive»[39]. Because this tort applies to intrusion into a private place, *it may be deduced that it would apply to computer files stored in a private «place»*. The jurisprudence, which has already applied this tort to telephone monitoring[40], to the recording of oral communications[41], and to the interception of personal mail[42], seems to authorize this broad interpretation. Anyone committing such an «offensive intrusion» on the Internet would consequently be obliged to compensate the victim who suffered the invasion of privacy. In certain cases, the common law privacy right could be used to protect some types of confidential communications between employees on the Internet. Here again, however, this privacy right comes into conflict with the employer's equally valid right to manage his or her business. Even if employees succeed in establishing the confidential nature of their messages and in proving that the messages are not simply the property of their employer, they would still have to prove that it was reasonable to expect that these messages were confidential and that interceptions by their employer were not excusable as a legitimate business practice[43].

It can be concluded, then, that the confidentiality of employee messages on the Internet will be difficult to protect from employers, who can invoke the numerous grounds and exceptions which we have mentioned as justification for the interception of communications. In any case, businesses wishing to systematically monitor the messages sent by their employees on the Internet should adopt and disseminate a company policy along these lines and should inform employees from the outset that they cannot expect any confidentiality whatsoever on the network, since all employee messages originating from company access links and circulating on the Internet are considered company records. Under American law it is essential to ensure that employees are aware of the possibility that messages may be monitored, and that this monitoring is undertaken for legitimate business reasons. Monitoring can consequently be considered justified and not arbitrary[44].

2. *Under European law*

As we have seen, section 8 of the *European Convention on Human Rights* protects privacy and the confidentiality of correspondence between Internet users[45] with regard to government authorities, but by virtue of its horizontal effect[46], it also applies to private parties such as employers[47], computer systems managers and service providers, who consequently must refrain from *all monitoring and interception*. Moreover, in certain recent judgments the European Court of Human Rights has considerably enlarged this protection as concerns relationships between private individuals, in that it has held that correspondence and telecommunications must be protected, regardless of whether or not information therein originates in private or in commercial and professional domains. Various types of conversation are thus considered correspondence, and are therefore protected independently of the privacy right[48].

Under French law, the protection of the confidentiality of files and dossiers as regards private parties on the Internet is guaranteed by several laws.

Section 25 of the law of July 10, 1991 on the confidentiality of correspondence via telecommunications provides for criminal sanctions[49] against any agent of the public operator, a network operator or a telecommunications service provider (such as an access provider, for example) *who violates the confidentiality of the correspondence* entrusted to the service in which he or she participates. Any voluntary acts on the part of such agents which tend to breach the confidentiality of correspondence and which are not justified by technical necessity are therefore prohibited, even if the contents of such correspondence are neither disclosed nor used.

Furthermore, section 323-3 of the French penal code, which was introduced by the law of January 5, 1988, punishes anyone who intentionally and without regard for the rights of others, either directly or indirectly introduces data into a computerized processing system, or deletes or modifies data contained therein, *or their processing or transmission.*

Finally, the French law of January 5, 1988 on computer fraud provides for the punishment of all unauthorized infiltration of a computer system by any means whatsoever, as is the case when fraud is perpetrated via a telecommunications network.

The various European legal systems sometimes make exceptions in favour of computer services administrators or employers, the scope of which varies from one state to another. For example, under French law, the criminal offence of violating the confidentiality of correspondence as applied to telecommunications *will not be incurred by computer services providers* if their intrusion is justified by technical necessity (as is the case of most intrusions necessary to the activity of an Internet access provider[50]). As concerns employer monitoring of employee Internet use, the principle stipulated by section 368 of the penal code bears noting - recording or simply listening to the words of a person *without his or her consent* constitutes an invasion of privacy susceptible to criminal sanction.

Under English law, the basic provision regarding the interception of information is the *Interception of Communications Act* of 1985[51], which criminally sanctions any person who intentionally intercepts a communication during its transmission by post or via a public telecommunications service (section 1).

3. *Netiquette, current practices and the use of technology to maintain confidentiality*

Current good cybermanners consider that an Internet user should not disclose personal information about other users. The community of Internet users calls such an «impolite» disclosure a «Nixon». Personal information includes any part of an e-mail or of an electronic address, or any other information of a personal nature. Among themselves, Internet users assume that all information is confidential. This assumption can be ignored only when a user is expressly informed by the person concerned that a particular piece of information is not confidential or when he or she is authorized to disclose the information. Finally, a user who receives a message intended for someone else must inform the sender of the transmission error or, if this fails, he or she must try to forward the message to the addressee indicated. Such cautious attitudes are courteous, and usually succeed in preventing legal difficulties[52].

Furthermore, it is important for users to be aware of how the services used operate from a technical point of view, so that they may prevent errors rather than be obliged to repair them. It is easier to take precautions destined to prevent the disclosure of personal information or production secrets *a priori* than it is to obtain damages *a posteriori*.

It is also important to realize that files containing e-mail can be deleted without actually being destroyed, and thus can be retrieved using file retrieval techniques. Some businesses systematically monitor employee e-mail, but others actually pay specialist companies to «unearth» old e-mail[53]. Consequently old e-mail messages may resurface on the desk of an employer or of a competitor. It is therefore imperative to avoid sending secret or compromising information by e-mail. For greater security, however, there is software available which can be used to permanently destroy or shred old files[54]. In the case of particularly delicate information, the user could also consider encrypting it.

II. The Internet and regulations regarding computerized processing of personal data

The collection and processing of personal data by computers rapidly came to be considered a serious threat to privacy. Everyone was on file with the police, with insurance companies, and with ill-intentioned competitors. The law could not long remain oblivious to these developments.

As a result, it seemed necessary to most of the states of the European Union and of North America, to the O.E.C.D.[55], the Council of Europe[56] and to the European Union, to respond to these developments by framing conditions governing the creation of such files, rather than by prohibiting them. A total ban on collating and using personal data was also to be avoided: privacy rights had to be reconciled with the right to information, which is derived from the principle of freedom of expression, and which is equally fundamental to a democracy.

This framework varies from one country to another as regards the rights granted to users, but also as regards protective techniques. In this respect, North America clearly differs from the European Union. In the United States and Canada, only computerized processing in the *public sector* is governed by a law, while the private sector is self-regulated. In the European Union, legal protection is provided in both the public and the private sectors.

Whether they derive from legislation or from self-regulation, these standards will be of great importance for the Internet. They confer rights upon users and netsurfers, and they limit the activities of certain types of firms on the Internet (for example, companies involved in telemarketing and in the constitution of consumer profiles). Service providers, newsgroup administrators, Web servers, and IAPs who create or hold personal data files are obliged to comply with these rules. Often data in the hands of network administrators and service providers may only be recorded and processed for the purpose of ensuring the proper functioning of the service, such as billing and system management, and electronic mailboxes for example. Without the authorization of the users concerned, the data cannot be used for other purposes, such as marketing, nor communicated to third parties. It is nonetheless advisable, in every case, to include provisions to this effect in service provision contracts.

A. *Under American and Canadian law*

American law does not regulate the creation of personal data computer files in the private sector, and it is not covered by the *ECPA*. On the other hand, the *Privacy Act of 1974* and the *Computer Matching and Privacy Protection Act of 1988* offer privacy protections regarding the computerized processing of personal data *in the public sector.*

The *Privacy Act* restricts the types of computerized data files which government bodies can create, and the use which they can make of them. A government body which constitutes personal data files is obliged, in particular, to limit the creation and maintenance of these files to that which is necessary to complete its mission, to gather information directly from the data subject, to inform the individual concerned of how this information is to be used, to keep accurate, relevant and updated records, and to implement reasonable security measures to protect the confidentiality of the data. Furthermore, no government body may disclose personal data in the absence of a request from or at least an authorization on the part of the data subject. Finally, the law gives individuals a right of access to data concerning them, as well as the right to copy, to contest and to correct such data.

In Canada, the *Privacy Act* [57] offers a similar protection *in the federal public sector*. The only personal information which a federal institution may collect is that which is directly related to its programs or activities (s. 4). According to section 5 of the *Act,* a federal institution is obliged to collect personal information concerning an individual from the data subject himself or herself whenever possible, and it is obliged to inform the individual from whom it collects personal data of the uses to which it is to be put. According to section 6(2), a federal institution is obliged to ensure, as far as possible, that the personal information it uses is updated, accurate and complete. Section 12(1) of the law gives the individual the right to have personal information concerning him or her sent to him or her upon request. He or she may also request the correction of incorrect or incomplete information concerning him or her (s. 12(2)).

Subject to certain exceptions, (ss. 7 and 8), the information collected may not be disclosed without the consent of the data subject. No federal legislation governs the creation and maintenance of personal data files in the private sector, but Québec[58], Ontario, Saskatchewan, British Columbia, Nova Scotia and Alberta have all adopted privacy protection legislation, which varies in scope.

These various laws then govern not only the conditions under which government authorities may use the Internet to create personal data files, but also the uses which may be made of such files, as well as the rights of the person on file.

B. In Europe

Due to their desire to comply with the 1981 *Council of Europe Convention*, which established the first principles of protection for the member countries of the Council of Europe, most of the states of the European Union have privacy protection legislation pertaining to computer files. These states must examine their regulations, and if necessary they must adapt them, within a period of three years[59], to conformity with the new *European directive 95/46 on the protection of physical persons as regards the processing of personal data and the free movement of data* (the «privacy» directive), adopted jointly by the Parliament and the Council on October 24, 1995[60].

Here again, the application of this new European directive protects:
- the creation of files from data collected via the Internet;
- the transfer via the Internet of personal data files;
- the grouping and interconnection of such files scattered around different computers connected to the Internet.

The terms of the directive, and particularly the notions of «personal data» and of «processing» are defined very broadly.

Personal data refers to all information concerning a physical person, directly or indirectly identified or identifiable. Any theoretical possibility of ascribing data to a particular person confers upon these data the character of personal data. A broker who disseminates photographs of residential buildings via the Internet consequently falls within the scope of application of the directive[61]. It also applies to digitized images and sounds. Furthermore, the directive defines processing as «any operation or series of operations carried out with or without the use of computerized procedures and applied to personal data, such as collection, recording, organization, storage, adaptation or modification, extraction, consultation, use, communication by transmission, broadcasting or any other means of data provision, matching or interconnection, as well as locking, deletion or destruction». Requesting information on the Internet, consulting personal data files, exchanging messages in newsgroups or on BBSs, in short a great many computer operations on the Internet could thus be considered as processing.

The new directive guarantees persons on file the following rights in particular:

- the right to know, when information is collected, the identity of the person collecting the information and the use to which the processed data will be put;
- the right to access the information stored in a file;
- the right to correct information in a file which is incomplete or inaccurate, etc.

Furthermore, *when a message containing personal data is transmitted* via a telecommunications service or e-mail, *it is the sender, and not the party offering the service, who is responsible for the processing.* The service provider, however, is responsible for processing additional personal data necessary to the operation of the service[62].

The person responsible for the processing, whoever this may be, must take appropriate technical and organizational measures to protect the personal data against destruction, loss, alteration, dissemination or unauthorized access, particularly when the processing involves transmitting data via a network[63].

C. *International transfers of personal data on the Internet*

We now come to the critical problem on the Internet of the almost instantaneous exporting of personal data from a country where privacy is well protected, to a country where it is less protected, and from where in no time at all data can be illegally broadcast throughout the world. Two international texts offer solutions to this problem.

On the one hand, the O.E.C.D. *Guidelines governing the protection of privacy and transborder flows of personal data* recognize the principle of equivalence. A member state of the O.E.C.D. can oppose the transmission of personal data to another member state if the latter does not offer a protection equivalent to its own (s. 19). The *Guidelines* specify, however, that member countries can establish this equivalence by means of self-regulation[64].

On the other hand, section 25 of the *new European directive* accepts the principle of the transfer to a third country of personal data, which is being processed or is to be processed after its transfer, *provided that the third country in question guarantees an adequate level of protection*. The adequacy of the level of protection is assessed by taking into account the nature of the data, the purpose and duration of the planned processing, the country of origin and of final destination, the general or sectorial rules in force in the third countries in question, and the security measures observed.

The application of these rules to the context of the Internet raises doubts as to the validity of certain international transfers of personal data already occurring on the Internet, and whose frequency is intensifying in tandem with the development of the network of networks.

To summarize...

 In *most* countries of the European Union and of North America, privacy quickly came to be seen as a value worthy of protection. The legal means of protecting it nonetheless varies from one country to another - in some countries, privacy is protected by law, while in others it is protected by jurisprudence. These general forms of protection carry penalties in the event of the dissemination of messages which may disclose information (text, images, etc.) constituting an invasion of privacy. In addition, privacy is protected against electronic monitoring both by government authorities and by private individuals. Finally, the processing of personal data, which represents a genuine threat to privacy, is strictly regulated (in both the public and private sectors under European law and in the public sector under American and Canadian law), or is subject to self-regulation (as regards the private sector in Canada and the United States).

 Private communications circulating on the Internet are protected from electronic monitoring by government authorities - usually a warrant is required. The *European Convention on Human Rights* places very strictly limits the cases where such monitoring can be organized by the national legal systems which are subject to it. American law, however, appears to authorize American law enforcement services to check, without a warrant, the identity of computers establishing a connection with a computer which is under surveillance, but not the content of the communications.

 The law usually punishes private individuals who electronically monitor communications on the Internet. There are, however, various exceptions under American and Canadian law and in certain European legal systems, such that this rule does not impede system operators (including, in particular, server and access provider administrators) from properly administrating their systems.

 There are also legal exceptions to the prohibition on electronic monitoring allowing employers to monitor employee use of the Internet. The scope of these exceptions, which are often based on the explicit or implicit authorization of the employee, varies considerably from one legal system to another, and we would strongly advise companies to inform themselves of the precise content of the national rules applicable to them before undertaking any electronic surveillance, even when employees have been clearly informed.

 Whether they derive from legislation or from self-regulation, standards governing privacy protection as regards computer filing are of great importance to the Internet community, because they confer rights upon individuals and specify to what extent and in what way companies can collect information from the Internet and create personal data files, what they can do with these files, and whether or not they can transfer these files via the network and export the data they contain. In particular, these standards govern the activities of all companies which use the Internet for telemarketing purposes, as well as the daily life of Internet access providers and servers.

chapter 5
The Internet and
commercial communication

Why ask questions?

A company's products and services can be brought to the attention of over 30 million users throughout the world through the appropriate use of each Internet application (Web, newsgroups and mailing lists). Advertising and marketing benefit from the network's size and interactivity. The Web is the application most widely used by companies wishing to establish a reputation on the Internet. It can be used to circulate advertising messages or market survey questionnaires. Even though attitudes on the Internet are progressing, only specific newsgroups and mailing lists welcome commercial or advertising messages. Companies must carefully identify these newsgroups and lists, because the virtual community condemns such practices via *flaming*. Furthermore, national legal systems regulate certain types of advertising disseminated on the Internet, the telemarketing practices which are developing, and the content of certain commercial offers.

What questions?

 Do current advertising regulations in American, Canadian and European law apply to the Internet?

 How can you undertake advertising or commercial telecanvassing on the Internet?

Introduction

The Internet allows advertisers to exploit various forms of commercial communication, such as advertising on the Web, direct marketing, and promotional offers[1]. These do not, however, escape regulation. North American and European law currently regulate both advertising and telemarketing on the Internet[2].

I. The Internet and the regulation of advertising in North America and in Europe

Although advertising is protected by the principle of freedom of expression, both under North American and Canadian law[3] and by the standards of the Council of Europe[4], national legal systems regulate certain types of advertising, notably as concerns the type of products being promoted, the content of the advertising message, and its audience or the methods used.

Although it is relatively easy to apply general advertising regulations (which apply to all mediums indifferently) to the Internet, it is difficult to subject it to specific regulations devised for other means of communication, such as those applicable to advertising on television, on the radio, or in the written press.

A. Applying the general rules

Certain common law advertising rules apply to the interactive services disseminated on the Internet with relative facility, since their purpose, regardless of the advertisement's medium, is to protect fundamental interests such as public order and public health, or to protect consumers. Advertising currently being developed on the Web will have to take into account these regulations destined to protect consumers, who might otherwise be easy targets.

It will be necessary to distinguish between regulations related to the nature of the product advertised, to the advertisement's audience, and to the advertising methods used[5].

1. Regulations related to the nature of the product

Several types of products or services (tobacco, financial services, medication, etc.) are subject to stringent national regulations. By way of example, we will focus on the rules governing tobacco and alcohol.

American and Canadian rules on tobacco and alcohol advertising are fairly comprehensive, since federal legislation is usually reinforced by legislation enacted by the states or provinces.

a. Tobacco

In Canada, the advertising of all tobacco products was entirely prohibited by the Tobacco Products Control Act until just recently[6]. This blanket prohibition was held to be unconstitutional by the Supreme Court of Canada, which considered it injurious to the freedom of commercial expression, and not justified despite the importance of its objective, namely the protection of public health[7].

In the United States, cigarette advertising is permitted, except on television and radio. As concerns these permissible forms of cigarette advertising, however, the advertiser must include public health warnings[8]. Advertising for other tobacco products is regulated at state level[9].

b. Alcohol

Excluding advertising on television and radio, alcohol advertising in Canada is regulated by the provinces, which have each adopted detailed outlines governing the various forms of alcohol advertising. Despite their differences, all of these outlines stipulate that printed or broadcast alcohol advertisements must be endorsed by the competent provincial Liquor Control Board[10]. Furthermore, advertisements likely to promote alcohol abuse are generally prohibited. In addition, alcohol advertisements may not target minors, and they may not suggest that the consumption of alcohol enhances social success.

In the United States, alcohol advertising is governed by the Federal Administration Act of 1935, which prohibits the use of misleading or indecent remarks in alcohol advertisements. Furthermore, advertisers (those responsible for the advertisement) must mention their names and addresses. The various state regulations both incorporate the federal regulations and add their own restrictions[11].

European national regulations generally impose the following restrictions on alcohol and tobacco advertising:
- ascribing therapeutic or physical qualities to alcohol or tobacco products, such as asserting that they promote a certain degree of

social ease, or that they have qualities related to sexual prowess, is prohibited
- advertisers are obligated to indicate the dangerous character of these products, notably the risks related to alcohol consumption in certain situations, such as when driving, for example.
- advertisers are obligated to indicate the quantities of harmful substances contained in these products.

2. Regulations related to the advertising audience

In order to protect the most vulnerable consumers, certain national regulations stipulate that advertising must not exert any pressure on the consumer, nor play on consumer fears or superstitions[12]. Similarly, in the majority of North American and European national legal systems, advertising aimed at children is regulated or even self-regulated, and sometimes very precisely[13].

3. Regulations related to the methods used: misleading and comparative advertising

In the intention of guaranteeing the accuracy of the advertising message conveyed to the consumer, misleading and comparative advertising is the subject of legislation both in North America and in Europe.

a. Misleading advertising

Misleading advertising is forbidden under American law on the basis of Article 5 of the Federal Trade Commission Act[14] (FTC), which prohibits unfair competition, unfair practices or acts, and misleading practices or acts[15]. Under American law, two elements are used to determine whether an advertisement is misleading: the content of the advertising message (namely the language used), the assertions made, and the nature of the transaction[16] on the one hand, and the way in which a reasonable consumer may perceive the advertising message on the other[17]. Evidently advertisers are less likely to be held liable for opinions than for statements of fact[18].

Under Canadian law, Article 7 of the «Trade marks» Act[19] prohibits false or misleading statements which tend to discredit a competitor, as well as acts which are contrary to sound commercial practices[20]. Article 52 of the «Trade marks» Act expressly prohibits misleading advertising and marketing[21]. The misleading character of an advertisement is determined in the same way as under American law, and covers both misleading statements, omissions, and opinions[22].

Misleading advertising is also regulated in European law. Any advertisement which in any way, and this includes its presentation, misleads or is likely to mislead its intended or actual audience, and which is likely to harm a competitor as a result of its misleading nature, is forbidden under European law[23]. The misleading nature of the advertisement is assessed on the basis of several elements, including:
- the characteristics of the goods or services promoted (availability, nature, performance, composition, method and date of manufacture or provision, appropriateness, uses, etc.);
- the price or the method of determining the price, and the conditions under which goods are to be supplied or services provided;
- the advertiser's qualities and rights.

b. Comparative advertising

In the United States, the FTC encourages comparative advertising because it believes that it promotes consumer information. Advertisements must, however, be substantiated - they must provide proof of the affirmations that they contain. Accordingly, they may not be either false or misleading[24].

Canadian law similarly permits comparative advertising, although here it is strictly framed. Both the Misleading Advertising Guidelines of Consumer and Corporate Affairs Canada (1991) and the Competition Act prohibit affirmations regarding the performance or efficiency of a product in the absence of official substantiation. An advertiser may not, for example, suggest that a particular product is generally superior to another if this superiority can only be verified in respect of certain precise uses[25]. The Canadian Code of Advertising Standards of the Canadian Advertising Foundation (1991) also prohibits comparative advertising which tends to discredit, denigrate or unfairly attack other products, services, advertisements or companies[26],or which exaggerates the nature or extent of differences between products, services, advertisements or companies.

The authorities of the European Union have made proposals[27] aimed at harmonizing comparative advertising practices within the Union under very strict conditions. At the moment, however, the national European regulations still apply. Consequently an advertiser in one member state could be informed by the authorities of another member state that his or her advertising on the Web is contrary to the comparative advertising laws of that state. This plethora of national laws is currently an obstacle to the free provision of advertising services within the Union. Advertisers wishing to launch a European advertising campaign on the Internet in compliance with the national laws and regulations of the various European states will have to either produce a different campaign for each state, or devise their campaigns in consideration of the requirements of the most restrictive of these legislations[28].

The vast array of national regulations governing comparative advertising, and presenting varying degrees of severity, could lead advertisers to take advantage of the open network which is the Internet in order to relocate advertising services so as to benefit from laws more lenient than those of their own country, while still targeting consumers in their own country. Within the European Union this practice, which constitutes a circumvention of the national law, has already been condemned. Member states whose nationals attempt to circumvent restrictive provisions may take measures to prevent service providers from shirking the professional rules of that state[29].

B. Advertising restrictions applicable to the Internet

The question which remains is that of whether or not advertising on the Internet can be subjected to the application of legal regimes devised specifically for other media, such as radio, television, or the written press.

Given the new role of the «consumer-surfer» and the new possibilities available to him or her, which render television or radio advertising law unsuitable because it was designed to protect a passive audience, we do not advocate this approach. On the Internet the consumer abandons the passive role in favour of the power of initiative: a simple click on the screen allows him or her to obtain additional information or to cause anything considered intrusive to disappear. The contact established between the consumer and the advertiser is also the result of a far more voluntary action on the part of the consumer-surfer, who decides to visit an advertisement on the Web.

A specific advertising law which takes into account the interactive role of the consumer could be developed. It should be inspired by the rules governing advertising in the written press, which are aimed at an active consumer (the reader), and which are therefore less restrictive. Its purpose should be to reconcile the needs of those who disseminate information and of the operators of the new services with consumer protection[30].

II. Telemarketing on the Internet

The Internet facilitates the accomplishment of two classic telemarketing operations - advertising telecanvassing (sending advertising messages to people's homes or places of work), and commercial telecanvassing (soliciting a person directly with a view to concluding a contract for the sale of goods or for the provision of services immediately[31]).

A. Internet and advertising telecanvassing

As regards advertising telecanvassing, in our opinion it is necessary to take stock of two advertising practices developed on the Internet, these being canvassing by electronic mail, and intrusion into newsgroups.

1. Solicitation via electronic mail

Sending advertising material by electronic mail is one of the most effective applications of advertising telecanvassing on the Internet. This practice offers the twofold advantage of reaching a consumer directly wherever he or she may be in the world, provided that the consumer has an electronic address, and of costing very little[32].

Sending advertising messages by ordinary mail (direct mailing) is tolerated by national legal systems to the extent that this technique does not constitute harassment, and insofar as these messages are not contrary to public order and to public health. We do not, however, believe that these legal regimes can serve as grounds for the authorization of advertising telecanvassing via electronic mail on the Internet. The situation on the Net in fact more closely resembles the sending of advertising messages by fax[33], where even unconsenting recipients bear the cost of the paper, and may be inconvenienced by occupation of their fax machines. People with e-mail addresses in some cases have to pay at least part of the cost of transmission in order to be able to read their mail. In addition, bearing in mind the storage capacity of electronic mailboxes, the repeated sending of e-mail advertising messages may cause the disappearance of other messages, or it may at least obstruct the consumer's electronic mailbox, thus causing damages.

Self-regulation provides a solution to some of these questions. Self-regulatory bodies which govern unsolicited advertising in general are found in many countries, and it would be perfectly feasible to apply some of these general standards to the context of the Internet[34]. On the other hand, some of the Acceptable Use Policies, rules elaborated by certain computer networks and which outline acceptable uses and behaviour on the network, specify that it is not acceptable to use the network to interfere with or disturb other users, or network services or equipment, and this includes the dissemination of unsolicited advertising[35].

2. Intrusion into newsgroups

Is an advertiser allowed to intrude into a newsgroup in order to insert an advertisement entirely unrelated to the newsgroup's subject of interest? This practice is not prohibited, to the extent of our knowledge, although it is annoying for newsgroup participants. On the other hand, good cybermanners and the acceptable use policies of certain networks or of the newsgroups themselves may regulate such behaviour if need be.

It should be noted that originally the Internet was an information network used exclusively by university, scientific and even military circles, and which tolerated no commercial intrusion of any kind. The «democratization» of the network has resulted in a relaxation of attitudes towards such practices. The fact remains, however, that advertising or commercial intrusions are prohibited in most cases, and are consequently perilous for a company's image. Such intrusions are prohibited by acceptable use policies, and more generally by good cybermanners, which usually forbid or advise against:

- sending mass messages to a large number of servers or newsgroups (thus obliging users to read the same message on different sites);
- posting advertising messages on newsgroups, unless the advertiser has targeted specific newsgroups likely to be interested in the products or services offered[36]. Even in this case, it is important to determine beforehand whether or not the users of these newsgroups are hostile to advertising in general.

Such advertising is risky for a company's image, because it may provoke a negative reaction on the part of network users. Rather than engaging in advertising practices which may jeopardise a company's image, advertisers on the Internet should consider creating their own tools. A subtle and effective strategy consists of making oneself heard and known through more informative means - internauts call this the schmooze. It can involve, for example, intelligent and relevant participation in discussion groups, or replying to questions posted on a Web server or in a newsgroup[37]. It is a more reliable method of establishing credibility on the network. Another way for an advertiser to integrate himself or herself into the structure of the Internet is to create a Web page on a server dealing with a subject which corresponds or is related to the subject of the advertisement. The Web page should be both simple and comprehensive, and it should offer additional advantages such as links with other servers likely to be of interest to users. In whatever form it takes, advertising on the Net will only be effective if it offers ample information free of charge, and if it remains brief and to the point without being commercially aggressive[38].

B. Internet and offers related to commercial telecanvassing

The Internet allows businesses and merchants to send commercial offers to targeted users. The law assesses these practices with particular attention to the way in which the offer endeavours to persuade the consumer to purchase the product or service. Thus advertisers can use the Internet to make offers, tailored to a consumers' particular interests, of advantages (items or services) related to the purchase of a product, or they can offer special prices on products or services. Another promotional technique which may be of interest to advertisers on the Net is that of contests, which attract public attention to a product.

These practices are subject to the application of regulations governing commercial offers which, for consumer protection purposes, notably stipulate the acceptable forms that an offer may take. In general, the advantages linked to the purchase of a product must be limited to items or services having a direct connection with the product. Contests are also heavily regulated, and must not resemble a lottery, which are almost always subject to very strict conditions.

Once again, the lack of harmonization between national legal systems creates an impediment to the launch of international advertising and commercial campaigns on the Internet. The European Union has tackled the problem by establishing[39] a dialogue with the various actors involved in commercial communication in Europe with the intention of creating a common regulatory and self-regulatory framework. Nonetheless, clearly a more global solution will have to be sought in an international context, probably that of the World Trade Organization (WTO), because the creation of a common framework would benefit not only advertisers, in the form of cost reductions and legal security, but also consumers, by offering them a wider choice of products and services as well as better information.

To summarize...

 Certain forms of protection provided for by the common law on advertising apply to the interactive services disseminated on the Internet, since their purpose is to protect fundamental interests (such as the public order, public health, or consumer protection), irrespective of the advertising media used. The advertising currently being developed on the Web must take into account these regulations aimed at protecting consumers who would otherwise likely be easy targets. These rules refer either to specific products and services (such as tobacco or financial services) or to advertising methods (such as comparative or misleading advertising) or to the protection of certain audiences.

 Companies currently carry out two traditional telemarketing operations via the Internet-advertising telecanvassing and commercial telecanvassing. Advertising telecanvassing, which has developed mainly via electronic mail (it is one of the most attractive forms of advertising for companies, given its extremely low cost), could be subject to certain regulations (for example, regulations relating to unsolicited faxes) or to certain forms of self-regulation. Furthermore, commercial telecanvassing is subject to the regulations on commercial offers (batch sales, contests).

chapter 6

Electronic commerce

Why ask questions?

The Internet is fundamentally changing international commerce by abolishing the borders separating companies from consumers, sellers from purchasers and service providers from clients, all of whom can now meet in virtual markets on the Internet which enjoy the benefits of suitable technical security, of a certain notoriety and of precise regulations. Companies can also develop their own sites. They can select the means of payment most suited to their needs and those of their customers. Even if e-money is still in its infancy, companies will soon be compelled to take it into consideration. The various transactions involved in electronic commerce are regulated by various laws, some of which include public order rules. Companies engaged in commerce on the Internet would be well advised to pay particular attention to consumer law.

What questions?

What is the legal status of an offer made on a Web page?

What is the importance of determining when and where a contract was concluded?

What services cannot be the object of a contract concluded via the Internet?

What is an electronic trading letter? How can this help you with commerce on the Internet?

What is the impact of consumer law on the Internet?

The use of credit cards without a code number is dangerous, but for whom?

How can the new commercial intermediaries such as First Virtual Holding facilitate and ensure the security of your payments via the Internet?

Does e-money already exist? Can you use it?

Introduction

The Internet, a network accessible to millions of users throughout the world, offers unique commercial potential. As a global storefront, it gives companies the opportunity to advertise and market their products at a low cost, as well as to carry out commercial transactions electronically. In both cases, the seller's target may be a private individual or a company.

Some believe that transactions which have developed and now occur frequently on the Internet, such as the sale of goods (clothes, CDs, software, books, etc.) or the provision of services (information research contracts), present risks linked to a lack of adequate security and confidentiality, as well as to the absence of any «paper» trail. It is said that trading on the Internet takes place in a legal vacuum, if not in complete anarchy. This is not at all the case. As we shall see, in addition to the rules governing evidence[1], *the conclusion of a contract* on the Internet is governed by both general rules and by rules which are specific to certain particular contracts.

Furthermore *payment on the Internet* (credit cards, electronic intermediaries, e-money) raises specific legal problems related to the time of payment, to the possibility of contesting a payment made (in the case of piracy for example), and consequently it raises consumer protection problems.

I. Concluding contracts via the Internet

A. General rules applicable to all contracts

1. The conclusion of contracts on the Internet via e-mail and via the Web

The Internet allows users to trade using various techniques, but we will restrain ourselves to an analysis of e-mail and of the Web. Firstly, we will outline the general rules of contract formation which apply to the Internet, followed by their specific application to the conclusion of contracts via e-mail or via the Web.

a. General rules governing the conclusion of contracts (on the Internet)

A contract concluded via the Internet is first and foremost a contract! This assertion is self-evident, and yet it is fraught with consequences, namely that legislation governing the conclusion of «traditional» or «classic» contracts will also apply to the Internet. Consequently in the United States the *Uniform Commercial Code (UCC)*[2] which governs contracts for the sale of moveables, and the *common law*[3], which governs the provision of services and transactions not covered by the definition of a sale, will govern the conclusion of contracts via the Internet. This is also true of the various European civil codes[4].

Under French law, a contract is established when an *offer* made by one party is *accepted* by another.

Under North American and English law, a contract is concluded when the parties show a voluntary and mutual intention to be bound by a set of terms[5]. Here as well an agreement is comprised of the offer made by one party and its acceptance, whether explicitly or implicitly, by the other party[6]. In order for a contract to be enforceable, however, North American and English law also require that an obligation consented by one person with regard to another must be based on a *valu-*

able consideration, which is a type of compensation whereby the co-contracting party to whom a party makes a contractual commitment «pays» for this commitment. The *consideration* must exist at the time of conclusion of the contract[7]. The principles elaborated by these different legal systems are thus very clear. All that remains, then, is to define the notions of offer and of acceptance.

Under French law, as under North American and English law, the *offer* is a unilateral declaration of willingness by which the party making the offer proposes the conclusion of a contract to one or more specific parties (for example, A makes an offer to his neighbour B), or to the «general public» (for example, A places a «For Sale» sign in front of his house). In order for its acceptance to constitute the formation of a contract, the offer must be sufficiently firm[8], precise[9] and unambiguous[10] (A offers to sell a car, identified by its serial number, to his neighbour B for a specified sum of money, payable within a week in accordance with specific terms and conditions). The acceptance is not subject to any other conditions as to its form[11].

This offer is effective only from the moment when the offeree is informed of it (for example, from the moment when A informs B, his neighbour, that he offers to sell him his car) and until the expiry of a period determined by the offeror (for example, A specifies in his offer to B that B has a week to decide whether or not he will accept the offer) or until the expiry of a «reasonable» delay[12].

Can an offer be revoked or «withdrawn»? French law permits withdrawal of an offer provided, of course, that the offer has not already been accepted[13]. English and North American law also permit revocation of an offer, even when it has been communicated, [14] provided that no *consideration* has changed hands.

Acceptance is the expression of the recipient's intention to purely and simply accept the offer, that is, without changing its terms[15] (B, the neighbour, accepts the specified car at the specified price, in accordance with the terms and conditions of payment proposed by A). Notification of acceptance must be given before the offer becomes null and void due to the expiry of the stipulated period of validity (B accepts after the one-week period) or due to its withdrawal by the offeror (A decides not to sell the car to B and informs him of this).

Can acceptance be implicit or must it always be explicit? As a general rule, the offeree cannot be bound by his or her silence[16], and thus the offeree who receives e-mail indicating that failure to reply within a certain period of time will be deemed to signify acceptance, is not obliged to reply. Acceptance may, however, be implicit in two situations.[17] First of all, acceptance may be implicit if the offer is made in the exclusive interest of the offeree (such as in the case of a gratuitous act, or an act which implies no obligation on the part of the offeree)[18], but this does not occur very frequently on the Internet. It may also be implicit when there is already a regular flow of business between the contracting parties[19] (companies with a permanent business relationship or which are already linked within the framework of a previous contract), which is an ordinary practice on the Internet. Whether it is explicit or tacit, acceptance is not subject to any conditions as to its form[20].

It is the *acceptance* which, in principle, signals the *birth of the contract,* and which irrevocably binds the parties. This principle must sometimes be qualified, as in cases where one or all of the parties can revoke their acceptance. In these cases the contract is not definitively concluded until the period allowed for revocation has elapsed (for example, the period within which a consumer may revoke a contract of sale concluded with an absent party, that is, concluded by parties not in one another's presence).

b. The application of these rules to electronic commerce via e-mail

The Internet constitutes the primary form of electronic commerce, and it allows businesses to contact targeted consumers or companies via e-mail. Either in a first transmission, or after a preliminary exchange, this mail may contain a commercial offer. The offeree reads the commercial offer at the earliest when he or she consults his or her mail box, and at the latest when he or she opens the mail already deposited in the mailbox. The offer will take effect from the moment that it is read by the offeree, and then it is up to the offeree to accept it by returning an e-mail of acceptance to the offeror. An electronic mail system is a perfectly appropriate means of sending commercial offers and acceptances, and thus of concluding contracts via the Internet.

c. The application of the rules to electronic commerce via the Web

Some Internet servers offer goods and services to the «general public» (*home shopping*) by means of attractive Web pages (usually on-screen catalogues) inviting users to conclude contracts with them by following a specified commercial procedure (notably by providing certain information, such as the user's name and e-mail address, for example). Since sellers present on the server cannot know in advance the name, financial situation, or even the number of users (risk of stock shortfalls) who will reply to their commercial proposals and who will conclude contracts, they would be well advised to specify, on the server, that the commercial proposals are not offers in the legal sense of the term, and cannot have any effect in law (for example, by including expressions such as: «not binding» or «subject to confirmation», etc.). They simply invite the other party to negotiate[21]. In this case, the consumer who completes the electronic order form indicates his or her will to enter into an undertaking, and thus establishes himself or herself as the offeror. The seller, by sending an e-mail of acceptance, becomes the accepting party. Unless the seller stipulates that he or she is not issuing an offer, most European and North American national legal systems will consider that a commercial offer has been made, and that its acceptance by the buyer on the Internet constitutes the conclusion of a legally binding contract[22].

2. The time and place of contract formation

Determining the time and place of contract formation is essential, since it identifies, among other things, the moment of the transfer of ownership (and of risk) in the event of a sale, as well as the law applicable to the contract and the jurisdiction competent to hear any disputes that may arise.

In principle, a contract is established *in the place where the parties are located and at the moment when both express their consent*. On the Internet, obviously the situation is complicated by the fact that the parties are not in the presence of one another. There is not, however, an infinite number of solutions regarding contracts concluded between absent parties, and national legal systems consider that a contract is established at one of the following moments and places:

a. Upon expedition of the acceptor's

Upon expedition of the acceptor's consent (expedition theory), for example, at the moment when the acceptor drafts an electronic mail message of acceptance (which he or she does not, perhaps, succeed in sending via the Internet).

b. Upon the sending of the acceptor's acceptance

Upon the sending of the acceptor's acceptance (transmission theory) - the contract is concluded at the moment when the electronic mail is sent by the acceptor (*send* function) or, in regards to commercial proposals made via on-screen catalogues on the Web, either when the buyer sends the information requested on the Web server (in cases where the seller's proposal may be considered as an offer), or when the seller returns confirmation of the order (see above regarding the question of when commercial proposals displayed on a server may not be considered offers).

c. Upon reception of acceptation by the offeror

Upon reception of acceptation by the offeror, even if he or she has not yet read it (reception theory). In our opinion, it is the receipt of the acceptance in the Internet access provider's mail box which should be taken into consideration, and not the «check mail» function in the individual mail box on the offeror's personal computer. In fact, the access provider's mail box is in itself a personal mail box having more in common with a post office box than with a post office sorting centre.

d. Upon the offeror's knowledge of the acceptation

Upon the offeror's knowledge of the acceptation (information theory). When the contract is concluded by an exchange of electronic mail, this knowledge presupposes that the mail has been received by the access provider, that the offeror has checked the mail box, and that he or she has read the acceptance message.

It is easy to imagine the numerous problems these various legal solutions may pose. Under the expedition theory, the offeror will find it difficult to prove that the acceptor drafted a mail accepting the offer, if the mail was not sent and consequently was not received. Under all of these theories, the loss of a message on the network, its return because of an incorrect address, or a computer transmission error are sources of innumerable uncertainties, which may possibly[23] be counteracted if the offeror, the acceptor and their respective suppliers systematically keep records, on a durable and inalterable medium, of the various messages sent and received. One thing is unfortunately certain - here more than anywhere else, the diversity of national legal systems[24] does nothing to simplify the situation of the contracting parties in the event of a dispute. As we will see, however, the *Vienna Convention* of April 11 1980 harmonized the various laws of the signatory states by adopting the reception theory as regards the international sale of goods[25] (see below).

3. *The validity of contracts concluded via the Internet*

Most national legal systems impose four conditions on the valid conclusion of a contract via the Internet (and on the valid conclusion of all other contracts): the *consent* and the *capacity* of the parties, and that the contract has a lawful *object* and *cause*[26][27]. The first three of these elements appear to us to present to us certain particularities on the Internet.

a. Consent

For a contract to be concluded on the Internet, it is essential for each party to manifest his or her free and informed *consent* to be bound by the agreement. In other words, this consent must exist and it must not be vitiated. Our discussion will be limited to certain consent problems specific to the Internet.

Consent is *vitiated* notably in cases of error or fraudulent representation, that is, when one of the parties committed an error or was deceived[28].

Error consists of an involuntary discrepancy between the actual wishes and the declared wishes of the party committing the error, which was not provoked by his or her co-contracting party. It may be significant enough to preclude consent by both parties to the same thing (error constituting an obstacle in French law or a lack of "meeting of the minds" in common law[29], such as when A intends to sell a book to B, while B intends to buy a CD), or it may only concern certain decisive elements of the contract[30]. For example, a user who replies via the Internet to an advertisement placed by a private individual and purchases an item from him or her, and who realizes upon delivery of the item that it is not what he or she expected or is not suitable for the use that he or she intended to make of it, may have the contract of sale annulled on grounds of error, provided that the error is excusable.

Fraudulent representation, on the other hand, consists of an intentional and malicious maneuver in the absence of which the contract would not have been concluded or would have been concluded under different conditions. This could be the case of a clearly misleading advertisement on the Internet, or of a promise made via e-mail of subsequent imaginary advantages, and made with the sole intention of convincing the other party to conclude the contract under these conditions. Such behaviour is punishable by the various legal systems[31] (depending on its effect and on the intention of the party committing the fraudulent representation), notably by the voiding of the contract, by actions for compensation (damages) if the contract is maintained[32], by particular civil actions providing for damages and interests or the nonperformance of the obligations of the victim of the fraudulent representation[33].

b. Legal capacity

Generally, contracts concluded by minors[34] are considered null and void[35]. Some legal systems do, however, recognize the validity of contracts aimed at obtaining items which are necessary for the daily life of a minor[36] (a minor could purchase newspaper articles on the Internet, for example).

For the moment, a problem arises when sellers or providers of telematic services cannot be certain that the user communicating with them is not a minor. For example, let us imagine that a minor subscribes to a pornographic server or to a stock market information service using his or her parents' credit card. Does this mean that the contract will inevitably be null and void and that the service provider will remain unpaid? In principle, parents are not contractually bound by obligations arising from contracts concluded by their under-age children[37].

In France, however, even supposing theft by a minor misappropriating his or her parents' credit card, the latter are nevertheless bound by the *contract* concluded by their child by virtue of the theory of appearance (to the supplier, the child appeared to be the card holder and therefore an adult). Under North American law, the minor may revoke a contract that he or she concluded in excess of what is permitted by law. Parties believing in good faith that they are concluding a contract with an adult, when in fact their contracting partner is a minor, could, however, hold the minor liable on the basis of a tort. Certain torts overlap with common law rules of contract, but the minor will only be liable on the basis of torts independent of the contract. This system aims to prevent the co-contracting party from compelling the minor to fulfill his or her contractual obligations on the basis of civil liability[38].

Parents therefore have a vested interest in supervising their children's use of the Internet, and thus in not installing an automatic version of their password (a password which the computer automatically feeds to the IAP when connecting).

c. The object of the contract

In the vast majority of national legal systems, the object of a contract (the prestations undertaken by the parties) must, among other things, be lawful and compliant with the public order and public morality. Companies should keep this in mind when marketing services which may not meet such criteria in certain countries (such as pornographic services or games, for example).

4. A master contract to facilitate concluding contracts via the Internet?

a. The master contract and its advantages

In order to avoid the majority of problems when concluding a contract on the Internet (often by means of a simple exchange of e-mail), parties wishing to maintain a genuine flow of business among themselves and consequently to conclude several contracts via the Internet, would be well advised to initially conclude a master contract. It would be preferable to draw up this contract in writing, and it should specify the terms and conditions governing any contracts which these same parties may conclude via the Internet. Although this solution offers a certain degree of legal security, its disadvantages are the creation of additional formalities, and its cost. Each individual party will have to assess the usefulness of such a master contract, specifically in consideration of the number of electronic contracts that he or she intends to conclude with the same co-contracting party.

Among other things, the master contract could specify:

1) the time and place of formation of future contracts concluded on the Internet;

2) the law applicable to the contract[39];
there is, however, a nuance to be made regarding this freedom of choice under North American law. In the United States, even though the freedom of contract principle allows contracting parties to choose the law applicable to the contract[40], the American courts have proven reluctant to accept the choice of a legal system which bears no relation or a rather tenuous relation to the transaction in question and which enables the parties to avoid the application of the legal provisions in force[41]. It is possible, then, that in these cases the choice of law may not be respected, and that the court will apply its own rules relating to conflicts of laws to determine which law is applicable to the contract. A similar approach exists under Canadian law-the courts are free to refuse the choice of a legal system which has no substantial connection with the commercial relationship in question.

3) methods of interpreting or fulfilling the agreement in the event of a dispute;

4) the admissibility and probative value of certain computer documents (for example, messages meeting certain conditions of form will be considered a signed «writing»[42]);

5) the jurisdiction having competence to settle disputes according to its own rules[43]. *Evidently, the parties will have to verify that the jurisdiction chosen is not subject to a public order rule which would forbid the application of the law they have selected for their contract.*

6) Finally, as for all contracts, the master contract may not contain any provisions which are contrary to the rules of public order of the applicable law.

b. A simplified form of the master contract: the electronic trading letter

A simplified form of the master contract is the electronic trading letter[44]. This basic master contract looks like a letter - as its name indicates - in which one party, usually a seller, offers another party, usually a buyer, general and often standard conditions for the conclusion of subsequent electronic contracts. The offeree simply has to sign a copy of the letter received and return it to the sender for a master contract to be legally concluded. Its purpose is to promote more spontaneous commerce (simplified form) without abandoning all legal guarantees.

This electronic trading letter may also be concluded by an exchange of electronic mail. This involves the same process of signing a master contract devised to govern subsequent contracts between the parties.

Finally, the trading letter may be displayed on a Web server, in which case it must be treated like any Web posting. The rule is that, unless otherwise indicated, and subject to a jurisprudential relaxation of the rules, this display constitutes an offer to contract and its acceptance forms the contract between the parties. It is useful, however, to distinguish two possible hypotheses. Either the server provides the co-contracting party with an occasion to indicate his or her agreement via the trading letter, for example by returning the letter after having signed it electronically, thereby expressly consenting to the master contract which is the electronic trading letter, or the server does not provide for this possibility but displays the trading letter in the course of all transactions on the Internet. In this latter hypothesis, the trading letter is no more or less than general conditions governing transactions concluded on the Internet, like the general conditions which may be printed on the reverse side of any contract concluded on paper, and there is no longer any question of signing a master agreement.

The advantages of speed and of facility offered by electronic forms of trading letters (e-mail exchanges or the offer of the letter on an Internet Web server) must be assessed in light of the risks that they entail. In this assessment, the parties will have to take into account the specific characteristics of their businesses, the various extraneous elements and, of course, the admissibility of computerized documents as a form of evidence pursuant to the applicable law of evidence and consumer protection law. These numerous difficulties[45] often outweigh the advantages of concluding a trading letter electronically via the Internet, as opposed to concluding it on paper.

5. *Contracts concluded via the Internet and consumer protection law*

As soon as a contract is concluded between a consumer and a trader[46] (to simplify matters), the transaction in question is quite minutely regulated by consumer protection law. Consumer protection is provided both by *general laws*[47] and by laws *specifically* applicable to long-distance selling[48], or to a certain product or service[49], which usually apply on the Internet as elsewhere. Failure to respect these laws is punishable in certain cases by the voiding of the transaction or by the non-application of the clause said to adversely affect the consumer.

For example, the consumer has the *right to repent*[50] within a certain delay and is often expressly protected against *abusive or unreasonable clauses*[51]. These laws may also contain particular warranty requirements, which may be impossible to contractually exclude, such as good title, suitability of goods for intended purposes, and merchantable quality, or an obligation to inform consumers of the guarantees offered by the seller[52]). There may also be a writing requirement regarding contracts concluded between a trader and a consumer, with a duplicate of this writing provided to the consumer[53]. Since the purpose of this rule is consumer protection, courts will often not be satisfied with computerized documents. In these cases, the trader is advised to send the written documents required by law to the consumer by conventional mail. Consumer protection laws may also stipulate that contracts concluded at a distance are deemed to be concluded at the address of the consumer[54] which has an interesting consequence: the competent court is that of the legal district in which the consumer is domiciled[55]. Finally, it is often stipulated that any ambiguities wills be interpreted in favour of the consumer[56].

These various national legal systems[57] obviously have a considerable influence on the conditions under which home shopping can be undertaken on the Internet.

B. Rules specific to certain contracts or to certain categories of contracts

1. Adhesion contracts

An adhesion contract is a contract in which all the conditions of the agreement are stipulated by one of the parties (insurance contracts, contracts with banks, or found in wholesale or retail trade are often of this nature), and the other party can only agree or refuse to sign the standard agreement. These are usually printed contracts in which not even the slightest clause can be modified or deleted subsequent to negotiation between the parties. A standard contract can thus be converted into an adhesion contract only if it is not considered amendable point by point. These contracts are already a common occurrence on the Internet. The general conditions of sale are displayed on the servers, and the visitor's only choice as the potential co-contracting party is to accept them or not to conclude the contract!

Evidently national legal systems reacted long ago to the appearance of adhesion contracts, which constitute an imbalance of power potentially threatening to the very spirit of contractual freedom, by protecting the weakest party to the contract. Most of these legal systems will apply to the Internet.

Under *American law*, the validity of adhesion contract provisions is assessed on the basis of the reasonableness of their terms[58]. When the party drafting the contract has reason to believe that the other party would not consent if he or she was aware of the existence of certain clauses, then these clauses are considered non-existent[59]. This rule is presumed to apply in the event of peculiar or abusive clauses, in the event of provisions which relieve of all substance the non-standardized clauses to which the co-contracting party had expressly agreed, or if they eliminate the main purpose of the transaction (for example, in the case of an Internet access contract, a clause banning all access to the network)[60].

An adhesion contract may also be considered unconscionable if, in addition to precluding any negotiation by the other party, it presents terms which are unreasonably favourable to the party drafting it (oppression of the other party, surprise or ridiculous terms)[61].

Under Québec law, the *Civil Code of Québec* stipulates that in regards to consumer or adhesion contracts, illegible or incomprehensible clauses are invalid if they adversely affect the adhering party and were not clearly explained at the time of contract formation[62]. All abusive clauses will be invalid, or the consumer will be able to obtain a reduction of the resultant obligations[63]. Finally, an adhesion contract must be interpreted in favour of the adhering party in case of ambiguity[64].

Under French law, provisions which have not been negotiated and which constitute abuse of the adhering party (for example, contracts stipulating that the supplier of a product or service does not guarantee against hidden defects[65]) are prohibited. The law of February 1, 1995[66], which applies to contracts of all forms[67] (and therefore to contracts concluded via the Internet), distinguishes between obscure clauses (ambiguous or incomprehensible) and abusive clauses (entailing a significant imbalance in the rights and obligations of the parties). It stipulates that in the event of doubt, obscure clauses shall be interpreted in favour of the consumer or non-professional[68] and that abusive clauses will be deemed void (but the contract itself remains valid as concerns provisions other than those deemed abusive, at least insofar as the contact can survive without them)[69].

2. Internet and international sales

In order to settle the numerous problems of international commerce, a *Convention* on international sales of goods was adopted in Vienna on April 11, 1980[70]. Its purpose was to establish uniform rules regarding international sales of goods. For a sale of goods to be covered by the *Convention*, certain conditions must be satisfied. These conditions are related to the international character of the sale (the buyer and the seller must be established in different states), to the nature of the contract (it must involve a sale as defined by the *Convention*), and to the object of the contract (the sale must concern movable goods). The *Convention* thus clearly applies to international sales concluded via older telematic technologies (telephone, telex, fax), and now applies fully to international sales concluded via the Internet. Since it is only binding on signatory states, unfortunately the *Convention* does not resolve problems involving contracts concluded between parties of whom at least one is established in a state that has not yet ratified it[71].

With a view to its application to the Internet, the following points from this *Convention* should be noted:

1) The sales contract does not necessarily have to be concluded or recorded in writing, and is not subject to *any other conditions of form*. It may be proved by all means, included by witnesses (s. 11).

2) The *offer* takes effect when it reaches the offeree. The offeror assumes the risk of loss during transmission of its proposal to conclude a contract if, for example, an offer sent by electronic mail is wrongly forwarded (s. 15).

3) *Receipt of the acceptation by the offeror* (reception theory, see above)[72], irrespective of its form[73], *signals the birth of the contract*. The *Convention* only governs the time of the formation of the contract, however, and is silent as to the place of its formation, which it considers to be of secondary importance.

3. EDI agreements on the Internet?

Specialized and closed networks offering a high level of security have allowed the development of *Electronic Data Interchange* (EDI). EDI consists of the computerized exchange of standardized and approved messages between computer applications by remote data processing. This transmission of data between computers on the basis of a common language permits commercial communication, and consequently *the conclusion of contracts, without any human intervention* (the computer managing the buyer's stock automatically orders goods from the seller when necessary, and the seller's computer automatically accepts and implements the order).

The Internet, whose role is that of open network, does not *a priori* offer the security required for the development of EDI practices. The low cost of Internet use, however, is a major advantage for small and medium-sized companies who cannot afford to subscribe to specialized networks and who, *in a more or less near future*, could gain access to the advantages of EDI in this way[74].

In order to facilitate recourse to these computerized practices, various international organizations or associations have drawn up standard EDI contracts.[75] With certain modifications, Internet users will be able to make use of these various legal instruments, all of which cover:

- technical standards applicable to messages;
- the operation and methods of transmission of messages;
- acknowledgments of receipt of messages;
- message processing;
- message security;
- message recording and storage;
- intervention by intermediaries (third-party certifiers);
- electronic transactions and the conclusion of contracts;
- the admissibility and probative value of messages;
- the protection of personal data;
- the applicable law;
- the resolution of disputes.

II. Payment via the Internet

Initially, even when a transaction was effected via the Internet, payment was external to the network, such as payment by *bank transfer*, for example. There was no real means of making payment via the Internet. Commerce on the network could not, however, develop on the basis of means so traditional and slow.

The need for speed led to the development of *payment by credit card* (Visa, Mastercard, American Express, etc.) on the network. The buyer would give the trader his or her credit card number and sometimes its date of expiry. This method, which is already used in telephone sales, gives rise to certain problems. In addition to the cost involved, it constitutes a threat to privacy (a person's purchases may be «tracked»). Furthermore, in the context of an open network like the Internet, payment by credit card creates risks linked to computer piracy of confidential data in circulation on the network. In order to overcome this disadvantage, and to reassure individual users, certain professional servers systematically encrypt these confidential data when they are transferred via the network.

Despite the reliability of encrypting credit card data, fear of piracy has led to the appearance of a second generation of Internet payment methods: *electronic payment*. From among the many systems which already exist (First Virtual Holdings Incorporated, Netcheque, Netchex, etc.), we have chosen to present the First Virtual system.

Finally, the third generation of Internet payment methods, and the most revolutionary one in the eyes of the public, is *virtual money (E-money)*. Stripped of the myths and the mediatization, the system is actually quite simple: the holder of a bank account «purchases» cyberdollars using real dollars! This is the type of system offered notably by DigiCash, CyberCash, Mondex, NetCash and E-cash. Our analysis of e-money will focus on the *Mark Twain* bank, which has been operating the DigiCash system since October 23, 1995.

A. Payment by ordinary credit card[76]

Using a credit card to pay on the Internet raises two legal questions: when is this payment made; and what are the risks involved in this transaction?

1. The moment of payment

It is sometimes important to determine the moment of payment, notably when a commercial offer displayed on a Web server is only valid for a specific period of time. Unfortunately, it is difficult to detect a uniform trend in this area, since national legal systems differ significantly. Some legal systems consider that payment is made when the client's account is debited, when the beneficiary's bank account is credited or when the beneficiary himself receives the payment, or when the beneficiary is informed of the transfer to his or her account[77]. Consequently, it is important to take into account the variety of possible solutions when transacting internationally on the Internet, and we strongly advise parties to inform themselves of the solutions provided for by the law applicable to the contract.

2. Using credit cards without a code number- dangerous, yes, but for whom?

Payment by credit card without a code number is risky. A trader cannot be certain that the client is indeed the holder of the card[78]. What happens in the event of piracy? Can a payment made by credit card on the Internet be contested? Within what period of time?

The answer to these questions can be found in the *contracts* concluded by the company issuing the credit card with the user («bearer agreement») and with traders («franchise agreement»), as well as in law.

a. Contractual solutions

With respect to credit card payments, three contracts co-exist:
- the contract between the trader and the consumer for the sale or provision of services;
- the *bearer agreement* between the issuer and the card holder;
- the *franchise agreement* between the issuer and the trader[79].

The *bearer agreement* usually *protects the credit institution against all claims*: The institution executes all transactions recorded and transmitted by the trader, even if there is no signature, and the consumer has no recourse against it[80].

Consumers who contest a debit are not, however, entirely powerless. In the *franchise agreement, the trader usually undertakes to bear all risks* should the client contest the debit, and expressly authorizes the credit institution to automatically debit its account for the amount of any transaction contested by the client, without any time limit[81].

It should be noted that the systems applicable in Europe and in North America are very similar, the only difference being that competition between the numerous North American banking institutions drives them to try to outbid one another as regards client protection. Some of them go so far as to act as conciliators in disputes between traders and dissatisfied clients.

Ultimately, it is these general clauses, applicable to all credit card payments, which efficiently protect the consumer paying by credit card on the Internet.

b. Legislative solutions

At the European level, a proposal is currently being prepared for a directive on consumer protection regarding contracts between absents[82], which evidently applies to the Internet, and which stipulates two basic principles. Firstly, it introduces a general consumer «*right of cancellation*», whereby a consumer can change his or her mind and cancel an order within a period of seven days from receipt of the product or service, regardless of the means of payment used. Secondly, if the consumer has made his or her purchase using a card without a code, *any payment which he or she contests is canceled*, unless the contestation is fraudulent. In transposing contractual principles to legislation, these provisions further reinforce consumer protection.

Until the adoption of this directive, the matter continues to be governed by the various national legal systems within the European Union[83]. Consequently, *in France*, the January 6, 1988 law on telepromotional campaigns which include an offer of sale, known as teleshopping, grants a period of seven days from delivery for the return of an order. This law refers only to sales of products, however, and excludes the provision of services and real estate transactions[84]. *In Germany*, the period of reflection is fourteen days. This protection results from the jurisprudence on telephone sales and is not laid down in any text. *In Italy*, paragraph 4 of section 36 of the law of June 11, 1971, No 426, on «commercial discipline» stipulates that when products ordered by correspondence do not correspond to the order, they must be replaced or a refund must be given. Finally, in *Great Britain*, the consumer has a period of fourteen days to change his or her mind and to return an order[85]. Furthermore, the *Consumer Credit Act* of 1974 fixes a ceiling of 50 pounds on the amount to be paid by the card holder in the event of fraudulent payment by credit card, the remainder being borne by the issuer[86].

Under North American law, several provisions also protect the consumer. First of all, under the ordinary rules of *common law*, the consumer can resiliate a contract at any time for reasons of error, fraudulent and innocent misrepresentation, duress, or unconscionableness or undue influence.

Secondly, the *Uniform Commercial Code* governing sales of goods also offers several forms of protection. According to section 2-601, if the goods delivered do not conform to that which is stipulated in the contract, the consumer has the option of returning them, subject to any contractual stipulations limiting the forms of redress offered to the buyer. Section 2-719 authorizes the seller to specify the forms of redress which he or she is bound to honour should the contract not be performed. In addition, the seller may also limit the damages that he or she may be obliged to pay, provided that this limit is not *unconscionable*. Thus the seller may, for example, stipulate that if the goods delivered do not conform, the buyer may require that they be replaced or repaired, but may not request a reimbursement. If, however, the redress foreseen prevents performance of the contract (because after repeated attempts the seller is not able to repair the goods, for example), the buyer may consider this clause void, and may request the redress provided for by section 2-712. This section stipulates that, in addition to reimbursement for the goods, the buyer may claim from the seller payment of the difference between the price agreed to by contract and the price paid to purchase similar replacement goods[87].

The seller may also limit the damages to which he or she may be bound, provided that this limitation is not *unconscionable* (abusive).

The aforementioned principles of common law are also applicable under Canadian law, and furthermore they are expressly foreseen by the *sales of goods acts* of each province. In addition, provincial consumer protection legislation usually allows the consumer a certain period of time within which he or she may change his or her mind. This period of time varies from one province to another, the shortest being two days (province of Ontario) and the longest being ten days (province of Newfoundland)[88].

B. The new electronic intermediaries and virtual money

1. First Virtual Holdings Incorporated or the new electronic intermediaries[89]

First Virtual Holdings is first and foremost an intermediary between buyers and sellers of electronic goods and services on the Internet. This system presupposes the conclusion of a contract between *First Virtual* and the buyer, and between *First Virtual* and the seller.

In the interests of security, the buyer informs *First Virtual* of his or her account number and credit card information via telephone or fax when concluding his or her contract. The buyer then receives a *Virtual-PIN*, a code which will serve to identify him or her in future transactions.

If he or she has an account in the United States and satisfies certain conditions, the seller may stock goods either on *First Virtual's*

WWW server or on his or her own WWW server. The buyer interested in purchasing an article offered on one of these servers informs the seller of his or her *Virtual-PIN*. The *First Virtual* server checks the validity of the account (accuracy of the card details).

For «*purchases» of information* (such as articles or photos, for example) available on its own server, *First Virtual* initially sends the buyer a copy of the selected article for examination. If after having examined it, the client confirms by electronic mail that he or she wishes to acquire the information, *First Virtual* invites him or her to pay, again by electronic mail. The buyer's credit institution credits the amount of the to *First Virtual*, which subtracts its commission (0.29$ + 2% of the amount of the transaction) and then pays the seller [90].

As concerns *purchases of goods offered directly on the seller's server,* however, trial examination is not possible. The buyer must send his or her *Virtual-PIN*, thus permitting the seller to be paid in advance. Once the payment has been confirmed by *First Virtual*, the seller undertakes to send the goods within twenty-four hours[91].

2. *DigiCash or E-money*

During an experimental phase, DigiCash carried out a test to check the viability of its system and to allow consumers to familiarize themselves with its operation. Over five thousand volunteers received a digital account with an initial capital of one hundred cyberdollars, or virtual money. With this capital, they could purchase goods and services, via the network, from a certain number of «stores» which had agreed to go along with the game, which is exactly what it was a game consisting of paying for goods and services using «virtual Monopoly money» without any real value. The aim of this initial phase was to convince real banks of the interest of such a system, and of the software developed by *DigiCash*.

The second phase began on October 23, 1995. Since this date, the *Mark Twain Bank*, an American institution, has been trying the system out by offering its customers the possibility of converting dollars into cyberbucks and vice versa. For example, a client can ask the *Mark Twain Bank* to convert one hundred dollars into cyberdollars in order to make a purchase on the Internet. The bank fulfills such requests by transferring the «electronic sum» to the customer's hard disk, turning it into a veritable wallet. Once this sum has been loaded,

the client can make purchases from traders who accept this virtual money[92]. The trader has two possibilities open to him or her - he or she can either load the sum onto his or her own hard disk, or it can be transferred directly to his or her account at the *Mark Twain Bank*.
Using software developed by *DigiCash* and a«*blind signature*» assigned to each virtual unit, the *Mark Twain Bank* checks all transactions to make sure that each virtual unit is used only once[93]. Each unit of this virtual money is in fact no more than a number which allows the bank to authenticate it in relation to other units[94], similar to the serial number on a bank note. They are thus no less than a dematerialized form of the dollar, like the tokens which can only be used in casinos[95].

3. The legal issues raised by the new electronic intermediaries and virtual money

a. Contracts and consumer protection

a.1. The competent court and applicable law
The *First Virtual* (FV) agreement stipulates that in the event of a dispute, the parties agree to bring the matter before the competent court in Wyoming[96], but it does not specify the applicable law.

As for the *Mark Twain Bank* (MT), its contract states that in the event of a dispute relating to the contract, the customer agrees to first submit the dispute to arbitration in accordance with Title 9 of the *United States Code* (*United States Arbitration Act*). Where the arbitration clause does not apply, the customer agrees to submit the dispute to a court in the state of Missouri, which will apply the regulations of the Federal Reserv, the federal laws, and subsidiarily, the internal laws of the state of Missouri[97].

These clauses seem to us to be perfectly acceptable, insofar as FV is based in Wyoming and MT in Missouri, which would exclude any arguments of extraneousness.

a.2. Consumer protection

1) Under American law
The contracts proposed by MT and FV contain several clauses which are worth examining in light of American law.

The MT contract stipulates, in particular, that the bank reserves the right to modify the conditions of the contract unilaterally, and that it will advise customers of this at least 10 days before such modifications take effect[98]. The FV contract also reserves FV's right to unilaterally modify the terms of a contract, and it does not mention any prior notice or term of prior notice requirement[99]. In any case, both the MT and FV contracts will have to respect the period required by the *Electronic Funds Transfer Act*[100] which stipulates that the bank must inform the consumer in writing of any modification in the terms and conditions of the contract at least 21 days before the entry into force of modifications which will result in an increase in consumer expenses or liabilities, or when they will limit the consumer's access to his or her own account.

The MT contract also contains a limitation on the bank's liability in the event of the unauthorized use of the customer's account. According to this clause, MT is not liable for unauthorized transactions on the customer's account, and consequently, the consumer is obliged to reimburse in full the amounts withdrawn. The contract proposed by FV contains a similar clause, according to which the consumer bears all liability for fraudulent use of his or her account[101]. Clauses such as these are clearly contrary to section 1693g of the *EFTA*, which limits consumer liability regarding unauthorized transactions to a ceiling of $50 US (which may increase to $500 US if the customer does not inform the bank within two days of the discovery of the loss or theft of his «*access device*») payable by the customer, the remainder being borne by the bank[102]. It should be noted, however, that the FV contract always requires a buyer to confirm his or her purchase via e-mail, and requires the buyer to guarantee that he or she is the only user of his or her account (*Virtual-PIN* confidentiality). Consequently if a buyer who discovers that his or her *Virtual-PIN* has been used by a third party does not notify FV of the fraudulent use, then he or she could be liable up to $500 US.

MT also significantly limits its liability for damages caused by the use of its software or for damages beyond its control[103]. American courts might consider these limits «*unconscionable*», particularly in the context of an adhesion contract. The same is true of the similar provisions found in the FV contract[104].

Finally, there is a contradiction in the FV contract between its clause Q8.2.2.1 (waiver of right to take legal action) and its clause Q11 (choice of law applicable in the event of legal action). This contradiction should be interpreted in favour of the buyer, especially since the buyer may not waive the protections offered by the *EFTA*[105], which include notably the right to take legal action.

2) *Under European law*

The new electronic intermediaries and new forms of banking applications are likely to develop in Europe, consequently examining the contracts proposed by *First Virtual*[106] (FV) and by the *Mark Twain Bank*[107] (MT) in the light of European law is by no means an indulgence.

In addition, it is not impossible that an American court, to which a dispute between FV or MT and a European consumer is referred, may consider that the relationship between the consumer and these professionals imbalanced, and that the legal system selected places the weaker party at a disadvantage. In this case an American judge may, in application of the rules of private international law, take European law into account, despite the choice of jurisdiction clause[108].

These contracts contain clauses which, according to the *European directive* on abusive clauses[109], may be considered abusive by the various European national legal systems and jurisdictions. This is also true of the MT provisions relating to unilateral modification of the contract, and which do not specify the conditions under which it may intervene[110], and of its disclaimer regarding software failure[111]. Similarly, the provisions of the FV contract[112], whereby the buyer waives his or her right to sue FV or any person linked to FV, is questionable under the same European standards, although it is to be noted that this same contract stipulates that in the event of a dispute the buyer must bring action before the court of Cheyenne in the State of Wyoming!

b. *Beyond contracts*

One of the purposes of electronic money is to ensure the confidentiality of financial transactions and the anonymity of the parties to a transaction. This confidentiality and this anonymity can, however, give rise to numerous abuses, such as money laundering or tax fraud. In order to avoid this, several countries have introduced «*reporting requirements*», which oblige financial institutions to reports to governmental authorities regarding certain financial transactions[113]. In the United States, for example, financial institutions may be compelled to provide the government with detailed information on certain types of transactions[114], either by law or pursuant to a *subpoena*[115]. The *Money Laundering Act* for example, requires that all transactions involving an amount in excess of $10,000 US be reported, and that a copy be kept of all transactions over $100 US[116].It is also worth considering the impact of fluctuations in exchange rates between the American dollar and European currencies in this virtual world based on the greenback[117].

Finally, the competition which currently prevails between the various private financial systems and institutions in the world of electronic money is evocative of the situation which existed in the United States in the 1860s before the creation of the *Federal Reserve*[118], when cheques endorsed by different financial institutions were in circulation simultaneously and consequently were not reliable. Electronic money raises a similar problem - who will guarantee its stability and its validity? Isn't monetary regulation[119], even when virtual, too important to be left in the hands of the private sector?

To summarize...

 Unless the seller specifies on his or her site that he or she is not issuing an offer (for example, by including expressions such as «not binding», or «subject to confirmation»), most national legal systems in Europe and in North America will consider that a commercial offer has been issued and that its acceptance by the buyer on the Internet constitutes a legally binding contract.

 Sales between parties not in the presence of one another via the Internet poses the thorny problem of ascertaining the time and place at which the contract was concluded, which determines the moment of transfer of ownership and risk, and in some cases the law applicable to the contract and the competent court. Unfortunately, national legal systems differ on this point.

 Most national legal systems prohibit both private individuals and companies, on the Internet as elsewhere, from making commitments which are contrary to public order or to public morality, thus rendering the object of the contract illegal.

 An electronic trading letter is a simplified master agreement in which one party, usually a seller, proposes to another party, usually a buyer, the general conditions for the conclusion of subsequent electronic contracts. The offeree need only sign a copy of the letter received and return it to the sender for a master agreement to be legally concluded. The advantages of speed and facility offered by electronic forms of the trading letter have to be assessed in light of the risks that they entail, in particular those related to the rules of evidence. On the other hand, when the trading letter is posted on a server's *home page*, it should be considered as the *general conditions* of the contract, often electronic, which the company proposes to conclude.

 Transactions on the Internet involving consumers are quite minutely regulated in American, Canadian and European consumer law.

 Contractual and legal credit card payment systems usually make the trader the bearer of risks of disputes with buyers (notably consumers) using these methods of payment on the Internet.

First Virtual Holdings is first and foremost an intermediary between buyers and sellers of electronic goods and services on the Internet. This system presupposes that the purchaser and the seller have each concluded a contract with *First Virtual*. In the interests of security, the buyer informs *First Virtual* of his or her account number and credit card information via telephone or fax when concluding his or her contract. The buyer then receives a *Virtual-PIN* - a code which will serve to identify him or her in future transactions. Should the purchaser be interested in an item offered on the seller's site, he or she informs the seller of his *Virtual PIN*. The *First Virtual* server will then check the validity of the account (in particular the accuracy of the card details).

 Currently only one American bank, the *Mark Twain Bank* has taken up the challenge of offering its customers the possibility of converting dollars into cyberbucks and vice versa using software developed by *Digicash*. The bank fulfills such requests by transferring the «electronic sum» to the customer's hard disk, turning it into a veritable wallet.

chapter 7

Cryptography

Why ask questions?

On the Internet, cryptography is necessary to ensure the privacy of messages between individuals, the authentication and integrity of certain information, the protection of commercial and industrial secrets, and the protection of intellectual property rights. Although it is indispensable for companies and private individuals, cryptography poses serious problems for government authorities, because it substantially restricts the investigative powers of law enforcement and intelligence services.

What questions?

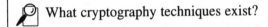 What cryptography techniques exist?

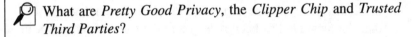 What are *Pretty Good Privacy*, the *Clipper Chip* and *Trusted Third Parties*?

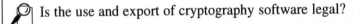 Is the use and export of cryptography software legal?

Introduction

One of the consequences of an open network such as the Internet are problems of security and of confidentiality. Given the increasing frequency of commercial transactions and of the transmission of sensitive information such as financial information or data protected by professional secrecy, users, authors and businesses want to be able to guarantee the security and confidentiality of their information. One of the safest means of doing this is to use cryptography, a technique based on a mathematical algorithm which transforms a message readable to all into a form which is unreadable to any user not in possession of a secret decryption key. In itself, cryptography is not new. Encryption techniques have existed since antiquity. They have been used most extensively on military and diplomatic information, such that they are often assimilated to the status of military material[1]. With the development of the Internet, cryptography has finally emerged from obscurity and is now available to a continually expanding public.

Cryptography can also be used to create digital signatures, to authenticate electronic messages and to verify their integrity (that is, that the message has been received in the same form as that in which it was sent, and that it comes from the source indicated) which, in the context of electronic business, is of vital importance.

From a government perspective, however, cryptography creates the dilemma of having to balance two important and contradictory political objectives. On the one hand, the government must allow the development of techniques destined to protect the confidentiality and security of information and, on the other hand, it must curb the proliferation of technologies which could weaken the surveillance capabilities of law enforcement agencies or intelligence services, since reliable encryption techniques can also be used in the transmission of illegal messages by criminal elements. Effective cryptography facilitates, for example, the transmission and dissemination with complete impunity of terrorist or pornographic messages.

I. Existing cryptographic technologies

There are essentially two distinct types of cryptography: those requiring the use of a private key and those using a public key.

Private key cryptography systems, such as the *Data Encryption Standard* (DES) developed by the American government, operate on the basis of one «private» key which is known to both the sender and the receiver of a message, and which is used both to encrypt and to decrypt the electronic message[2]. The use of private key cryptography means that a person receiving encrypted messages from twenty different people has to use twenty different keys. It also, however, means that the secret key, which must necessarily be communicated from one party to the other, could get lost and could be obtained by a third party. Furthermore, when two people are using the same key it is impossible to guarantee the authenticity of an electronic signature, because there is always a risk that the signature has been forged by the other party.

Public key cryptography, which was developed in 1977 under the name *RSA* (acronym composed of the initials of its inventors, Rivest, Shamir and Adleman) involves the use of two keys, one of which is private and one of which is public. A user who wants to encrypt a message has his or her own private key which can be used to encrypt the message on the basis of unique criteria (thus making it possible to identify this person) and a public key which he or she transmits to all those with whom he or she intends to communicate encrypted messages. By means of a user's public key, members of the general public can also encrypt messages which this user alone will be able to decrypt.

Public key cryptography has the advantage of being efficient, since each user uses only one key to encrypt and to decrypt all the messages that he or she sends or receives. It also has the very great advantage of being secure. Since the public key can only be used to decrypt messages encrypted by the user's private key, it is possible to authenticate the digital signature such that it cannot be repudiated by the user. The only security problem which may arise concerns the authenticity of the public key, or the guarantee that the public key actually comes from the user to whom it is supposed to belong and has not been forged. This problem can be resolved by the creation of a certification authority which issues and tracks public keys, and can therefore guarantee third parties of the authenticity of a user's public key[3].

II. Pretty Good Privacy, the Clipper Chip and Trusted Third Parties

Pretty Good Privacy (PGP) is cryptography software which uses *RSA*. It was created by Phil Zimmermann in 1991 and is distributed free of charge on the Internet. It is in the process of becoming the cryptography software most widely used by private individuals, and some consider it to be virtually impregnable[4]. It was partly in response to the propagation of *PGP* that the Clinton Administration in the United States unveiled in«April of 1993 its «escrowed encryption» project, also known as «Clipper» or the «Clipper chip». This *Escrowed Encryption Standard (EES)* uses a classified symmetrical algorithm developed by the *National Security Agency (NSA)*, and it is only available on *hardware*.

The term *escrowed encryption* originates in the fact that two government agencies, the *National Institute of Standards and Technology (NIST)* and the *Department of Treasury,* each hold half of each key installed on *hardware*[5]. If necessary, and upon due authorization, a law-enforcement agent could obtain each half of the key and decrypt any message encrypted using *Clipper*. In February of 1994, the *Department of Commerce* declared that *EES* constitutes a federal cryptography standard for unclassified information[6]. The fact that the American government has ordered significant numbers of Clipper devices, and their installation in communication equipment such as fax machines, telephones and modems[7], have contributed to the broad distribution of *EES* and to its promotion to the rank of a national standard.

The *Clipper chip* has, however, encountered substantial opposition. The role played by the *NSA*, the fact that government agencies hold the key, its installation in telecommunications equipment, and in particular the possibility that it may become the only legal cryptography technique, have given rise to fears that the American government will unduly control the transmission of information[8].

Finally, a European Directive currently being drafted could compel the member states of the European Union to create a network of «Trusted Third Parties». These «Trusted Third Parties» would hold the private keys of those using encryption programs and, upon authorization by a judge, would transmit the encryption keys to law enforcement authorities in order to enable them to decrypt intercepted messages suspected of being of a criminal nature[9].

III. Is the use and export of cryptography and PGP legal?

A. In North America

The use of cryptography is authorized within the United States and Canada. For reasons of national security, however, the *export* of cryptography software from the United States and Canada is subject to regulation. Cryptography software is in fact included in the *United States Munitions List*, which is part of the *International Traffic Arms Regulations (ITAR)*[10] governing munitions exports in the United States and Canada[11]. More specifically, it would appear that cryptography software, technical data on cryptography and encrypted data may be considered as weapons whose export is illegal if it is not authorized by the American *Department of State*. It should be noted that the disclosure or transfer of technical data to a foreigner, whether this person is resident on American territory or elsewhere[12], constitutes export. Consequently, although the use of *PGP* is legal in the United States and Canada, the act by an American or Canadian user of making this software available on Internet servers may be considered an illegal arms export, since non-American users or users residing outside of the United States or Canada can easily download it.

DES cryptography, for its part, can be used in overseas communications only between American firms and their American-owned overseas subsidiaries. *RC2* and *RC4*, the newest public key cryptography techniques, contain applications which cannot be used in any overseas communications, not even those addressed to subsidiaries[13]. Thus the legality of exporting cryptography software used on the Internet or of transmitting encrypted data via the Internet depends on the type of cryptography used, on the country from which and to which the software and the data are exported, on the person for whom they are intended in some cases and, finally, on the status of persons implicated in the export. An electronic message encrypted and sent by an overseas American, or sent to certain non-American inhabitants of the United States, could constitute an infringement of the *State Department* rules governing the sale of arms[14].

Finally, irrespective of national regulations, some service providers stipulate restrictions regarding the type of information transmitted via their networks. It is therefore necessary to be informed of their rules regarding the transfer of encrypted data, even when such transfer occurs entirely within national borders.

B. In Europe

Most of the member States of the European Union regulate *exports* of encryption programs[15]. These laws assimilate cryptographic techniques to armaments, and therefore subject their export to licensing requirements. In essence, these laws are based on the rules adopted within the COCOM (Coordinating Committee for Multilateral Export Controls), an international organization whose task was to coordinate and limit exports of sensitive material from member countries during the Cold War, and which was disbanded in 1994. Most of the states which were members of this Committee (virtually all of the members of the European Union) have maintained these export licensing regimes for weaponry (which includes cryptography, at least as regards high-level protection programs)[16]. On the basis of this legislation, the unauthorized export of sophisticated encryption software, for example by allowing it to be downloaded by an overseas Internet user, is prohibited.

A European Union Council Regulation of December 19, 1994 institutes a regime of Community control over exports *having either civilian or military uses*[17], which covers notably cryptography equipment, units and components[18]. As regards the *use* of cryptography programs in European Union countries, only[19] two countries have licensing regimes or declaration requirements, these being France[20] and, to a certain extent, Belgium[21]. A bill along these lines was tabled in the Netherlands in 1994, but was abandoned after having been severely criticized[22]. The German government is also preparing a bill regulating the use of cryptography[23].

In *France*[24,] the supply, operation or use[25] of cryptography equipment or services are subject to a twofold regime for each user:
  - there must be prior declaration by the user if the aim of the equipment or services is to authenticate or to verify the integrity of a message;
  - the user must obtain prior authorization in order to fully decrypt or encrypt a message.

The declaration and the request for authorization should be submitted at least one month prior to any use of cryptographic materials.

This twofold system may be made simpler and less cumbersome when a general declaration of use has been made by a supplier or by a user of encryption equipment, in which equipment users or categories of equipment users are specified. In this case, within certain limits, no declaration or application for authorization need be submitted when the software changes user.

It would appear that the French administration (the interministerial delegation responsible for the security of information systems) tends to authorize only cryptography programs of low or medium protection levels, which thus would foreclose upon any general use of PGP[26].

In *Belgium,* a law adopted on December 21, 1994 allows the Ministry of Telecommunications to order the disconnection of equipment from the public telecommunications infrastructure if it proves to be disrupting the effectiveness of the legal surveillance of private telecommunications. It seems that this measure could be applied to encryption methods used on the Internet. Users of such methods therefore run the risk of having their telephone lines disconnected[27].

To summarize...-

 Basically, there are two distinct types of cryptography techniques - those requiring the use of the same private key (such as the Data Encryption Standard) by the sender and by the receiver, and those which use a public and private key (such as RSA), where the user encrypt a message using his or her private key and transmits his to her public key to all those to whom he or she wishes to send messages. This latter system forms the basis of the most user-friendly and widely used software program of all those found and distributed on the Internet: P.G.P. (Pretty Good Privacy).

 Pretty Good Privacy (PGP) is cryptography software which uses the RSA, and which is considered to be virtually inviolable. To combat what is, both for the American government and for its law enforcement services, a monitoring problem, the American government chose to promote an escrowed encryption system - the Clipper Chip - which is «controlled» by two governmental agencies. A European directive currently being drafted could impose a network of Trusted Third Parties who would hold the private keys of all users and who could, in certain circumstances, and with the authorization of the judge, forward these keys to law enforcement authorities.

 Under American and Canadian law, the use of cryptography is legal within the United States and Canada, but the export of such software and of encrypted data is subject to stringent regulation, for reasons of national security. Forwarding this software or data to foreign countries via the Internet may be considered illegal arms export. Most of the member States of the European Union also regulate exports of cryptography software considered to be military equipment. Otherwise, only France and Belgium regulate the use of cryptography, and in very different ways.

chapter 8

Crime

Why ask questions?

The cost of computer crime runs into billions of dollars every year. Multinational and large-scale companies are, of course, the target of *hackers* and industrial spies. Every day, 72,000 attempts are made to gain illegal access to the Internet. Companies will have to take into account the fact that most computer crime is committed by employees.

What questions?

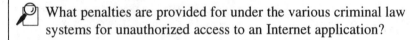 What penalties are provided for under the various criminal law systems for unauthorized access to an Internet application?

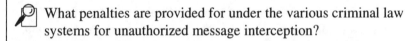 What penalties are provided for under the various criminal law systems for unauthorized message interception?

Can acts or the dissemination of material causing damage on the Internet be punished under criminal law?

Introduction

Two types of offence can be committed on the Internet - conventional offences for which the Internet is merely a means of communication like any other (non-computer crime on the Internet), and offences which involve using the network and computing tools for reprehensible purposes (computer crime on the Internet). In this chapter, we will restrain ourselves to a consideration of computer crime on the Internet. This does not mean, however, that the network is free of non-computer crime. Alongside drug trafficking and the transmission of instructions relating to terrorist attacks and mafia activities, a great deal of pornographic material is circulated on the network[1]. The reason for this is notably the lucrative nature of the pornographic services available on the Internet via the Usenet and WWW protocols, and on BBSs[2]. Apart from being an attack on public order and public morality, the circulation of pornographic material also raises the issue of its accessibility to minors. Nonetheless, the need to make choices and the significant volume of computer crime on the Internet lead us to focus our attention here.

As concerns computer crime, we will consider three categories of computing behaviour[3] susceptible of adversely affecting Internet users.

Unauthorized acces is often the first step in any offence, and refers to a user who without authorization deliberately connects to a network, a server or a file (for example, an e-mailbox), or who makes the connection by accident but voluntarily decides to maintain it.

Harmful acts or the circulation of harmful material. Once he or she has entered a server, the offender can steal files, copy them or circulate harmful information such as viruses or worms. Although such behaviour does not fall within any precisely defined legal category, it is often classified either as piracy (appropriation, removal and use of data without its owner's knowledge) or as sabotage (alteration, modification or destruction of data or software, the effect of which is to paralyse the computing activity of the system or of the server on the Internet).

Unauthorized interception. In this case, the hacker detects electronic pulses transmitted via the Internet and obtains information not intended for him or her. When such interception occurs outside of any unauthorized access, it is extremely difficult to locate.

The most recent statistics on this form of computer crime on the Internet are enlightening: 72,000 attempts to gain unlawful access are said to occur every day[4]. More generally, and according figures cited by Glenn D. Backer in 1993, over 1,000 viruses had already been identified and he estimated that six new viruses appeared every day[5]. The number of these fraudulent operations gives us some idea of the computing and economic harm that they engender, and of the need for an appropriate reaction.

This level of criminality can be explained in part by the difficulties involved in its repression at an international level in general, and on the Internet in particular. The first of these difficulties lies in *detecting the fraud and in locating its perpetrator.* Although acts of computer sabotage occur rapidly and are frequently quickly discovered due to the dysfunctions they cause, the same cannot be said of unauthorized access or of unauthorized interception, and of piracy. Furthermore, the wide variety of interventions on the Internet (users, access providers, servers, server system operators, etc.) do not make it any easier to determine who is criminally liable. Thus a user who deliberately circulates a virus on an F.T.P. server may be liable, but in some cases the F.T.P. server may also be liable. Finally, international computer crime is developing along with the Internet. Users are scattered all over the world and there is consequently a very strong probability that an offender and a victim will be subject to different national laws. Although international judicial cooperation agreements and bilateral extradition treaties are attempting to remedy some of the difficulties caused by international crime, unfortunately these possibilities are limited[6].

Evidently the law is not ignorant of this spiralling rise in international crime. In addition to international initiatives[7], both American and Canadian law, as well as the legal systems of the vast majority of European countries have criminalized the three types of computing behaviour referred to above, namely unauthorized access, the circulation of harmful material and unauthorized interception.

I. American law[8]

At the federal level, this being the only level to be considered here, the *Computer Fraud and Abuse Act*[9] covers offences affecting the computing systems of the federal government on the one hand, and those requiring the use of computers located in more than one American state on the other. Evidently communications via the Internet usually satisfy this latter condition, and consequently the *Computer Fraud and Abuse Act* is frequently applied.

Unauthorized access to a computer system is one of the major issues dealt with by the *Computer Fraud and Abuse Act*. Under certain conditions, which we cannot fully elaborate here, unauthorized access or access in excess of limited authorization is criminalized. It is necessary, in all cases, to prove that the intruder intended to transgress the computer system's barriers. It follows, then, that such barriers must exist and that the user should have been aware of them. In practical terms, the user would have encountered a request for a password, or a sufficiently clear indication that the site in question was private. A password request may be inadequate if the log-in password is circulated on the Internet by the network controller. The same is true if this request does not aim to select users, such as is the case of password requests which require only an electronic address or the word «guest» as a reply. Subject to these reservations, this criminalization covers both unauthorized access to the services of an IAP and unauthorized access to paying or non-paying Internet Web servers. The *Act*s also creates two offences aimed at curbing the *propagation of viruses and other malevolent computer programs, as well as sabotage*[10], provided that the damage amounts to more than $1000 in American funds within a period of one year (or that health services are affected). A university student who had circulated a worm on the Internet was convicted under a previous version of this law[11].

On the other hand, the criminal liability of a server administrator who allows software programs to be exchanged between users, or the criminal liability of one of these users, can only be invoked when they participate in the propagation of viruses and other malevolent computer programs if they were aware of the content of the transmission and its consequences.

Finally, the *Electronic Communications Privacy Act* [12] criminalizes access to private electronic communciations or their unauthorized interception. The protection accorded is greater as regards the interception of a direct communication such as a «chat» (a direct conversation by electronic means in which each participant replies to the other in near real time) than as regards the interception of a deferred communication such as electronic mail. The implementation of this protection will furthermore be more difficult as regards Internet applications which allow anyone to participate in a discussion (sites permitting public «chats» between Internet users or «Usenet» groups, for example). It is not impossible, however, for this protection to be invoked in the event of the interception of a message sent to a limited-access discussion group.

II. Canadian law[13]

Unauthorized use of a computer is, of course, at the top of the list of behaviour criminalized under Canadian law and which can be used to denounce criminal use of the Internet. This offence is committed notably when an offender obtains services or functions from a computer illegally, or uses a computer to commit a computer crime[14]. Such acts must be committed without any possibility of belief on the part of the user (appearance) that he or she was acting in colour of right. Here again, system operators thus have a vested interest in adopting security measures destined to protect the private sectors of a site, and especially to clearly indicate on their site that these private sectors are off limits to users. Since the offence involves unauthorized use rather than unauthorized access, it is possible to suppress a user who exceeds the limits established by a service. As the offence covers use of functions, it also indirectly allows the suppression of illegal data appropriation on the Internet. Intruders attempting to appropriate data will necessarily first have to arrange the communication of the data via the computing system. In so doing, they use telematic or computer services without authorization.

The crime of *computer wrongdoing* covers not only the simple destruction or modification of data, but also all acts which render the data useless or which temporarily or permanently interrupt or disrupt access to the data[15]. This offence can be used to convict both the authors of direct and harmful attacks on the Internet, and the authors of viruses or worms. As is the case under American law, another user or server who participates in circulating malevolent software can only be considered criminally liable if they were aware of the presence of the virus, of its nature and of its harmful effect.

The interception of private messages, including telecommunications messages, is also a criminal offence in Canada, insofar as the hacker in question could reasonably have expected the intercepted message to be confidential[16].

III. European national legal systems

Most European countries have in the past ten years or so done their utmost to bring within the auspices of criminal law conduct such as the fraudulent accessing of computer systems or the fraudulent maintaining of such access, the dissemination of viruses, or the interception of computer messages.

Faced with judicial reluctance to apply «conventional» criminal provisions to conduct such as that described above, and given the extent of the phenomenon of computer crime, national legislatures have considered this issue, referring where necessary to the work of the Council of Europe[17], and have adopted (often cumulatively) specific provisions relating to the computing aspects of «conventional» criminal offences, or provisions creating new offences.

For example, the French law of January 5, 1988[18] adds to the French penal code a chapter on computer crime[19] which criminalizes, among other things, fraudulent access to or maintaining fraudulent access to a computer system, and which stipulates a minimum fine of FRF 100,000 for such offences. Dishonest users could incur criminal liability on this basis, possibly at the initiative of an *access provider* or a server (Art. 323-1). Introducing a virus is also subject to punishment and anyone committing this crime risks three years imprisonment and a fine of FRF 300,000, not to mention possibly dramatic civil consequences (Art. 323-2)! Fraudulently intercepting messages can also give rise to penalties ranging from three months' to three years imprisonment and to a fine of between FRF 2,000 and

FRF 5,000 (Art. 323-3). It should be noted, however, that this law of January 5, 1988 does not solve every problem, and certain injurious conducts, such as the fraudulent copying and re-using of a file where the copying does not alter the original file and the copier has not fraudulently accessed the system, are not covered by any of the punishable offences foreseen by this law[20].

English law also punishes deliberate unauthorized access to a computer system by a fine and a term of imprisonment of no more than six months, in cases of «simple» access, and by a fine and a term of imprisonment which may be as long as five years, if access was gained in order to commit more serious offences such as theft or blackmail. Introducing a virus into a computer system or, more generally, any deliberate act which results in the unauthorized modification of a computer is punishable by a fine and a term of imprisonment of up to five years[21]. The notion of modification covers any addition, alteration or deletion of data, and will be considered illegal if the person committing the act was not so authorized or did not have the approval of anyone with such authorization[22]. Finally, the deliberate interception of telephone communications or of communications effected via a public telecommunications system may lead to penalties consisting of fines and a term of imprisonment of no more than two years[23].

It is not possible, in the context of this discussion, to analyze the computer crime laws of all of the European countries. Provisions similar to those of French and English law mentioned above exist in most western countries, although evidently the approaches adopted sometimes vary, particularly as regards the point at which the various legislatures consider that illegal access, to take but one example, should be subject to *criminal* sanctions.

All of these different approaches, however, are inspired by the same concern to make electronic communications, transactions and exchanges as reliable as possible. There is no doubt that these new laws provide effective penalties for most of the crime committed via the Internet.

To summarize...

 Unauthorized access to a computer system or overstepping restricted authorization can carry criminal liability, under both American and Canadian law and under most of the European legal systems.

 Intercepting private or confidential electronic messages is a criminal offence under American, Canadian and European law. Direct communications (such as the *chat function*) benefit from greater protection in this respect than deferred communications (such as. electronic mail).

 Most acts undertaken or material distributed on the Internet which cause damage can be punished in criminal law, such as piracy, sabotage or more specifically the dissemination of malicious software (such as viruses or worms).

chapter 9

Liability on the Internet

Why ask questions?

Before establishing a presence on the *Internet*, and every year thereafter, a company's budget forecast should factor in the cost of liability that may be incurred, at least in terms of risk (profits and losses). Businesses should compare the cost of the risk with that of the technical (software, etc.) and legal investments (drafting of an *acceptable use policy*, contract analysis, legal audit, insurance, etc.) involved in avoiding or reducing this risk. The user will suffer a financial loss if he or she is sentenced under civil law. In addition, apart from having to pay compensation, companies may suffer other financial loss resulting from an action in liability, namely the financial loss incurred by harm done to their corporate image. Finally, company managers, like users, may incur criminal liability in some cases.

What questions?

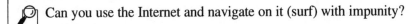 Can you use the Internet and navigate on it (surf) with impunity?

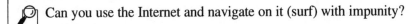 Can companies be held liable for the actions of their employees on the Internet?

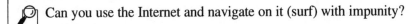 What penalties are imposed by law if you fail to respect it?

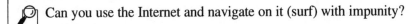 In what cases do you incur criminal liability?

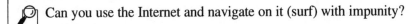 How can a company protect itself against the risk of liability?

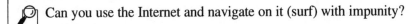 Can users (companies or a private individuals) take legal action against their access provider?

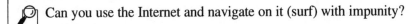 Can you take legal action against a server on the Internet?

Introduction

The various «actors» on the Internet (users, servers, access providers, etc.) are responsible for their conduct on the network. If they commit a criminal offence (such as libel or breach of public order), then the state could hold them *criminally liable*. Furthermore, if the conduct of one of these actors harms another, the latter could claim civil compensation, usually in a financial form (civil liability), either on the basis of a contract concluded between them (*contractual civil liability*), or on the basis of general principles or specific liability provisions (*extra-contractual civil liability*). A «player» on the network may, of course, incur civil and criminal liability simultaneously. Civil liability is in fact frequently incurred as a result of an offence committed on the Internet (such as libel, forgery, credit card number piracy and the use of pirated numbers, or the propagation of a virus).

One of the main difficulties in establishing liability on the Internet consists of locating the perpetrator of the damage. This difficulty is now leading some to recommend that, in the event of damages, action systematically be taken against Internet servers and access providers rather than against the perpetrator him or herself.

Compensation for damage caused by an Internet actor will usually consist of a sum of money paid to the victim (compensatory damages). Sometimes if an item is disseminated which seriously harms a right or a freedom, *action to restrain interference* may be taken, ordering the perpetrator of the act to cease distribution immediately, for example on his or her Web server. Furthermore, if incorrect or calumnious information is disseminated, the *right to reply* can, in some cases, provide an acceptable form of redress[1]. Application of the right of response foreseen for the written press could oblige the administrator of a Web page on which someone has been maligned to insert a reply by the victim, insofar as this reply is not contrary to public morality, public order, the law or the legitimate interests of third parties[2]. It is reassuring to note that this right of reply will not often need to be requested *through legal channels,* since the principle behind certain Internet applications (discussion groups, for example) is to allow everyone to reply to everyone else.

I. The framework of liability on the Internet

A. The various actors of Internet liability

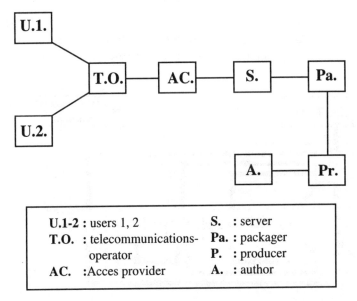

U.1-2 : users 1, 2	**S.** : server
T.O. : telecommunications- operator	**Pa.** : packager
	P. : producer
AC. :Acces provider	**A.** : author

The above diagram illustrates the various actors involved on the Internet, or more precisely the various functions which can be executed there. One person can actually perform several functions at the same time. Thus a user is also the author of the messages that he or she posts in discussion groups. He or she may also produce «multimedia» documents disseminated on the Web and why not act as a server at the same time. Consequently, establishing the civil and criminal liability of an Internet actor implies analyzing the function and role which he or she assumes on the Internet at a given moment, rather than the first or most obvious categorization.

The logic behind this general diagram is the logic of dissemination. Via an access provider and using the channel of a telecommunications operator, user no.1 accesses servers containing material which in some cases has been produced by producers, assembled by packagers, and often contains creations by authors. Via certain applications (such as discussion groups), this user can contact other users (user n°2, for example).

For reasons of facility and particularly in the interests of legal security, it is important to know which relations are governed by the application of a contract.

B. Contractual liability

1. The various contractual relations between Internet actors

Several of the relations between Internet players are governed by contract. These can be indicated as follows on the diagram of Internet actors:

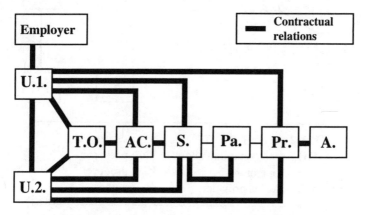

a. The various contractual relations between Internet actors

a.1. Contractual relations between an access provider and subscribers

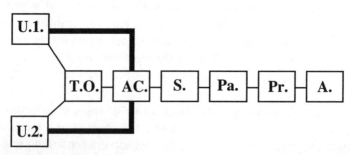

The contracts concluded between an access provider and a user can stipulate the respective obligations of the parties, their prerogatives and the limits within which they may act, but also exceptions to or restrictions on their liability (for example, excluding or limiting the liability of an access provider in the event of technical problems inherent in the telecommunications networks used). Even if this contract is strictly basic, it will generally form the foundation of any legal action the user may take, if the access provider either fails to provide the user with access to the Internet or discontinues this access, or if this access does not correspond to the services proposed. Thus the user could take action against his or her access provider if his or her password is used illegally by proving, for example, that the access provider did not provide proper protection for this information, which is by its very nature confidential. Consequently, we cannot advise access providers strongly enough to either encrypt the password files (PSSWD files), or to protect access to these files in a different way for example, by using the «firewall» technique (a detection function which permits only the entry and exit of data approved by the system).

a.2. Contractual relations between a server and the access provider who disseminates it or provides it with permanent access

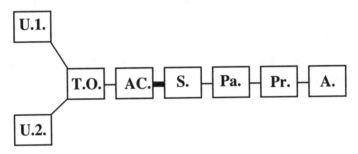

The contract concluded between the server and the access provider who disseminates his or her service will govern most of the relations between the two. For example, this contract may stipulate that the server cannot accept the Web pages of another server without the authorization of the access provider.

a.3. Contractual relations between a producer, particularly a professional producer, and the server who disseminates its products

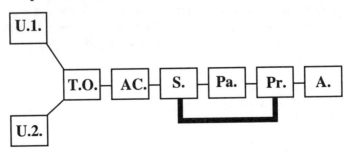

The relationship between a producer and a server who stores his or her material is usually based on a contract. This contract will thus form the basis of their respective liability.

a.4. Contractual relations between certain servers or professional producers and their users

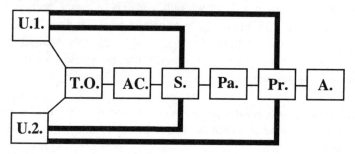

If a server or the producer of a database has concluded a contract for the provision of services with a user, the latter may hold them liable on this basis. We would advise servers and producers to check in particular the quality and lawfulness of the information they disseminate on the Internet.

a.5. Contractual relations between authors and producers

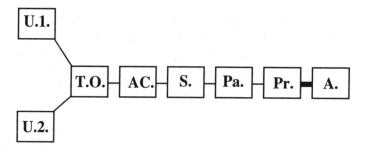

Authors and producers establish relations with one another, and particularly the conditions under which the work created may be disseminated via the Internet, by means of a contract, usually a contract for the assignment of intellectual property rights.

a.6. Contractual relations between users

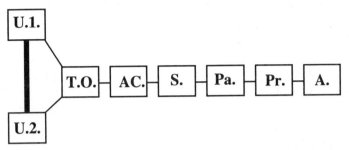

In certain cases, relations between users may be governed by a contract, for example, in the event of a sale between Internet users.

a.7 The employer's liability for employee conduct on the Internet

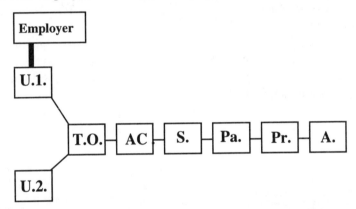

The main problem an employer risks facing when employees use the Internet, both under French law[3], and under American[4] and Canadian[5] or English law[6], is liability for an offence committed by an employee in the exercise of his or her functions and particularly in the workplace. Generally, the employer is liable for those who work under his or her orders and can only evade this liability in certain specific cases stipulated by national legal systems. Thus in certain cases an employer can escape liability by proving that the act in question constitutes gross negligence (sabotage, hijacking of files), or a serious offence (unauthorized access to protected files), or that it has been expressly forbidden in the employment contract (for example, by means of an *Acceptable Use Policy*). Although the employer is liable for employee activities, the latter obviously remain responsible for their own offences. Hence the victim of a forgery can often take action against the employee or the employer, or both.

b. Contractual relations in the field of the provision of professional information, publishing, and production

b.1. The provision of professional information

Contractual relations (legal diagrams) must be distinguished from the technical procedure used to access the information (technical diagrams) in the field of the provision of professional information:

Technical diagrams: *Legal diagrams:*

$$U \leftrightarrow AP \leftrightarrow S \leftrightarrow P$$

$$U \blacksquare P$$
$$\blacksquare \quad \blacksquare$$
$$AP \quad S$$

The user uses his access provider to access a Web server (usually), who disseminates the professional information of a producer against payment.

-The user concludes a contract with the access provider to gain access to the Internet.;

-once he «reaches» a server, he signs a contract with the producer, who undertakes to supply information;

-said producer has already concluded a contract with the server (who is usually an access provider), whereby the latter disseminates the information.

b.2. The fields of publishing and production on the Internet

Contractual relations (legal diagrams) must be distinguished from the technical procedure used to access information (technical diagram) in the field of publishing on the Internet:

Technical diagrams	*Legal diagrams*
$U \leftrightarrow AP \leftrightarrow S \leftrightarrow P$	$U \blacksquare\ P \blacksquare\ S$
The user uses an access provider to gain access via a server to the «products» of another producer (articles, books, databases, music, etc.)	The user concludes a contract with a producer who disseminates his products on the Internet[7] himself.
$U \leftrightarrow AP \leftrightarrow S \leftrightarrow P$	$U \blacksquare\ A \blacksquare\ S$
The user uses an access provider to gain access via a server to the creations or documents of an author. The development of the Internet has meant that authors will become their own «producers or publishers».	The user concludes a contract with an author who, in the same way as the producer in the previous case, has already concluded a contract with a server for the dissemination of his work.

2. *Liability clauses*

Clearly, the majority of the actors on the Internet wish to avoid, or at to least substantially restrict their own liability, and at the same time often extend that of their contracting partner. The most influential partner in the negotiations will usually include in the contract clauses which are likely to promote his or her own interests. It is, therefore, important to know to what extent clauses which limit, deny, or extend liability are valid. There is no doubt as to the lawfulness of clauses extending liability. This is also true of clauses restricting liability, which are admitted in French[8], American[9], Canadian[10] and English law[11], but within certain limits. Thus under most European and North American legal systems, an offender cannot escape liability for misrepresentation or for an offence against public order provisions (for example, consumer protection) or criminal provisions (for example, an access provider cannot contractually evade his liability vis-à-vis the user if he deliberately propagates a virus). Similarly, a party may not agree to a clause which would result in obliterating the very essence of the obligation[12]. An access provider cannot, therefore, deny *all liability* vis-à-vis a subscriber.

In any case, a certain degree of moderation must be observed. Hence an access provider who, in addition to general access to the Internet also provides access to his or her own electronic message base or server, will be well advised to provide for a general disclaimer of liability for information that users may gather on the Internet (Web servers, discussion groups, etc.), but to acknowledge liability regarding the content of the information over which he or she has control (such as that circulating via his or her Web server, or his or her own message bases over which he or she exercises control).

II. *Invoking the liability of the various players*

We will consider in turn the liability of users, servers and of access providers, authors and telecommunications operators. In each case and in the interests of clarity, the various forms of liability will be classified in terms of the party who can invoke them (liability of the server invoked by a user or the holder of intellectual property rights, for example), although this classification is only relevant when considering civil liability.

A. The user's liability

1. Liability invoked by another user

There are numerous possibilities for disputes between Internet users. A user can fraudulently employ the password of another user in order to access the Internet, or pirate a credit card number, commit an act of defamation, intercept private messages, or disseminate viruses. All of the harmful acts which a user can carry out using any Internet application (*e-mail, Newsgroup, etc.*) justify the invocation of his or her liability by the victim under French law. Under Anglo-Saxon law, however, liability can only be invoked in such cases if there is a law or a *tort* providing for the redress of injury.

We shall consider in particular the liability of the user in the event of defamation or the invasion of privacy.

a. Liability for defamation

Defamation can give rise to criminal and civil liability on the part of the author under American, Canadian[13], French and English law. Thus, under French law, in cases of defamation the author will be held liable on the basis of criminal law, and compensation for the injury suffered could be obtained under the terms of section 1382 of the civil code.

In England[14], the first case of defamation on the Internet which gave rise to legal proceedings occurred in December 1993, when Dr Laurence Godfrey instituted proceedings against Dr Phillip Hallam-Baker for «libel or alternatively slander[15] in respect of articles posted on the USENET computer network»[16].

b. Liability for invasion of privacy

As we have seen[17], an Internet user who intercepts the contents of private communications or who accesses private zones of computers belonging to other users may be held liable. Similarly, failure to comply with privacy protection provisions regarding computer filing is punishable under criminal and civil law. Finally, in most national legal systems, the dissemination of a message damaging to the privacy of another will be punished under civil law[18].

2. Liability invoked by the access provider or the server

Access providers or servers may wish to invoke the liability of a user because he or she *gains unauthorized access to the system* (for example, the user has not paid or it is a private network), because the user exceeds his or her lawful access (for example, access outside of the fixed time limits); or because he or she *causes damage upon access* (by disseminating a virus, for example). The server could also reproach the user for illicitly copying works disseminated on the server or for re-using the server's databases for commercial purposes. Similarly, the access provider could reproach the user for pirating password files.

As we have seen, these potential situations can be settled under the terms of a contract which may stipulate, for example, that the user may not re-use the database made available to him or her by the server, or reproduce the works disseminated, or pass on information thus obtained to third parties. This is the basis on which servers or access providers could take action against users. Failing this, in addition to action in civil liability, servers and access providers may invoke as appropriate the special regulations on unlawful access to information systems[19], and the protection of intellectual property rights.

3. Liability invoked by the copyright holder

The copyright holder can take action against the user for having infringed his or her copyright, for example by rebroadcasting his or her works on the Internet without authorization[20]. Such infringements give rise to criminal as well as civil liability under American[21], Canadian[22], English[23] and French law[24] (action for forgery).

B. Liability of the server and the access provider

Can Internet servers and access providers be held liable for the information which circulates «via them and with their assistance»? This question has frequently been raised by the media. Even today, it is still the subject of fierce debate in France[25]. The reply must be qualified: it is possible to hold a server or an access provider liable for the message which they helped to circulate, but to different degrees.

We will only consider server and access provider participation in the *public dissemination* of information (for example, via a Web server or a Newsgroup)[26].

In the absence of any laws specifically regulating certain forms of liability, the general systems of civil and criminal liability could be applied, as could the editorial liability of these servers and access providers in certain cases. The importance of establishing this distinction between common law liability and editorial liability varies from one country to another. Under American law, it is easy to see why this is important-a primary publisher bears greater liability since he or she is presumed to be aware of what he or she publishes (familiarity).

Under French law, the main consequence of editorial liability is that the publisher bears criminal liability for the acts of the author even before the latter, and even if the author is known (cascade system).

1. Liability invoked by the user

a. «Editorial» liability

a.1. «Editorial» liability under American and Canadian law

An access provider or a server can be likened to a publisher by analogy to the system of liability applicable to the written press. In the context of his or her editorial liability, an Internet access provider or server can be likened either to a so-called primary publisher or to a distributor.

1) Liability as a «primary» publisher

As is the case with any publisher, a server and infrequently an access provider could incur liability if they exceed the limits of their freedom of the press, for example by disseminating pornographic information or information inciting others to commit illegal activities. They must, however, have been aware of the content of the offensive message before disseminating it[27]. Since a primary publisher, unlike a secondary publisher, is always presumed to be familiar with the material which he or she publishes (since he or she claims a certain degree of control over this material[28]), he or she will easily incur liability for certain types of advertising circulated in his or her newspaper or magazine[29], such as false or misleading advertising, for example[30].

But when should a server or an access provider be considered a primary publisher? One common sense criterion comes immediately to mind-when the previous behaviour of the server or the access provider demonstrates the role of primary publisher (they have already acted as publishers, for example, by censoring messages).

In the case of *Stratton Oakmonth, Inc.* v. *Prodigy*, the court adopted another interesting criterion. It concluded that Prodigy was a primary publisher because its publications specified, as an «advertising» argument aimed at families, that offensive material had been removed from its system and that Prodigy used a monitoring software program which automatically filtered mailings in order to detect offensive vocabulary[31]. Editorial liability is thus more likely to be incurred under American law if the server and the access provider have themselves emphasized the control that they exercise.

2) Liability as a distributor or «secondary publisher»

Servers or access providers who act simply as technical intermediaries, that is, who merely distribute information without exercising any editorial control as such, are not usually obliged to examine the content of the messages they circulate[32]. They can only incur liability if they were aware or should reasonably have been aware of the message, taking into account the size of the server's or access provider's computing equipment, and the degree of control that they exercise as a result[33].

In the case of *Cubby Inc* v. *CompuServe*, the court decided that *CompuServe*, which is both an access provider and a server, could be likened to an electronic book shop or library engaged in a gainful activity. Consequently, *CompuServe* had the choice of whether or not to make the offensive periodical available to the public, but once it had made the decision, it no longer had any editorial control over the content of the periodical. The court found that a computer data base was the functional equivalent of a news distributor or a public library, and that accordingly, in the interests of not hindering the circulation of information, it should only be subject to the criterion of the knowledge which a reasonable person could be expected to have[34]. To conclude, let us say that just as we feel that it is legitimate for a Web server to incur liability as a primary publisher, so we feel that is it reasonable, under American law, for an access provider—in his or her capacity as an access provider—to be considered a simple distributor.

a.2. Editorial liability under French law

Servers or in rare cases access providers involved in the public distribution of information on the Internet, could in certain circumstances be considered publishers, and could therefore be subject to a system of strict liability stipulated by the law of July 29, 1881 relating to the written press, but also by the legislation of March 11 1957 on literary and artistic property, amended and supplemented by the law of July 3, 1985[35].

The written press was regulated under French law shortly after it appeared, owing to its «capacity to disseminate information». This was also the case concerning radio, television, and Minitel. Today it is the Internet's turn. While waiting for the legislature to enact a law specific to the Internet, or for jurisprudence to be established, it seems that certain public Internet applications can be linked to the law on the press[36]. In fact, everything which is regulated by the law of 1881 can be found on the Internet, such as books, articles, newspapers and magazines, or periodical texts which may unfortunately contain defamatory, provocative or insulting messages or even banned publications[37]. Consequently, if committed on the Internet, these various infringements of the law of 1881 could entail a criminal sentence imposed upon the party qualified as the publisher. Under French law, beyond the legal definitions established by the laws of 1881 and 1957, which are strongly imbued with the law on intellectual property and publishing contracts, the publisher may be considered as the party who *takes responsibility for the publication and distribution* of copies of a work which is the product of the author's own imagination. This could be the server or the access provider, depending on the role that they have assumed on the Internet. In this case, the server or the access provider could therefore be considered criminally liable as the main perpetrator of the offence. Moreover, they could incur serious civil liability, as can clearly be seen from the recent «wild carrots and hemlock» case[38].

a.3. «Editorial» liability under English law

When access providers or servers exercise a certain degree of control over the information, they may be held liable for defamation (as publishers), or for false information. Even though they have to be legally considered publishers only as regards defamation, and may incur liability for false information on the basis of the *tort of negligence* whether or not they are publishers, we have decided to consider these two issues under the heading of editorial liability. These two actions in fact always refer to a certain level of control which access providers and servers must exercise in respect of the content of the information and the messages which they distribute.

1) Liability for defamation

-Liability as a publisher

Under English law, on the basis of the *«tort of defamation»*[39], anyone taking part in the dissemination of defamatory messages will be held liable in the same way as the author[40]. Hence, in addition to the author himself or herself, the publisher, the printer, the distributors or the sellers may also be held liable.

In order to exonerate themselves of liability, those accused of defamation will, in principle only, have recourse to the means of defence granted to the author. As a result, they will not be considered liable if they can prove that the statement is true, or that it constitutes a *fair comment*[41], that is, the honest expression of an opinion, even if this opinion is unjust or exaggerated, provided that it is based on existing facts and is void of any malicious intent[42].

In the world of the Internet, in the event of the publication of a defamatory message on a Web page or in a Newsgroup, the servers and access providers could—depending on their activity—be compared to a publisher, a printer, a distributor or a seller[43]. It is up to the judge to assess this qualification, taking into account the degree of control over the content of the information exercised by these Internet actors[44]. Thus it is probable that servers who regularly check all the messages they distribute will be considered publishers, and will accordingly incur liability. The same will probably apply to servers who run moderate discussion groups, and to access providers whose network, in terms of size, can reasonably be effectively checked pertaining to the content of the messages circulating on it[45].

-Liability as a distributor
The system of liability imposed upon those who are likened to the author of the defamation, such as publishers, is fairly severe. Hence, in the *Defamation Act* of 1952 *(innocent defamation)*, English law provided for a system of lesser liability for those who only play a secondary role in the distribution of a defamatory message. This system is very useful on the Internet, since it does not seem fair to impose editorial liability on an access provider or on the manager of a system or network whose size renders it impossible, in practical terms, to check all of the messages (the major F.T.P. servers or less moderate discussion groups, for example). Consequently, access providers and servers considered as simple intermediaries could be likened to a distributor, and thus be subject to the less severe system of the *Defamation Act*[46]. The effect of this classification, as regards their liability for defamation, is simple: once they have been classified as distributors, servers and access providers can escape liability by proving that they were not aware that the content of the message they were disseminating was defamatory and that this «ignorance» was not due to negligence on their part[47].

2) Liability for disseminating false information
In terms of the provision of professional information, relations between the server and the user are usually regulated by a contract. Thus, if the server disseminates false information, the user can invoke his or her liability on the basis of this contract.

If there is no contract, a service provider may nonetheless incur liability for the dissemination of false information on the Internet[48], probably on the basis of the *tort of negligence*. This system of civil liability is applied differently, depending on whether the damage is material (physical) or purely economic. The publication of information on the Internet can give rise to both types of damage.

Information which causes *physical damage* falls under the common system of the tort of negligence[49]. For a person to be considered liable on the basis of this tort, it is first of all necessary to prove the existence of a duty of care between the parties in the type of situation envisaged. Secondly, it must be shown that the party in question has not demonstrated the degree of care usually required in this type of situation and that damage has been suffered. Finally, it must be shown that there is a causal link between the default and the damage. The *Clayton* v. *Woodman & Son (Builders) Ltd.*[50] decision opened up the way in this matter, by admitting the claim of a worker against an architect in respect of harm he had suffered as a result of following incorrect instructions given him by the latter. As far as we are aware, there are no English decisions dealing with the liability of the publisher in the event of false or incorrect information which may cause physical harm. The main difficulty here is that of proving *the existence of a duty of care* on the part of the publisher vis-à-vis his or her readers[51]. This duty can only exist if it can fairly, justly and reasonably be imposed in the context of the relationship in question. However, it is possible to envisage that in certain cases, an access provider or a server may incur liability on this basis for the dissemination of information which may cause physical harm to a person who uses it believing it to be true (such as a user who makes a bomb on the basis of information obtained on the Internet, and is injured in consequence).

The courts adopt a different approach regarding incorrect information which causes only *purely economic damage*. In this case, for liability to be incurred, in addition to proving the duty of care between the parties, it is also necessary to show that there is a special relationship (a relationship of closeness) between the person providing the information and the person using it. This additional condition limits the application of redress in respect of *negligent misstatement* [52] to situations in which the party providing the information supplies specific, incorrect information intended for persons whose problems or needs he or she is familiar with. On the Internet, this type of liability is thus difficult to envisage when information is disseminated to the general public. It could only be incurred if information is disseminated on the basis of the needs of a particular user. However, it should be noted that certain authors advocate extending the application of this system so that all information providers incur liability, even if the information is not provided for a specific reason of which they are aware[53].

b. Recourses which do not fall within the regime of editorial liability

b.1. Under North American law

As we have already seen, in order to take into account the new problems of liability posed by the development of information technology, which it is sometimes difficult to cover under common law *torts*, the legislatures of these countries have adopted specific regulations pertaining to information technology, often dealing with it under criminal law. Some of these laws also provide for civil recourse.

1) Liability for invasion of privacy

Users may complain that a private communication has been intercepted by an access provider (violation of e-mail, for example) or a server (monitoring by a B.B.S. administrator, for example). Although certain types of conduct are subject to punishment in criminal law, under American law, as we have seen[54], technical service providers still have a considerable margin of manoeuvre to carry out their task. The regulations protecting privacy in respect of the computer processing of personal data of course also apply to the activity of Internet access providers and servers.

2) Liability for incorrectly labeled files

Another problem specific to the roles of access providers and servers as intermediaries on the Internet is that of whether or not they are liable for the correct, clear, and exact labeling of the files on their computer systems[55]. It would appear that under American law, access providers and servers can be held liable for incorrect labeling due either to their own negligence, or to that of other users. They could, therefore, be held liable if a child inadvertently downloaded material which could be emotionally upsetting[56] as a result of incorrect labeling. Although the parents of the child naturally have a duty of supervision, the liability of the manager of the computer system in this area will once again be determined on the basis of the criterion of what is «reasonable»[57]. It would, therefore, be useful for the system manager to be aware of client expectations, and to include a clause in the contract with his or her client covering this issue.

3) Liability for viruses and malicious software

Evidently anyone who disseminates a virus is liable for this action and for the damage caused by the virus, but it is sometimes difficult to identify or locate these people. In most cases the user will thus be able to invoke the liability of the access provider or the server if a malicious program (a virus or a worm, for example.) from the Internet infects his or her computer system.

Such recourse by clients will be based on their contract, particularly if it stipulates that a continuous service will be provided and if this service is interrupted by the malevolent program[58]. In the absence of a contract, access providers and servers could incur liability on the basis of *the tort of negligence*. The degree of diligence which access providers and servers are supposed to demonstrate has not, however, been precisely defined. It is nonetheless probable that an access provider or a server who does not take precautions to ward off the threat of a virus (frequent checks using an anti-virus system) on the site visited could incur liability. Since the firewall[59] practice is also widely used, access providers or servers who do not have a firewall to protect their clients, or who do not explain to users how to install a firewall, could incur liability under many legal systems if damage is caused to users transiting via their sites. Similarly, on the basis of this *tort of negligence*, an access provider or a server who does not protect client passwords could be compelled to compensate them in the absence of a contract.

The user cannot, however, invoke the liability of the access provider or the server (and consequently avoid liability himself or herself) if he or she has not shown reasonable diligence and if his or her acts have harmed the operator (for example, if the user chooses a password which is too simple or if he or she writes it down or leaves it next to his computer[60]).

b.2. Under French law

Apart from any particular criminal legislation, anyone who suffers damage of whatever nature can under French law invoke the liability of the person who caused the damage on the basis of the general principle of civil liability provided for by section 1382 ff. of the civil code. It is simply necessary to establish the existence of damage suffered by a victim, a fault on the part of the author, and a causal link in order for the author of the damage to be compelled to compensate the victim. Further to the application of this rule, under these conditions access providers or servers are liable for any shortcoming in respect of normally diligent behaviour, without it being necessary to demonstrate that this shortcoming falls within the application of a specific civil action (such as *tort*). This is convenient for the user, who can invoke the liability of the access provider or server, particularly if his or her privacy is invaded, if his or her site is infected by a virus, or he or she suffers damages as a result of incorrect file labeling.

1) Liability for invasion of privacy

As under North American law, intercepting electronic communications and gaining unauthorized access to computer files are criminal offences under French law. French law also protects privacy with regard to the processing of personal data. In addition, on the basis of the principles of civil liability and of the protection of privacy[61], servers and access providers can incur liability if they invade the privacy of a user. Such an invasion of privacy may result from the dissemination on a Web server of information revealing details of the life of a private person, or of public figures to a certain extent, without their consent.

2) Liability for the dissemination of malicious software

As under American law, the user can invoke the contractual or extra-contractual civil liability of an access provider or server if a malicious program (such as a virus or a worm) from the Internet has infected his or her computing system as a result of negligence on their part.

3) Liability for incorrectly labeled files

Access providers and servers could be held liable for incorrect labeling due to their negligence.

4) Civil liability for the content of information (apart from editorial liability)

When a publisher has committed a harmful act which does not fall within the framework of the law of 1881, recourse is still possible if, for example, he or she has been guilty of negligence in monitoring the content of his or her publications.

b.3. Under English law

Under English law, there is no general principle of liability comparable with section 1382 of the French civil code. The matter is governed by the *torts of common law* which constitute a catalogue of *actions in tort* and which, when the case in question satisfies the conditions for the application of a *tort* (*tort of negligence, tort of nuisance, tort of defamation*, for example[62]), can be used to obtain civil redress. It would seem that by analogy, it is possible to apply some of these actions to disputes caused by the network of networks, specifically those in which access providers and servers incur liability.

1) Liability for invasion of privacy

It should be remembered that under English law, the interception of electronic communications and unauthorized access carries criminal punishment, but the national legal system does not comprise a general principle on the protection of privacy which could be invoked if messages threatening privacy are disseminated. Access providers and servers are, of course, always subject to the application of the rules protecting privacy with regard to computer filing[63].

2) Liability for the dissemination of viruses, damage caused by hackers and incorrectly labeled files

Under English law, the user may bring an action for liability against access providers or servers for damage caused by viruses, hackers or incorrect file labeling on the basis of *tort of negligence*[64], provided that the access providers or servers in question were aware of the risk of damage (even if they did not commit the act in question themselves), and did nothing to avoid it (such as a server who, aware of the risk of contamination by existing viruses, does not take the precaution of installing an anti-virus program and launching it regularly on his or her site).

It should also be remembered that liability incurred in respect of the dissemination of a virus may also be criminal[65] under English law.

2. Liability invoked by the author

Internet access providers or servers can also incur liability if they take part in the dissemination or distribution of forged works. This liability can be all the more easily incurred under American and

English law[66] since the infringement does not involve any requirements as to intent or even knowledge[67].

Thus in the case of *Playboy Enterprises Inc.* v. *Frena*, a B.B.S.
computer system manager who allowed users to access his servers
and message bases in return for payment was held liable for the
distribution of unauthorized copies of images protected by *copyright*. The system manager claimed that he had not placed the
images himself and was not aware of the infringement. The court
ruled that knowledge was not a requirement when determining the
existence of an infringement of *copyright*[68]. The sub-committee of
the Canadian Advisory Committee on the Information
Superhighway (CCAI) advocates that system operators should
only be held liable for the unauthorized distribution of protected
material on their systems if they were aware of the material in
question, and did not take reasonable measures to withdraw it from
their systems. The extent of the defence remains ambiguous, however, since it is not easy to ascertain whether a system operator is
or is not obliged to set up an inspection system to seek out material which could be covered by *copyright* protection, or whether it is
enough simply to remove it further to a complaint or when the
material is observed by chance[69]. Consequently, it would appear at
the moment that access providers and servers run a serious risk of
incurring liability, in the event of copyright infringements occurring on their systems under Canadian law as well, irrespective of
whether or not they were aware of the offence.

C. Author's liability

Authors on the Internet will incur liability for the content of messages which they claim are their own[70]. In particular, they could be
held liable for the offence of provoking racial hatred[71], or crimes
and misdemeanors[72], offences against the President of the Republic
or foreign Heads of State, acts which undermine the authority of
the law, the forbidden dissemination of information on adoption or
suicide, the dissemination of pornographic services, defamation or
insult[73], invasion of privacy, infringement of copyright or violations of public order and public morality[74], false advertising[75], or
the dissemination of false news[76]...

Similarly, an author who provides incorrect information could be held liable, as was established by jurisprudence in the wild carrots and hemlock case[77].

D. *The liability of telecommunications operators*

Telecommunications operators who convey information, and in particular, who establish the connection between the access provider and the user, rarely incur liability[78]. However, there may be occasions when this situation may arise, such as in the event of a technical alteration or the loss of messages while being transmitted via the network[79].

To summarize...

 The various «players» on the Internet (private individuals, companies, authors, producers, access providers, servers, telecommunications operators) may incur civil and criminal liability for their conduct on the Internet.

 Companies are liable vis-à-vis third parties for certain behaviour on the part of employees «in the execution of their functions» on the Internet (this concept varies from one legal system to another).

 The regulations which apply to the Internet foresee either sentences to pay compensation or criminal sentences.

 The «players» on the Internet could, depending on the various national legal systems, be subject to criminal penalties in the following cases in particular: defamation, insults, invasion of privacy, breach of the public order or of public morality; misleading advertising, forgery, piracy, unauthorized access, dissemination of viruses, credit card piracy, etc.

 An economically powerful «player» on the Internet (for example, an access provider, a server or a company) can protect itself from civil liability vis-à-vis co-contracting parties by including liability disclaimers in contracts. The validity of such clauses usually depends on their scope and on the context of the contract. Businesses would also be well advised to draft an *acceptable use policy* (describing acceptable employee conduct), and to attach it to employment contacts and post it at the workplace.

 User recourse against his or her access provider will be based mainly on the services subscription contract between them. Depending on the various national legal systems, the access provider could incur extra contractual liability, in particular for invasions of privacy (for example, violation of the rules concerning the computerized filing), or for the dissemination of malicious software. Depending on the various legal systems, the access provider will sometimes agree to accept liability as a distributor and on rare occasions as a publisher.

Relations between users and non-professional servers on the Internet are rarely contractual. These servers (which may be company servers) are thus most frequently liable on an extra-contractual basis in the same cases as the access provider, but also sometimes in cases of incorrectly labeled files and the dissemination or incorrect data. Professional servers can usually be held liable thanks to the existence of a contract for the provision of services between the server and a user. Finally, depending on the degree of control that they exercise over the content of the information on the server, Internet servers may also be liable as «publishers».

chapter 10
Evidence

Why ask questions?

Companies involved in commerce on the Internet sometimes need to prove their claims in a court of law. For example, they may need to provide evidence that a contract has been concluded or that a software package has been delivered on the network of networks. As regards contractual relationships, various hypotheses are possible (*home shopping*, agreements between companies, etc.) Companies are confronted with evidence law requirements stipulating the conditions under which a computer document can be produced as evidence in court. Consequently it is easier for companies to take into account the requirements of this law and its impact, notably regarding the choice of certain computing equipment or the need for written documents, before beginning their activities on the Internet, rather than to discover the practical implications of these rules during legal proceedings. This legal security often, however, involves additional costs (such as the purchase of optical disks, or the conclusion of evidence agreements, particularly between professionals.).

What questions?

What happens if you are unable to prove in court an act concluded via the Internet or a fact which occurred on the Internet?

What are the main rules of evidence under French law?

What are the main rules of evidence under English law?

What are the main rules of evidence under American and Canadian law?

How can difficulties be prevented rather than «cured»?

Introduction

We have now reached the final chapter of this section devoted to describing the content of Internet law. Although Internet law exists, not all of its players apply it or interpret it in the same way, and some intentionally choose to disrespect it. Consequently, daily life abounds with disputes, particularly among companies, among private individuals, or between companies and private individuals. Where they cannot settle their disputes amicably or through arbitration, it is the legal system which decides.

In this phase of legal activity, Internet actors will have to explain the nature of their dispute to the judge, and they will have to convince him or her. They will have to *prove* facts, exercise their rights and *prove* contracts. Most of the «events» which they will relate will have occurred on the network («I was the victim of defamation in such and such a forum», «I received a virus while downloading this software», «the commercial offer circulated on such and such a Web server misled me», «he failed to respect the contract that we concluded by e-mail on such and such a date», «there is an illegal copy of one of my works on such and such a newsgroup»).

This brings us to a sizeable difficulty and to a crucial moment. The difficulty is sizeable because Internet actors must demonstrate the legitimacy of their claim before a judge and in accordance with established *rules of evidence*. Not everything is admissible evidence in the eyes of the court. Submitting electronic mail is not permitted in some cases, for example, and P.G.P. signatures are not always accepted. The moment is crucial because, if a party fails to prove a fact or a contract to the judge, he or she will exclude it from consideration when deciding the case!

The following paragraphs explain the essential elements of civil and commercial law rules of evidence (we will refrain from considering criminal rules of evidence here) in North America and in two different European legal systems (France and England). We would advise readers unwilling to devote themselves to the technical analysis which follows to nonetheless glance at the last section of this chapter («Caution is essential»), where they will find practical tips for Internet users (for example, store computer data on a durable and inalterable medium such as an optical disk) which will facilitate proving a claim in the event of a dispute.

I. In Europe

A. French law

In French civil law[1,] proof of *facts* [2], such as the issuance or receipt of a message, or the publication of a Web page, is different from proof of juridical acts[3], which covers, for example, payments made or contracts concluded via the Internet[4]. We have chosen to focus our analysis of the evidentiary rules concerning juridical acts on proving *contracts* (sales contracts concluded via the Internet, for example), but the reader should keep in mind that these rules are of broader application. As we shall see, French commercial law[5] does not acknowledge this distinction between proof of facts and proof of juridical acts, which we will nonetheless retain for pedagogical reasons.

1. Proof of facts

How can the sending or reception of e-mail, the circulation of certain remarks on the Web, or the provenance of a message from a given person be proven before a judge? Both civil and commercial law in France stipulate that evidence of all of these facts is unrestricted and that they may therefore be proven by any legal means[6,] A computer file or a print-out of a document circulating on the Internet could then validly be produced in court. It is up to the judge to decide whether or not the computer documents submitted constitute evidence of the fact in question. Evidently, the greater the certainty, reliability[7], durability or inalterability of the computer medium submitted as evidence, the greater is the likelihood of its acceptance by the judge (admissibility), and of its privileging in relation to other evidence (probative value). To satisfy these criteria, Internet users and especially companies are recommended to make frequent and even systematic use of an electronic signature and of a reliable system of storage on an inalterable medium (*see below*, «*Caution is essential*»).

2. Proof of contracts

Proving a contract concluded via the Internet differs depending on whether it is to be proven in the context of a civil or a commercial dispute. It is thus imperative, both for users and for companies, to be informed as to which rules of evidence apply to them. In this respect, four hypotheses beg consideration. When a contract is concluded between a *private individual and a trader*[8],the private individual may prove the existence or performance of the contract in accordance with the rules of commercial law (by any legal means), while the trader will be subject to the stricter rules of civil law, which requires, for example, a signed writing for all contracts worth more than 5,000FRF. Contracts *between private individuals* will be proven in accordance with civil law rules. Finally, the parties to a contract concluded *between traders* are governed by commercial law rules of evidence.

a. Civil law proof of contracts concluded via the Internet

French civil law privileges writings over every other type of evidence (thus a writing has greater probative value than other evidence), and requires a signed and original writing as proof of a contract worth more than 5,000FRF. Only a writing will constitute admissible evidence. The reasoning behind this dual rule is simple: to date, writings have been considered the most reliable evidence. It is not, however, difficult to imagine the difficulties provoked by this rule, both for private individuals and for companies concluding contracts via the Internet.

Rather than analyzing the rule (the writing requirement) and then analyzing its exceptions, we prefer a more practical and pragmatic approach. First of all, we will identify the situations in which *a writing is not required*. The exceptions to the writing requirement rule have a scope of application so broad that Internet users will rarely encounter any real problems in proving a contract concluded on the network, except in the case of contracts of great value. Secondly, we will attempt to explain *to what extent a computer document circulating on the Internet could be considered a signed and original writing*.

a.1. Contracts which need not be proven by a writing, and which facilitate use of the Internet

1) Contracts worth less than 5,000FRF

When the value of the contract is less than 5,000FRF, which is frequently the case on the Internet[9] (for example, in the case of contracts of sale of products such as CDs, books, or clothes), the

French *Civil Code*[10] stipulates that evidence is unrestricted, in other words these contracts may be proven by any legal means, including evidence in the form of computer documents circulating on the Internet. As is the case when proving facts, what is important is to convince the judge, and the use of durable, reliable and inalterable computer media, such as the systematic storage of electronic mail data on optical disks, will help.

2) A party produces «a commencement of proof in writing»

A judge may take into consideration an unsigned writing which is not an original (see below) if it satisfies two conditions. On the one hand, it must «emanate from the adverse party»[11] and on the other hand, it must give an indication of the probable existence of the fact or legal act in question. Subject to these two conditions, a judge may accord to this writing the particular status of a commencement of proof in writing.

It is important to note that this rule does not exist simply for the pleasure of civil law theoreticians. It is important on the Internet, because the print-out of e-mail or of a Web page which a party wishes to use in a lawsuit against its sender or distributor could be qualified as a commencement of proof in writing, and would consequently be admissible as such. In order to facilitate the production of evidence in the absence of a signed and original writing, jurisprudence[12] has considerably broadened the notion of a commencement of proof in writing[13], although it must nonetheless be supported by complementary elements[14], such as computer documents, for example.

3) Certain common practices which preclude the drafting of a writing

The existence of a common practice allows a party to admit into evidence a computerized document (such as an electronic mailbox) as evidence of a contract if the party has been materially or morally prevented from producing a «writing» as a result of that practice[15], that is, if requiring a co-contracting party to conclude a contract in writing is inconceivable under current Internet practices. Are current practices on the Internet widespread and well established enough to preclude a party from requiring a writing of the other party, even as regards a contract of considerable value? We do not think that this is yet the case, but it is certain that for reasons of cost, speed, and efficiency, network practices will tend more and more to avoid written documents.

4) Admission

The commencement of performance of a contract concluded via the Internet (such as the dispatching of goods, or payment) is considered an extrajudicial admission constituting valid proof of the existence of the contract[16.] Here again a party need not produce any signed and original writing in order for a judge to allow his or her claim.

a.2. Contracts which must be proven by a writing-Internet and the signed and original writing requirement

The presentation - which we intended to be reassuring - of cases in which a party could prove a contract concluded via the Internet without a signed and original writing, and thus by means of computer data produced via the Internet and printed out on a printer, should not make us lose sight of the principle laid down in section 1341 of the French *Civil Code* which requires a *written, signed and original contract*[17] (as opposed to a commencement of proof in writing) in order *to prove any contract worth more than 5,000FRF*. This raises the question, then, of whether or not a computer document circulating on the Internet may, under certain conditions, be considered a signed and original writing under French civil law.

1) A signed writing?

The signature has always fulfilled a two-fold purpose - on the one hand, the contracting party identifies himself or herself, and on the other hand, he or she expresses approval of the content of the contract. In our opinion, there would be no formal obstacle to the acceptance of an electronic signature (such as a signature created using P.G.P. encryption) in French civil law, since it fulfils the two functions of a conventional signature. A party could therefore present the other party's encrypted acceptance, which he or she would have decrypted using the public key, as computer evidence of a contract concluded via the Internet. This operation unequivocally proves the identity and consent of the second party. Let us consider a case in which party A sends party B a contract to sign. B types in a consent formula and then indicates his consent to the contract as a whole by encrypting the entire contract using his private key. Since the only way of decrypting this acceptance is to use B's public key, it is clear that the acceptance could only have been encrypted using B's private key. A is thus in possession of adequate proof of B's expression of his consent.

A	**B**
sends the contract, encrypted, to B	decrypts it to see whether he agrees, then takes A's encrypted version, indicates his consent by typing in a consent formula, encrypts it in turn and sends it to C

C decrypts the contract using B's key, sees B's consent, then re-decrypts the message already decrypted once using A's key, and therefore sees A's consent. After having seen these two expressions of consent, C takes the initial version that he received and which was twice encrypted, by A and then by B, indicates his agreement, encrypts it using his key, and returns the entire document to A. Using this procedure, A could produce the electronic document in court and prove to a judge that the three parties have indicated their agreement.

This solution is also possible in the case of a contract between three parties. Let us consider the creation of an original document. Unfortunately, no jurisprudence to date has either confirmed or invalidated this position. A ruling from the Montpellier court of appeal recognized the validity of an electronically signed computer document, on the grounds that the user had used his card and his secret code simultaneously, which constitutes a twofold operation whereby the user can both identify himself and indicate his consent[18]. This decision was pronounced, however, in the context of a dispute implicating the rules of unrestricted evidence (contract worth less than 5,000FRF), and in no way did it accord to electronic signatures a value equivalent to manuscript signatures. While awaiting firm jurisprudential guidelines, parties would therefore be well advised, where possible, to expressly stipulate in writing in a master contract or by means of an evidence agreement that the electronic signature (created using encryption, for example) affixed to documents transmitted via the Internet shall have the same legal value as a manuscript signature.

2) An original?

For a copy to have the same weight as an original, it must bear the signature of all parties to the contract and the signature of the parties against whom the writing is being used. In addition, when contracts create obligations and rights on behalf of various parties (which is often the case, for example, as regards sales concluded via the Internet), the law requires the signature of as many originals as there are parties to the contract[19]. The essential and practical difference between an original and a copy is that the signature on a copy is not original, and is rather a copy of the original. Transposed to the Internet, the problem is obvious. If, after having successfully encrypted a document with his co-contracting party B (such that both of them have «signed» the document, which has thus been encrypted twice), A keeps the original of this file and sends a copy to B, then A is in possession of an original and B of a copy. It is important to note that the fact that the two documents, the original and the copy, are strictly identical is not proof that they constitute two originals since, as we have just seen, two identical documents can be obtained by producing an original and copying it digitally. What, then is the solution to proving that as many originals have been produced as there are parties to a contract concluded on the Internet? The contracting parties need only «sign» the various originals using their respective private encrypting keys, but in a different order on each original (in the same way as the signature on conventional original documents is never exactly the same from on document to another, nor is it affixed in exactly the same place on the various originals). If the judge must always use the same decrypting keys, but in a different order, he or she can thus be certain that he or she is in the presence of originals only.

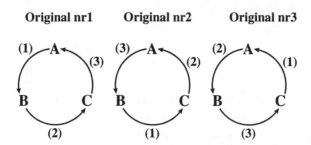

Original nr1   Original nr2   Original nr3

Order of signature: (1), (2), (3)

Let us take a practical look at how to produce three originals using this method. All that is required is to use the same technique three times, in a different order.

It is also interesting to note that the original writing requirement is sometimes waived[20] under French law in favour of a «faithful and lasting» copy which replaces the original if it[21] has been destroyed, and if the copy is a faithful reproduction of it[22]. If certain contracts signed using encryption techniques may be considered originals, as we suggest, then a faithful and lasting copy of these electronically signed contracts could be conserved by storing a copy of the encrypted originals on a reliable computer back-up medium, such as *CD WORM* or optical disk.

b. Proving commercial contracts concluded on the Internet

The difficulty of procuring writings has led the government[23] to introduce liberalized rules of evidence for commercial matters, and which apply to contracts. The parties to a contract thus have a considerable margin of manoeuvre: the contract may be proven by any legal means[24], as is the case for facts under civil law[25] and, once again, it may be proven using computer documents circulating on the Internet. It should be noted that written computer documents can take the place of a daybook or balance book. They must in this case be identified, numbered and dated from their inception, using means which will constitute convincing evidence[26].

B. England (and Wales)

English evidence law concerning transactions effected via the Internet is governed by the *Civil Evidence Act* of 1995[27], which will probably take effect in June of 1996. Under the former system, which is still applicable at the time this book goes to press and which we have decided not to describe, the admissibility before a judge of computer documents like those originating on the Internet (such as e-mail or newsgroup messages stored on hard drive or disk, as well as print-outs from a Web page) could be contested under English law. Difficulties arose from the application of two general exclusionary rules, namely the *best evidence rule* and the *hearsay rule*[28]. The new system considerably simplifies proof by means of computer documents[29] and is consequently very important[30] for Internet users.

1. The admissibility of Internet computer documents

According to the new regime created by the *Civil Evidence Act* of 1995, no computer document[31] is inadmissible as such. All e-mail, newsgroup messages, or Web pages circulated on the Internet and saved on computer or disk will constitute admissible evidence. This applies also to the computerized copy or to the print-out of digital documents circulating on the Internet.

On the other hand, these documents will have to be *authenticated* by a procedure which will vary depending on whether the party submitting evidence exercises a «*business*» (see below) or belongs to a *public authority*, or does not fall into either of these two categories. Furthermore, although all computer documents circulating on the Internet are in themselves admissible, provided that they are authenticated, we will see that they do not necessarily have the same *probative value* in the eyes of the court.

2. The authentication of computer documents: business and public authority or not?

a. Business and public authority

The *Civil Evidence Act* of 1995 facilitates the proving of facts on the Internet or the proving of contracts concluded via the Internet by «*businessmen*» and by public authorities. Their «records» can serve as evidence (broadly interpreted, «records» refers to most computer records stored on computers connected to the Internet, such as an e-mailbox, or the computer files of commercial servers on the Internet, for example). To be considered a *businessman* by English law, one need only exercise an activity for a certain period of time, even without intending to make a profit, and no distinction is made between a company and a physical person. The most minor of activities undertaken on the Internet should therefore benefit from this regime.

In practice, the law requires that a «*businessman*», in the sense defined above, who wishes to prove something using a computer document, must be issued a certificate by a person responsible for the activities that he or she wishes to prove (a sales manager, for example), or responsible for the records attesting to the fact that the computer documents submitted into evidence originated from these records (a computer services manager, for example) .

The absence of data entry into a computer record can also be proven (this was difficult under the *Civil Evidence Act* of 1968[32]). Thus if a customer declares that he or she has paid for a service or product by credit card, an *officer* (the person responsible for payments, for example) of the seller who disputes this payment will be able to certify, by means of an affidavit, that the records are regularly updated, and this can be used as evidence that the payment has not been made. If he or she runs a business, however, the customer will be able to produce his or her own records, and then it is the judge who will decide.

b. What about Internet users who cannot be described as businessmen or public authorities?

As regards Internet users who are not considered businessmen or public authorities by English law, such as an ordinary consumer for example, a computer document must be authenticated in accordance with standards which will be determined by the courts. The courts will probably continue to assess the authenticity of computer documents as before. For a document to be deemed authentic, it will usually be necessary to prove its origin, the nature of its issuance and the identity of the author or issuer. It will also be necessary to prove that the computer system, as well as the receiving computer, were operating correctly[33].

c. The probative value of Internet computer documents

Under English law, convincing the judge requires *tipping the balance of probabilities in one's favour*[34], the occurrence of the fact or act in question must be more probable than improbable[35]. In particular, judges will assess the circumstances surrounding evidence and which may lead to its being considered reasonably reliable. This is why a private individual or a business operating on the Internet has a vested interest in using computer systems which allow the conservation of valid proof on lasting and ideally inalterable media. In the event of a dispute, they will be able to produce evidence more persuasive in the eyes of the court.

When assessing the probative value of an Internet computer document, however, a judge will take into consideration the reasonableness and practicality, for the party submitting the computer document into evidence, of calling in the author of the statement contained in the document as a witness (in most cases this will be the author of the message)[36]. Furthermore, the computer document will be considered more reliable if it was produced at a point in time proximate to the fact or act to be proven. Similarly, a document reproduced several times within the network or within a company will be less secure than a document stored immediately upon receipt. The fact that one or several persons involved in the production or storage of the computer document may have reason to conceal or distort the facts could also have an effect.

II. In North America

The points common to American and Canadian evidence law are explained below. It is nonetheless important to note that *rules of evidence law vary from one state or province to another, and from one jurisdiction to another* (federal, state, administrative).

How can one know whether or not, under American or Canadian law, electronic mail, a message from a newsgroup saved on hard drive or a print-out from a Web page may produced as evidence in court? In general, and setting aside the rules governing proof of certain specific operations on the Internet (C.), the response to this question presupposes a two-fold enquiry:

a) is the evidence provided by the computer document from the Internet *relevant*[37] to the dispute? It will be considered relevant to the dispute only if the party submitting it can prove *the authenticity*[38] *of the Internet computer document* (A).

b) is the computer document admissible under the *hearsay rule* and under the *best evidence rule*, which explicitly exclude[39] evidence in the form of computer documents? (B)

A. *The Internet computer document must be authenticated*

Establishing the authenticity of an electronic message or of a computer document circulating on the Internet firstly involves proving *its origin* (that it comes from the source indicated, such as a particular Web address, for example), and then by proving *its integrity* (that it is a recording or an exact reproduction of the message sent or, in more flexible terms, that it is probable that the message has not been modified)[40]. The authenticity of electronic messages circulating on the Internet may be proven by any means, such as by testimony regarding the circumstances surrounding the message in question, the internal features of the message, or by a demonstration of the procedure used to produce the message[41]. It should also be noted that, in practice, the courts do not encourage pointless debates on questions of authenticity[42].

Apart from this rule, whereby all documents to be produced in court must be authenticated, in various American states or Canadian provinces there are old laws, the *statutes of frauds*, which require that certain types of documents be signed in order to be enforceable. As we have already indicated, the purpose of this requirement is very similar to a certain extent. Its purpose is to identify the source (the person who signs it) and to indicate that person's agreement with the content of the document. These laws date back to a time when the conventional signature, in ink and on paper, was the most reliable and commonly used means of ensuring the authenticity of a document. Despite its outdatedness in the era of computerization, networks and the electronic signature, these laws are still in force in some jurisdictions.

In practice, however, these statutory signature requirements should not pose any problems for businesses and private individuals operating on the Internet. The types of contract for which these laws require a signature are rarely concluded via the Internet. These are mainly contracts carried out by the executors of wills and by administrators, personal surety agreements, real property transfers, contracts which may not be performed during the first year, agreements in consideration of marriage and brokerage contracts in certain states.

In the rare cases where a business or a private individual is in one of these situations (for example, a business which electronically concludes a contract which may not be performed during the first year following its conclusion), a question arises: when a particular jurisdiction imposes a statutory signature requirement, can an Internet computer document satisfy it, by means of an electronic signature created using P.G.P. encryption, for example?

In order to reply to this question, it should first of all be noted that American courts *have adopted a broad interpretation of the statutes of frauds signature requirements*[43]. Courts have accepted typed names and stamps as signatures. They have even recognized that signatures need not necessarily be in ink[44]. In *Watson* v. *Tom Growney Equipment Ltd.*, for example, the court accepted that a typed name on a purchase order constituted the required signature. The courts have also accepted names on postal telegrams[45], leading some authors to argue that all electronic characters, even those not protected by security or reliability measures such as encryption, may adequately authenticate a message[46][47].

Given this relatively liberal interpretation of the signature requirement, and despite the argument of some authors according to which only a signature «likely to attest to a link with the signatory»[48] or a signature created in application of reasonable security measures represents sufficient authentication of a message[49], it seems to us that the P.G.P. signature process will satisfy these requirements on the Internet in most cases.

First of all, it must be remembered that a business or a private individual who concludes a contract on the Internet rarely falls within the scope of application of the *statutes of frauds* (which require a signature). Secondly, in the rare cases where these *statutes of frauds* apply to contracts concluded via the Internet, electronic signatures will usually fulfill the statutory signature requirement. When the signature has been encrypted (using P.G.P., for example), it has a very good chance of convincing even the most recalcitrant of judges.

In addition, certain laws clearly stipulate, either explicitly or implicitly, that the signature may be an electronic signature. In the state of Utah, when a public key encryption technique approved by a governmentally licensed body responsible for certifying public keys is employed in the creation of the computerized document[50], the electronic signature affixed to the computerized document is presumed to constitute consent to the content of the message[51], and the document accordingly signed is held to be as valid as a «paper» document[52].

Consequently in the state of Utah, an Internet user - whether private or professional - may be sure that his or her computerized document (if it has been encrypted using a public key encryption technique approved by a governmentally licensed body responsible for certifying public keys) will be admissible as evidence of the contract concluded.

Under Québec law, nothing in the definition of signature found in the *Civil Code of Québec* seems to exclude electronic signatures. It may therefore be presumed, even if it is not *expressly* stipulated, that an electronic signature would be admissible in all cases where a signature is required[53].

B. Does an Internet computer document constitute both an exception to the hearsay rule and to the best evidence rule?

Both American and Canadian rules of evidence originate in English *common law*, and under both American and Canadian law, the Internet user must take account of two venerable common law rules: the *best evidence rule* and the *hearsay rule*. The application of each of these two rules of law, which concern the content of a document[54], would in principle result in the exclusion of evidence in the form of computer documents or print-outs of such computer documents. As we will see, however, in most cases these two rules pose very few problems for Internet users, firstly because they have been codified in statutory form by the *Federal Rules of Evidence* in the United States and by the *Evidence Act* in Canada, which has updated them to take computerized documents into account in certain cases, and secondly because there are exceptions to these two rules, and areas in which their application has been relaxed.

1. The best evidence rule and the hearsay rule[55]

The *best evidence rule* obliges the judge to take into consideration only the best evidence that a party can possibly submit, this being the original document[56]. According to this rule, electronic acceptance by e-mail of a commercial offer could not be proved by a print-out of the electronic mail, which is only a copy of an original made up of electronic data, nor by any presentation of the electronic data itself, since it is unintelligible without the help of a computer.

The *hearsay rule* prohibits the admission into evidence of a document, notably a computer document, if the author of this document does not have personal knowledge of its content[57]. The rule is based on the principle that a party has the right to cross-examine the other party's witnesses. When it is a document that a party wishes to present, this right to cross-examine the other party is exercised with respect to the author of the document. This is why the rule requires two things - the testimony of the document's author, and that the document's author has personal knowledge of its contents. This rule clearly does not pose any problem regarding the admissibility of Internet computer documents produced by an independent user working alone and perfectly aware of the content of each of the messages he or she sends. In the context of business activities, however, let us consider the following hypothesis. If a secretary enters into a computer and sends by electronic mail a text in which his or her employer accepts a contractual offer, then the secretary is the author of the computer document, yet has no personal knowledge of its contents, in this case, the acceptance of a contractual offer. Consequently, the secretary may not testify as to its content. Nor may the employer testify, since despite his or her personal knowledge of the content of the document, he or she is not the «author» in the mechanical sense of the term (he or she did not create the document with his or her own hand). The computer document could not then serve as evidence, because it is not possible for its «author» to testify regarding his or her personal knowledge of its content. Unfortunately, on the Internet, situations in which several people contribute to the creation of a computer document are relatively frequent, particularly in companies. *In principle* then, the *hearsay rule* prevents the admissibility of these computer documents. However, the situation is not that serious since, as we will see, there is an exception to this rule which could frequently apply to businesses operating on the Internet.

2. Exceptions to the best evidence rule which allow the admission of computer documents

Fortunately for Internet users, the *best evidence rule* will not in most cases, pose any problems, for several reasons.

First of all, the *Federal Rules of Evidence*, federal legislation which attempts to harmonize the rules of evidence in the United States and which has been adopted by the majority of American states[58], stipulate that electronic records or any other form of data compilation constitute «writings»[59], and that a *printed document* which is a *faithful reproduction* of electronic data constitutes an «original»[60]. According to this rule, then, a party could admit into evidence a printed version of electronic data, such as a print-out of a Web page or of e-mail. The best evidence rule is thus now likely to pose problems only in jurisdictions where these provisions of the *Federal Rules of Evidence* have not been adopted. Even in these jurisdictions, the effect of the best evidence rule is usually not to exclude evidence but rather to establish a hierarchy of probative value, according to which the best evidence will have greater probative value than «secondary» evidence[61]. Furthermore, American courts tend towards an *evolutive interpretation of the rules of evidence, so as to take into account the realities of the business world and of professional practices*[62].

3. Exceptions to the hearsay rule which allow the admission of computer documents

Under American and Canadian law, the most important exception to the *hearsay rule* for Internet users concerns records, memos, reports or data compilations created in the ordinary course of business (*business record exception*)[63].

Under American law, a computer document circulating on the Internet *which has been created during the normal course of a company's business* (or that of an institution, association or profession, etc.) is admissible evidence insofar as it is introduced into evidence by the person or persons familiar with the data recording and storage system, who must testify regarding the reliability of the computer system. This person may be a computer expert, if the company has one, but it may also be the secretary, if he or she is sufficiently familiar with the system and its reliability. There is no obligation to carry out any particular technical examination of the computer system[64], and the argument that the computer may not have been very reliable will have no bearing on the admissibility of the computer documents, but only on the probative value to be accorded these documents[65].

Very similarly, under Canadian law section 30 of the *Evidence Act* provides an exception to the *hearsay rule* as regards documents (which include computerized documents) created in the ordinary course of a company's business. According to the interpretation adopted by the Canadian courts, a document created in the ordinary course of business (the dispatching of one of many e-mails from the company's «sales» department, for example) will be admissible evidence upon testimony by the person who mechanically created it. It is not necessary for this person to have personal knowledge of the contents of the document. Consequently the secretary who sent the e-mail, without having personal knowledge of its contents, can nonetheless testify and the document will be admissible as evidence.

C. Specific legal regimes

As concerns the sale of goods via the Internet, in the United States and in Canada it is necessary to take into account the sales of goods acts applicable in the various Canadian provinces and American states. Under American law, these rules of evidence have been harmonized to a relative extent by the *Uniform Commercial Code (UCC)*. Internet users should realize that a writing will be necessary in order to prove the sale of certain goods (according to the *UCC*, items which at the time of sale are moveable, specified and existent[66]) having a value in excess of $500 US. The sale of a car, of software or of a newspaper or magazine subscription (worth more than $500 US) concluded by e-mail or via a Web page, for example, can only be proven by means of a writing. As regards items which are not «goods», a writing will be required if their value exceeds $5000 US (these cases, such as investment securities for example, are more rare)[67]. Under the *UCC*, a «writing» comprises all intentional processes aimed at creating a tangible form[68], and the courts have ruled that a writing must be visible to the eye and durable[69].

III. Caution is essential

A. The evidence agreement: «yes, but...»

Parties which frequently trade with one another will, of course, be well advised to conclude an evidence agreement in writing, in which they will stipulate that, regardless of their national rules of evidence, they undertake to acknowledge as evidence the Internet files or electronic messages which comply with criteria established by the parties (types of evidence, methods of implementation, guaranteed security measures, filing and production in the event of an incident). The advantage of an evidence agreement for companies is that it harmonizes the rules of evidence applicable, particularly when exchanges take place between parties subject to the jurisdiction of a legal system hostile to the admissibility of computer evidence.

Evidence agreements, which can be used to resolve a great many problems between regular trading partners, are unfortunately not a panacea for at least two reasons. First of all, in practical terms they cover only a few circumstances. It is inconceivable for all Internet users to conclude evidence agreements with one another when they are in some sense contrary to the spirit of a telematic network open to the general public, and on which transactions are totally dematerialized. Secondly, even where it would be practically possible, national legal systems treat evidence agreements differently. Thus American and Canadian law[70] admit the validity of evidence agreements[71], provided that they do not infringe rules of public order (which may vary from one jurisdiction to another). These regimes are therefore much less flexible than that of French law,[72] which allows parties to freely define their agreement.

Consequently, before accepting or proposing an evidence agreement, businesses should inform themselves of the evidence law applicable to them.

B. *Use reliable techniques, as well as durable and preferably inalterable media*

A message circulating on the Internet may be modified before or after it is dispatched. The use of a special editing format (*Portable Document Format*) preventing the modification of a written document once it has been recorded, makes it possible to constitute in advance evidence which will be more convincing in court. This is also true of the use of a CD-WORM («write once read many» optical disk) which can be written upon only once, although the writing need not occur all at the same time.

Users wishing to identify themselves on the Internet are thus strongly advised to use the most technically reliable means of authentication, such as cryptography, a secret code (a personal password specific to each user, which can be used to confirm the user's identity upon accessing his or her access provider), or the penop strategy (a new technique involving the use of an electronic pencil)[73].

Partners in electronic commerce on the Internet will also have recourse to the services of a *third-party certifier* who will act as an «electronic notary»[74]. In the event of a dispute regarding the content of a message, the parties will refer to these electronic «minutes».

To summarize...

 If you are unable to prove in court an act concluded via the Internet or a fact which occurred on the Internet, the judge will not be obliged to take this act or fact into consideration when passing judgment.

 Under French law, proving facts (such as the distribution of electronic mail or the circulation of Web pages) differs from proving contracts concluded via the Internet. Proof of facts, in civil and commercial matters, can be provided by any legal means and therefore by computer documents. This is also true of commercial contracts concluded via the Internet. As regard civil matters, contracts need not be proven by a signed, original writing if the contract is worth less than 5,000FRF, if there is a commencement of evidence in writing, in the case of common practices or of an admission by the adverse party. On the other hand, a signed original writing is required for all other contracts. Whether or not an electronically signed computer document can be considered a signed, original writing is a debated question. Technology allows a level of reliability equal to that of a signed and original writing, but attitudes have yet to change...

 According to the new regime in English law (to take effect shortly), no computer documents are inadmissible as such. All electronic mail, *Newsgroup* messages or Web page computer recordings circulated on the Internet are admissible evidence. This is also true of a computerized copy or a print-out of digital documents circulating on the Internet. These documents will, however, have to be authenticated, by different procedures depending on whether or not the party producing the evidence exercises a *business* (a concept broader than the ordinary sense of the words) or belongs to a public authority. Furthermore, although all computer documents circulating on the Internet are admissible as such, provided they can be authenticated, they will not necessarily have the same weight in the eyes of the court (probative value).

Under American and Canadian law, the rules of evidence vary depending on the state or province and the jurisdiction concerned. Generally speaking, a party may produce a computer document on two conditions-the document must relevant (and in particular authenticated), and it must be covered by one of the exceptions to two rules which constitute obstacles to evidence in the form of computer documents (the best evidence rule and the hearsay rule). Producing computer documents created during the normal course of a company's activities has been facilitated by such exceptions. Finally, as regards sales of goods via the Internet, the legislation of the Canadian provinces and of the American states (*sales of goods acts*) must be taken into account.

 Legal and technical «means» can be used to anticipate and to alleviate the difficulties involved in producing evidence in the event of a dispute. Thus the parties to a contract can sign evidence agreements on paper. Furthermore, the use of reliable recording techniques - techniques which prevent the subsequent modification of a recorded computer document - allow the production of most convincing evidence. These techniques involve either a special form of recording (*Portable Document Format*) or a specific medium (CD-WORM).

part three

Twenty business contracts for the Internet

1. Internet access provider agreement

2. Internet system operator agreement

3. Supply of information agreement

4. Internet publishing agreement

5. Online space «rental» and related services agreement

6. Online advertising agreement

7. Online brokerage agreement

8. Agreement for the «rental» of online advertising space

9. Online multimedia product development agreement

10. Online market survey agreement

11. Online distribution agreement

12. Web page development and maintenance agreement

13. Online research agreement

14. Online lobbying and marketing agreement

15. Online forum participant agreement

16. Agreement for online database access

17. Master retail sales agreement

18. Electronic commerce agreement between professionals

19. Certifying authority agreement

20. Acceptable use policy

1. INTERNET ACCESS PROVIDER AGREEMENT

Any person or business wishing to connect to the Internet must retain the services of an Internet access provider. The access provider provides access to the Internet and directs user communications to the appropriate server. It also allocates a certain amount of «disk space» to each user such that his or her files, electronic messages, or home page may be temporarily or permanently stored. Often the user is also given access to a news server by which he or she can participate in various electronic discussion forums.

In general, the following terms and conditions tend to favour the Internet access provider. The user may want to obtain more specific commitments from the access provider regarding the technical characteristics of the service (for example the number of users per modem), or regarding the level of confidentiality which can be expected. If the user has sufficient bargaining power he or she may negotiate a higher ceiling on the financial liability of the Internet access provider for system failures due to negligence on the part of the access provider, its employees and agents.

SERVICES
- Description of the type of Internet access: speed of communication, type of communication channel (digital or analog), dial-up or leased line, access to a news server and to an electronic mailbox.
- Description of additional services such as user support lines, or local chat areas.
- Provision permitting the access provider to alter characteristics of the services offered.

PRICE
- Fee for Internet access.
- Specification of additional charges for use in excess of allocated limits or for the use of additional services.
- Method of payment and billing (ex. automatic billing of the user's credit card).
- Provision allowing the access provider to modify prices upon prior notice to the user.

CONDITIONS OF ACCESS TO SERVICES
- Limit on the number of users per account or other limits to access.

USER CONDUCT
- Description of expected user conduct when accessing the Internet.
- List of types of prohibited conduct: disrespect of freedom of expression, of privacy, of the confidentiality of certain information, of the security measures of an information system, and illegal activity in general. A separate provision containing several examples of prohibited activities is preferable.
- Obligation to conform to the rules of netiquette and to the acceptable use policies of frequented networks.

PRIVACY AND CONFIDENTIALITY
Description of the level of privacy accorded to communications:
- right of the access provider to screen messages or at least its limited right to view messages when there is reason to believe that all or part of the electronic communications relate to illegal activity.
- right of the access provider to access any communications stored on the system when the proper management of the system so requires.
- obligation of the user to preserve the confidentiality of his or her password.

ACCESS PROVIDER CONTROL
- Right of the access provider to edit the content of documents stored on its information system by the user and accessible via the Internet (such as a home page).
- Right of the access provider to exclude users who do not abide by the rules of participation established by a local message base.
- Right of the access provider to freely choose the newsgroups to be distributed by its news server. Access providers should be aware that such control over their systems may be interpreted as editorial control.

COPYRIGHT
- Definition of the status of copyright in messages posted on message bases maintained by the access provider: are they retained by the user or granted in whole or in part to the access provider?

LIMITATION OF ACCESS PROVIDER LIABILITY
- No access provider liability for damages suffered or losses incurred while using the services provided, or limitation of liability to a specific amount.

- No liability for interruptions in access to the Internet, or a description of minimal standards of performance.
- Determination of a fixed ceiling of liability.
- Indemnification of the access provider against claims by third parties relating to the user's conduct on the Internet or to messages transmitted by the user via the Internet.
- No liability for loss of data stored on the access provider's system, or limitation of the access provider's obligation to make back-up copies of data.
- No liability for disclosure of the confidential data stored on the access provider's system, or limitation of the access provider's obligation to preserve the confidentiality of data (it should be noted that all applicable regulations concerning the protection of personal data must be taken into account in drafting this clause).

TERM AND TERMINATION
- Duration and renewal of the contract.
- Right of either party to terminate the contract upon notice and term of prior notice.
- Immediate termination in case of nonperformance of contract (including both the absence of performance and insufficient performance) by the user.
- Right of the access provider upon termination of the contract to erase the «disk space» allotted to the user.

EVIDENCE
- Computer records stored on a durable and inalterable medium on the access provider's system shall be accepted as evidence of communications, contracts and payments made between the parties.

FORCE MAJEURE

CHOICE OF APPLICABLE LAW AND JURISDICTION

2. INTERNET SYSTEM OPERATOR AGREEMENT

A business setting up a server on the Internet will often hire a system operator to carry out all or part of the daily operations. The system operator may be hired, for example, to administrate a specified number of message areas (newsgroups, listservers, chat areas, etc.), where he or she acts as a moderator or as an editor. The system operator will then often act as a moderator. The system operator is usually granted the power to take disciplinary action notably against users who disregard the rules of the message base or, more generally, against users disrespecting the law, acceptable use policies or netiquette.

The drafting of the agreement is relatively neutral. The system operator may, however, want to limit the server administrator's right to terminate the agreement. If the system operator is well known and the server wishes to exploit the operator's name for marketing purposes, then the agreement should be drafted differently. The administrator of the server should in this case obtain the right to use the system operator's name and likeness in promotional material. The system operator, for his or her part, could obtain better financial compensation and a share of copyright in his or her own messages.

SERVICES
- Description of the discussion area or the message base to be administrated by the system operator.
- Description of the system operator's duties: information monitoring and control, application of server policies, placement of liability disclaimers, server promotion, etc.
- Provision stipulating that the contract must be fulfilled by the system operator personally.
- Definition of the relationship between the server administrator and the system operator: provision of services by an independent contractor.

REMUNERATION
- Method of remuneration for services rendered: monthly fee, percentage of revenues generated by the exploitation of a discussion area or message base, or any other mutually acceptable method of remuneration.

ACCESS
- Free access to the discussion area or to the message area is granted to the system operator exclusively for his or her personal or professional use.

COPYRIGHT
- Assignment of all or part of the rights to works created by the system operator in the execution of his or her functions.

CONFIDENTIAL INFORMATION
- Determination of information deemed by the parties to be confidential: client or user identity, business contacts, internal structure of the message base or of servers.
- Duration of the stipulated confidentiality.
- Liability of the system operator in case of the disclosure of confidential information.

TERM AND TERMINATION
- Duration of agreement and renewal.
- Right of either party to terminate the contract upon notice and term of prior notice.
- Immediate termination following notice in case of nonperformance of contract by the operator.
- No solicitation of the server's clients, employees or agents for a certain period of time after termination of the contract.

INDEMNITY
- Indemnification of the server by the system operator for any claims by third parties related to infringements of intellectual property rights or grossly negligent acts committed by the system operator in the execution of his or her functions.

EVIDENCE
- Computer records stored in reasonably secure conditions on the computer system of either party shall be accepted as evidence of communications, contracts and payments made between the parties.
- Records shall be presumed to have been stored in reasonably secure conditions if the documents are systematically recorded on a durable and inalterable medium.

FORCE MAJEURE

CHOICE OF APPLICABLE LAW AND JURISDICTION

3. SUPPLY OF INFORMATION AGREEMENT

Many businesses which gather information or which produce print publications are expanding onto the Internet. They will usually want to avoid the costs involved in creating and maintaining an on-line database and thus may wish to grant Internet exploitation rights to a business already established on the Internet. Usually this established business acts only as a distributor and does not edit the information. Any editing that may be done will be limited to changing the format of the data files for technical reasons.

An essential part of this agreement concerns the liability that may be incurred for inaccurate or outdated information. If the risk of liability remains with the information provider, or even if the information provider shares the risk, it should examine the standard terms and conditions in contracts between the online server and users. If the limitation of liability clauses and the restrictions on information use in contracts between the online server and users are not sufficiently broad, the information provider should specify in its contract with the server the particular elements which it requires the server to include in the standard terms and conditions of its contracts with users.

NATURE OF THE AGREEMENT
- Grant to the server of universal license to copy, distribute, transmit and provide access to the database or to the publications via the Internet or other similar networks.
- Right of the server to reformat data, or obligation of the server to preserve the data's original format.
- Scope and content of the license granted to the server or to users of the database or of the publications.

PRICE AND PAYMENT
- Percentage of revenues collected by the server to be paid to the information provider.
- Date of payment and the content of sales reports which must be transmitted to the information provider.

DELIVERY
- Time, periodicity and means of transmitting the contents of the database or of the publications and updates.

RECORDS
- Server's obligation to keep, on a durable and inalterable medium, a complete record of transactions.
- Information provider's right to examine the records and procedures for the examination of records, or its right to engage at its own expense a third party for the purpose of conducting an audit.

SERVER OBLIGATIONS
- Description of the services which must be offered to users by the server, including technical support to be offered to users during their use of the database.
- Description of the content of contracts to be concluded between the server and users.
- Obligation of the server to market, advertise and promote the database.
- Right of prior approval regarding all advertising material granted to the information provider.

INTELLECTUAL PROPERTY RIGHTS
- The information provider retains all rights on the database.
- Obligation of the server to advise the information provider of any infringing actions of which it is aware.

WARRANTIES
- The information provider guarantees that its database or its publications do not infringe the intellectual property rights, personality rights (notably privacy rights), or any other rights of any third parties, and that in general its contents are legal.
- Disclaimer of all access provider liability with regards to the information contained in the database, or limitation of the degree of care that may be expected of the information provider in verifying the factual accuracy of the information supplied and in updating the information.
- Indemnification of the server by the information provider for any claims by third parties relating to the information provider's warranties.

TERM AND TERMINATION
- Duration of the agreement and renewal.
- Right of either party to terminate the contract upon notice and term of prior notice.
- Immediate termination in case of nonperformance of contract.
- Server obligations after termination of the contract concerning the copy of the database in its possession.

EVIDENCE

- Computer records stored in reasonably secure conditions on the computer system of either party shall be accepted as evidence of communications, contracts and payments made between the parties.
- Records shall be presumed to have been stored in reasonably secure conditions if the documents are systematically recorded on a durable and inalterable medium.

FORCE MAJEURE

CHOICE OF APPLICABLE LAW AND JURISDICTION

4. INTERNET PUBLISHING AGREEMENT

Publishers can now directly sell electronic publications on the Internet. The possibility of constantly updating these publications, and of electronically linking them to other publications on the Internet by means of «hypertext» links, creates new business opportunities. The need for a constant relationship with the author (updates and complements) implies the need for the agreement to include particular measures destined to assure the continuity and even the development of the publication.

This agreement tends to favour the publisher. An author may thus try to negotiate broader rights regarding the development and final production of an electronic document, particularly in cases where the publication will be updated. On the other hand, certain national laws governing publishing contracts written on paper could be declared applicable to these new publishing contracts.

NATURE OF THE AGREEMENT
- Publication of a designated work on the Internet.
- All costs of publication are to be borne by the publisher.

COPYRIGHT
- Assignment of the rights of reproduction, transmission and distribution of the work on the Internet and on related networks.
- Acquisition of the additional rights of publication and distribution on paper and on CD-ROM, or the option to acquire these rights within a specified term.

EDITORIAL CONTROL
- Right of the publisher to edit the work in order to correct the style, language and any factual inaccuracies.

TRANSMISSION OF THE WORK AND UPDATES
- Deadline for receipt of «final draft» and consequences of late delivery.
- Obligation to provide periodic updates of the work, or the publisher's right to hire a third party to accomplish such work.
- Obligation of the publisher to incorporate such updates into the «publication».

PRODUCTION OF THE ELECTRONIC DOCUMENT
- The publisher alone determines all material aspects of the electronic publication, such as its format, fonts, graphics, photographs, animation, film and video sequences, soundtrack, etc.
- The publisher determines the final title of work.
- Obligation of the publisher to obtain the authorizations necessary in order to link the electronic publication to other documents on the Internet (permission of the owner of intellectual property rights for each publication linked).
- Right of the author to «hypertext» links from the electronic publication to his or her own home page.

PUBLICATION
- Deadline by which the publisher must make available a preliminary version of the electronic publication.
- Delay in which the author must approve the electronic publication and submit any corrections that he or she may wish to make.
- Deadline by which the publisher must make available online the definitive version of the electronic publication.

MARKETING AND ADVERTISING
- Obligation of the publisher to advertise the electronic publication in Internet search engines and indexes, to create a promotional page on the Internet, to create and administrate discussion groups or regarding any other advertising methods agreed to by the parties.
- Extent of the obligation to advertise and promote the electronic publication in non-electronic media.
- Extent of the author's obligation to cooperate in the promotion of the electronic publication.

ROYALTIES OR FLAT FEE
- Royalties to be paid to the author for publication on the Internet: a percentage of revenues or a flat fee.

PAYMENT AND RECORDS
- Payment dates for the royalties.
- Publisher's obligation to keep proper records, on a durable and inalterable medium, of all transactions related to the electronic publication.
- Right of the author to examine the records or to have the records examined by means of an audit at his or her own expense.
- Extent of the author's right to access online sales logs, possibly with an obligation to preserve the confidentiality of this information.

WARRANTIES
- Warranty by the author that the work does not infringe the rights, notably the intellectual property rights, of any third parties, and more generally that its contents are not illegal.
- Indemnification of the publisher for any claims by third parties in relation to the author's warranty.

TERM AND TERMINATION
- Duration of the agreement and renewal.
- Right of either party, upon notice and term of prior notice, to terminate the agreement for causes specified in relation to each party, such as the liquidation of the electronic publisher, for example.
- Immediate termination without notice in case of nonperformance of contract.

EVIDENCE
- Computer records stored in reasonably secure conditions on the computer system of either party shall be accepted as evidence of communications, contracts and payments made between the parties.
- Records shall be presumed to have been stored in reasonably secure conditions if the documents are systematically recorded on a durable and inalterable medium.

FORCE MAJEURE

CHOICE OF APPLICABLE LAW AND JURISDICTION

5. ONLINE SPACE «RENTAL» AND RELATED SERVICES AGREEMENT

Many businesses want to have complete control over what they are selling or publishing on the Internet but do not have the technical expertise or equipment to create and maintain their own server. They may thus want to «rent» disk space from a server already distributing information on the Internet. Businesses in this situation should consider concluding an online space rental agreement or a related services agreement. The agreement proposed here bears some similarity to rental agreements for commercial space in that it provides for the making available of an online «space» with a virtual storefront. It is also, however, an agreement for the provision of services.

One of the central purposes of this agreement is to clearly define the extent of the services to be provided by the «lessor» of online space. A technical description of these services could thus be incorporated into the agreement as a schedule. The «lessee» should also try to obtain specific commitments regarding the performance of any software provided with the space and guarantees regarding the accessibility of the leased space. The «lessor» who owns a virtual shopping center may already have developed software for taking orders, for administrating message bases, or other types of software, and a license for their use must be included in the agreement.

If any software or visual elements are to be developed by the «lessor», a technical description of the software or of the visual elements should be agreed to and integrated in the agreement as a schedule.

RESOURCES
- Precise description of «disk spaces» offered for rent, as distinguished by the type of service offered (file library, discussion area, electronic mail account), and including their sizes and capacities.
- Option to «lease» additional space.
- Description of the «lessee's» access to other areas and services of the «lessor's» system and at what cost.

SERVICES

Description of the services provided by the «lessor»:
- the granting and repeal of user access authorization;
- compilation of access records;
- maintenance of back-up copies of the «lessee's» files;
- security measures and measures destined to preserve the confidentiality of the names of users frequenting the rented zone, as well as of messages and files stored in the rented area;
- technical assistance offered by the «lessor» as concerns setting up the «lessee's disk space» (the range of services provided will be greater if the «lessor» is responsible for developing software);
- number of hours of training provided by the lessor to the «lessee's» personnel;
- right of the «lessor» to change system specifications upon prior notice;
- date when the «rented» space is to be operational;
- possibly the establishment of approval procedures, particularly if the «lessor» is responsible for developing graphics or software.

INTELLECTUAL PROPERTY

- If software is provided by the «lessor», the terms of the license should be stated, as well as an obligation to preserve the confidentiality of the source code.
- If any other type of copyrightable material is provided by the «lessor», the agreement should define whether or not licence is granted to the «lessee».

PRICE AND PAYMENT

- The agreement will determine the prices of the different services and the royalties due for assignments of intellectual property rights, such as charges for the setup of the rented zone, use of this zone, the development of material, assignment of licenses for software, maintenance of the site, additional services and consultations, etc.
- Periodicity and method of payment.

LIMITS TO USE

- Obligation of the «lessee» to comply with the rules of the server which may, for example, limit the right to modify system parameters, establish codes of conduct regarding commercial transactions with customers or concerning advertising, privacy, the respect of intellectual property rights, etc.
- Right of the «lessor» to change the rules.

- The «lessee» is solely responsible for all information and, more broadly, for all content made available on or transmitted via the leased space, by its own hand or by that of its users.
- The «lessee» does not have the right to «sublet» all or part of the «rented space». If, however, this right is to be accorded, the agreement should specify precise conditions of «sublet».

CONFIDENTIALITY
- Level of confidentiality offered by the «lessor» as regards each specific part of the «rented» space.
- Right of the lessor to monitor use of the «rented» space.
- Mutual obligation not to disclose confidential information and definition of what information is to be considered confidential.
- Right of the «lessor» to procure from the lessee any encryption key in the «lessee's» possession and used in the «rented» space, when such is necessary for legitimate monitoring purposes as required by law and by the present agreement.

WARRANTIES
- The «lessee» guarantees that his or her activities and any material used or provided for use in the «rented» space are not illegal and do not violate rights of third parties.
- The «lessee» will indemnify the «lessor» for any claim by third parties related to the «lessee's» use of or activities in the «rented space».
- The «lessor» guarantees the «lessee» that any software provided is maintained by competent personnel, whether employees or independent consultants.

DISCLAIMER
- The «lessor» offers no warranty for services rendered or software provided.
- Or the «lessor» guarantees services rendered and software provided, in which case the agreement specifies the level of care, competence or performance which the «lessee» may rightfully expect.
- Or no liability of the «lessor» (or limitation of the «lessor's» liability) regarding system failures or other interruptions of service.
- Or determination of the maximum number of hours per month or per week during which the system may be out of service.

INDEMNITY
- Indemnification and defense against any claims by third parties relating to warranties or representations specified in the agreement.

NO SOLICITATION
- For a defined period of time no party may solicit the employees or consultants of the other party.

NO PARTNERSHIP
- Statement to the effect that the parties are fully independent of each other.

TERM AND TERMINATION
- Duration of agreement and renewal.
- Immediate termination for nonperformance of contract or for unjustifiable peril to the lessor's system caused by the «lessee».

EVIDENCE
- Computer records stored in reasonably secure conditions on the computer system of either party shall be accepted as evidence of communications, contracts and payments made between the parties.
- Records shall be presumed to have been stored in reasonably secure conditions if the documents are systematically recorded on a durable and inalterable medium.

FORCE MAJEURE

CHOICE OF APPLICABLE LAW AND JURISDICTION

6. ONLINE ADVERTISING AGREEMENT

Businesses will want to contact users online in order to promote their products. Similarly, businesses which already sell their products directly via the Internet may want to find innovative or more efficient ways of attracting buyers to their server. These businesses will want to contract with an advertising agency so as to develop a comprehensive Internet advertising strategy. Businesses should take care to select an advertising agency capable of fully exploiting the interactive potential of the Internet.

The parties will necessarily have to take into consideration the problem of the lack of harmonization of advertising regulation. The Internet enables the advertiser to communicate a message to many countries but it also multiplies the number of laws that may apply to a single message.

SERVICES
- Research of competitors on the Internet.
- Creation and accomplishment of an Internet advertising campaign.
- Finding and «renting» of appropriate advertising space or the creation of new spaces for diffusing the advertiser's message.
- Development of interactive concepts in order to attract users to the advertiser's Internet site.

REMITTANCE OF MATERIAL
- The agreement determines the time and manner of remittance of material necessary to the preparation of the advertising campaign by the advertiser to the advertising agency.

ACCEPTANCE
- The advertiser's approval of each stage of the campaign is required before the campaign may be launched.

AGREEMENTS WITH THIRD PARTIES
- Power of the advertising agency to rent advertising space on Internet Web servers selected and approved by the advertiser .
- Power of the advertising agency, upon approval by the advertiser, to sign contracts for the hiring of Web page designers, for the «purchase» of a domain name, and for the hiring of one or more system operators to administrate Internet forums.

PAYMENT
- Method and frequency of reimbursement of costs incurred.
- Method and frequency of payment of commissions due to the advertising agency.

ADVERTISING CAMPAIGN FOLLOW-UP
- The advertising agency must ensure that the campaign is satisfactorily carried out on the Internet.
- The advertising agency must take action, if necessary, against suppliers of materials or services participating in the advertising campaign.
- The advertising agency will prepare an electronic advertising campaign portfolio and submit it to the advertiser within a reasonable time before the end of the campaign.
- Campaign efficiency test results or progress reports may be made available online via a confidential account provided to the advertiser.

CONTROL OF COSTS
- Obligation of the advertising agency to verify and pay all bills presented by suppliers relating to the campaign.

NETIQUETTE
- Obligation to comply with the rules of netiquette when sending messages or establishing a presence on the Internet.
- Liability or limitation of liability of the advertising agency for any damages to the reputation or clientele of the advertiser as a result of the transgression of these rules.

CONFIDENTIALITY
- Obligation of the advertising agency to preserve the confidentiality of any information provided by the advertiser and not destined for publication.
- Obligation of the advertising agency to take adequate measures of security as regards the protection of confidential information on its system.
- Description of security measures to be undertaken when transmitting documents between the parties and approving advertising material (which may, for example, involve the use of encryption).

ILLEGALITY AND DUTY TO INFORM
- Duty of the advertising agency to advise the advertiser of restrictions on advertising imposed by law or self-regulation. If the advertiser chooses to ignore such information, the advertising agency has the right to unilaterally terminate the agreement.

- Obligation of each party to inform the other of any investigation by a national governmental authority or self-regulatory body.
- Identity of the party who shall bear the cost of modifying the advertising campaign to ensure compliance with the Law.

INTELLECTUAL PROPERTY

- The advertising agency assigns to the advertiser all intellectual property rights to documents executed and distributed on the Internet.
- The agreement will specify which party is responsible for obtaining the intellectual property rights belonging to third parties where necessary to the accomplishment of the advertising campaign.

TERM AND TERMINATION

- Duration of agreement and renewal.
- Right of either party to terminate the agreement upon notice and term of prior notice.
- Immediate termination for nonperformance of contract or for specific causes (insolvency, liquidation, etc.). In case of this right of termination being exercised by the advertiser, the agreement should stipulate the advertising agency's obligation to transfer its rights and obligations arising from contracts concluded with suppliers to a new advertising agency designated by the advertiser.
- Right of the advertiser to terminate the agreement and obligation of the advertising agency to transfer contracts with suppliers to the new advertising agency.

EVIDENCE

- Computer records stored in reasonably secure conditions on the computer system of either party shall be accepted as evidence of communications, contracts and payments made between the parties.
- Records shall be presumed to have been stored in reasonably secure conditions if the documents are systematically recorded on a durable and inalterable medium.

FORCE MAJEURE

CHOICE OF APPLICABLE LAW AND JURISDICTION

7. ONLINE BROKERAGE AGREEMENT

Because of its international scale, the Internet can be used as a means of reaching buyers in new markets. An online broker can assist businesses in researching and contacting potential buyers and sellers in the appropriate regions of the Internet. The initial approach would be made by the broker who would inform the potential buyer of the nature of the goods offered for sale on the Internet by his or her client, for example. Once the potential buyer manifests an interest in the products offered, the broker would arrange for the buyer and the seller to communicate either via the Internet, or via conventional means (conventional means are preferable when the contract must necessarily be concluded on paper, for example for evidentiary reasons).

A business should ascertain, amongst other things, that there is no potential conflict between its Internet broker and other brokers operating in specific countries. In order to avoid such conflict, the contract should list all contracts that a firm has already signed with brokers. It should also stipulate that the «electronic» broker may not sell in the countries or zones implicated. If the sale or the import and export of the product is subject to restrictions in certain countries, the agreement should clearly define the responsibilities of each party. Furthermore, if the parties are aware at the time of signing of the agreement that the sale of a product may be illegal in certain countries, the agreement should either prohibit the broker from contacting buyers in those countries or it should stipulate that illicit contracts will not be pursued.

SERVICES
- Description of the products or services to be promoted by the broker.
- Definition of the territorial scope of the contract: application limited to specific territories or application to all of the Internet.
- Obligation to dispose of sufficient competent personnel, during a specific period of time, in order to respond to queries by potential customers.

MINIMAL EFFORTS
- Description of the minimum number of electronic messages which the broker must send per month, and of the minimal Internet presence

which the broker must develop by means of a Web site, including any required interactive features of the Web site.
- Obligation of the broker to maintain, for a specified period of time and on a durable and inalterable medium, an electronic record of communications with potential clients.
- Right of access by the client to such records upon prior notice.
- Obligation of the broker to provide such records to the client in the event of litigation implicating potential buyers.

WEB PRESENCE
- Obligation of the broker to develop a Web presence in cooperation with the client, or to integrate the client's products and services in the broker's Web site.
- Right of the client to approve all materials before making them available on a Web site.

RIGHT OF INFORMATION
- Obligation of the client to adequately inform the broker concerning the product or service.
- Obligation of the broker to preserve the confidentiality of information provided by the client and specifically designated as confidential.

NEGOTIATION AND CONCLUSION OF CONTRACTS
- Extent of the broker's power to negotiate contracts with potential clients.
- Contracts are to be concluded directly with the client and payments are to be made directly to the client.

NETIQUETTE, ILLEGALITY AND LIABILITY
- Obligation of the broker to comply with the rules of netiquette when sending messages or creating a Web presence on the Internet.
- Liability or limitation of liability for any damages to the reputation or clientele of the client.
- Obligation of the broker to respect applicable laws. Indemnification of the client in case of nonperformance of this obligation.

NOTIFICATION
- Obligation of the client to notify the broker of any commercial transaction concluded during the contract period or during a specified period of time after termination of the contract.
- Description of the security measures to be employed when transmitting such information via electronic mail.

COMMISSIONS AND ADVANCES
- Amount and method of payment of advances, if any.
- Commission for each contract concluded, determined on the basis of a percentage of the value of the transaction.
- Right of the broker to keep all or part of the advance not compensated upon termination of the contract.

WARRANTIES
- The client warrants that he or she has the right to conclude the agreement and that the agreement does not come into conflict with any other prior agreements, notably those concluded in other countries.
- Indemnification and protection of the broker against any claim by third parties related to these warranties.

SURVIVAL OF CERTAIN OBLIGATIONS
- The client must remunerate the broker in relation to all contracts concluded as a result of the broker's intervention, including those concluded within a certain delay after termination of the agreement.
- Obligation of the broker, after termination of the agreement, to archive records of communications and to cooperate with the client in case of litigation.

EVIDENCE
- Computer records stored in reasonably secure conditions on the computer system of either party shall be accepted as evidence of communications, contracts and payments made between the parties.
- Records shall be presumed to have been stored in reasonably secure conditions if the documents are systematically recorded on a durable and inalterable medium.

TERM AND TERMINATION
- Duration of the agreement and renewal.
- Termination upon notice and term of prior notice.

FORCE MAJEURE

CHOICE OF APPLICABLE LAW AND JURISDICTION

8. AGREEMENT FOR THE «RENTAL» OF ONLINE ADVERTISING SPACE

Many commercial and noncommercial Internet servers attract a considerable number of users to certain of their sites. As a means of financing their operations, these servers may offer advertising space to businesses or they may try to attract a single sponsor. One of the most notable advantages of advertising on the Internet is that it escapes some of the physical constraints of traditional forms of advertising. It is, for example, much easier to modify advertising content or to place many different advertisements in the same space at different times. It is also possible to integrate interactive components or to link the advertising directly to the advertiser's home page. Finally, the low cost of this method of advertising is one of its most attractive features.

Because of the constant evolution of most Internet sites, it is important for the sponsor or advertiser to clearly define the degree of prominence that the advertisement is to have on the site at all times. The server may wish to conserve the right to remove an advertisement or to modify it in the event of illegal content.

SERVICES
- «Rental» of advertising space on an Internet server in order to promote a product, a service or a cause.

PLACEMENT OF ADVERTISING MATERIAL
- Obligation to mention the sponsor and to integrate the sponsor's logo (or advertisement), for a determined period of time, on the site and in the message bases maintained by the server.
- Obligation to display the advertisement in a predetermined space and, if the advertisement is not permanently placed, indication of the frequency at which it is to appear and the schedule of its appearances in a given time zone.
- If any changes are made to the site during the course of the agreement, obligation to maintain the level of prominence of the space rented (determined on the basis of technical criteria established by the parties).
- Obligation to link with the sponsor's or the advertiser's home page.
- Description of any interactive services required.

- Obligation of the server to supply the required interactive services, by developing software or by acquiring a licence of intellectual property rights to existing software as necessary.

SUBMISSION OF MATERIAL

- Description of the manner and format in which the sponsor or advertiser must transmit the logo, promotional text, or advertisement.
- Maximum size of the graphic and textual elements to be submitted.
- Obligation of the server to conserve in their original form the elements submitted by the advertiser or sponsor, or right of the server to modify them.
- Manner, delay, and limits regarding the updating of the advertising on the site.

COPYRIGHT

- The sponsor or advertiser licenses the server to reproduce, distribute and transmit the advertising material on its site.
- The sponsor or advertiser owns the intellectual property rights on software created exclusively for its use by the server. This clause will be necessary when such is not foreseen by law.

PAYMENT

- Price of service and of the development of interactive elements.
- Method and periodicity of payment when payment is made by installments.

WARRANTY AND LIMITATION OF LIABILITY

- The advertiser or sponsor guarantees the server that the material submitted does not violate the rights of any third parties and is not illegal. Indemnification of the server for any claim by third parties related to this warranty.
- Liability of the server for interruptions of service may be limited to the price paid for the rental of advertising space for the duration of such interruption.

TERM AND TERMINATION

- Duration of the agreement and renewal.
- Right of either party to terminate the agreement upon notice and term of prior notice.

EVIDENCE

- Computer records stored in reasonably secure conditions on the computer system of either party shall be accepted as evidence of communications, contracts and payments made between the parties.

- Records shall be presumed to have been stored in reasonably secure conditions if the documents are systematically recorded on a durable and inalterable medium.

FORCE MAJEURE

CHOICE OF APPLICABLE LAW AND JURISDICTION

9. ONLINE MULTIMEDIA PRODUCT DEVELOPMENT AGREEMENT

As users are more and more able to transfer large amounts of data quickly, the demand for interactive multimedia products will be greater. This agreement consists of a joint venture between a software developer and an online server for the purposes of producing and marketing a multimedia product. If one of the two parties has more financial means than the other, it could simply engage the other party as a subcontractor.

This agreement favours the software developer, since it is the software developer here who defines the content of the product in the last instance, and who controls the services offered by the online server.

NATURE OF THE AGREEMENT
- Description of the nature and characteristics of the interactive product to be developed, notably of its scenario.
- Determination of the field of exploitation covered by the agreement, presumably the Internet, and the possibility of licensing to third parties.

MATERIAL
- Obligation of the software developer to acquire the rights required for the development of the product (rights to texts, images and sounds).

DEVELOPMENT
- Development of the software required by the software developer, and the server's obligation of full cooperation.
- Joint development of the software necessary for interfacing with the Internet.
- Schedule for the performance of each party's contribution to the development phase.

COMMERCIAL EXPLOITATION
- Minimal technical specifications of the server's computer system and telecommunications capabilities.
- Obligation to upgrade the system specifications in order to meet demand (the parties could include more specific indications regarding the performance of the server's system).

- Obligation of the server to conclude maintenance contracts regarding its computer equipment or to dispose of sufficiently qualified and competent personnel.
- Respective rights of the server and of the software developer to determine the marketing of the product and the name or trademark to be used.
- Obligation of the server to advertise the product on the Internet, to create a promotional Web page, to create and administrate discussion areas about the product and to place the product on Internet search and indexing engines.
- Cooperation of the parties in the establishment of a customer help line, to be made operational by the server.
- Obligation of the server to link product sites with the software developer's home page.

RECORDS AND AUDITING
- Obligation of the server to establish and keep accurate records, on a durable and inalterable medium, of transactions with customers.
- Right of the software developer to have the records inspected or verified and to an online access to these records.
- Right of the software developer to have the records audited at his or her own expense.

INTELLECTUAL PROPERTY RIGHTS
- The software developer retains ownership of copyright in the product.
- Where not foreseen by law, the contract should stipulate that the software developer conserves all intellectual property rights and industrial rights in the software, except as regards interface software jointly developed by the parties, in which both parties will equally share property rights.

CONFIDENTIALITY AND SECURITY
- Obligation of the server to provide secure and trustworthy methods of payment for customers.
- Obligation of the server to use appropriate means to preserve the confidentiality of source code and of the commercial information stored on the server's system.
- Survival of the obligation of confidentiality after termination of the agreement.

PAYMENT
- Determination of the percentage of revenues that the server must pay to the software developer.
- Periodicity and method of payment.
- Transmission of the contents of sales reports to the software developer.

MAINTENANCE, UPGRADE AND FURTHER DEVELOPMENT
- Obligation of the software developer to continue the development and perfecting of the product after its marketing.
- Obligation of the server to maintain and upgrade the product in a timely manner.

TERM AND TERMINATION
- Duration of the agreement and renewal.
- Right of either party to terminate the agreement without notice in case of insolvency, liquidation, etc., or in the event of nonperformance of contract by the other party.

WARRANTIES AND DISCLAIMERS
- The software developer guarantees the server that the software and materials incorporated into the product do not infringe the rights, and particularly the intellectual property rights, of third parties, and that the product's contents are not illegal.
- The software developer will indemnify the server for any claims for infringements of the rights of third parties.
- The developer does not guarantee the performance of the product on the Internet, or the developer guarantees a minimum standard of product performance on the Internet, using technical criteria to be determined by the parties.

EVIDENCE
- Computer records stored in reasonably secure conditions on the computer system of either party shall be accepted as evidence of communications, contracts and payments made between the parties.
- Records shall be presumed to have been stored in reasonably secure conditions if the documents are systematically recorded on a durable and inalterable medium.

FORCE MAJEURE

CHOICE OF APPLICABLE LAW AND JURISDICTION

10. ONLINE MARKET SURVEY AGREEMENT

In order to determine a product's potential market on the Internet, it can be useful to survey the opinions and preferences of Internet users. Gathering user responses efficiently and rapidly requires a method of attracting users to a site and of inciting them to complete a questionnaire. Many businesses will choose to have this task handled by an outside firm familiar with the network, such as an Internet market survey firm.

This agreement is relatively straightforward. As a precautionary measure, however, before concluding the agreement the parties should examine the applicable law relating to computer-matched personal data, which could apply to their agreement.

SERVICES
- Determination of the product's potential market by research accomplished via online questionnaires.
- Compilation of answers received. If the client wishes the market survey firm to analyze the data or to present it in a particular manner, this obligation should also be included here.
- Deadline for the completion of the market study.

PRESENTATION OF THE QUESTIONNAIRE
- Obligation of the client to transmit the questionnaire within a certain delay.
- Obligation of the market study firm to develop a Web site and to render it accessible via the Internet upon prior approval by the client.
- Obligation to promote the site by placing it in the appropriate Internet indexes and search tools.

IDENTIFICATION OF CLIENT
- Disclosure or non-disclosure on the promotional Web site of the client's identity.
- The client grants to the market survey firm license to use the client's intellectual property rights and trademark rights as required by the study.

PAYMENT
- Method, amount, and time of payment of the market survey firm's commission.

INFORMATION SUPPLIED BY CLIENT
- Obligation of the market survey firm to preserve the confidentiality of information supplied by the client and not destined for distribution on the Internet.
- Survival of this obligation after termination of the agreement.

RECORDS
- Obligation to conserve, on a durable and inalterable medium, data concerning user accesses to the Web sites on which the questionnaires are placed.
- Right of the client to access and to examine these records, and the manner in which this right may be exercised.

DATA COMPILATIONS
- The agreement determines the ownership of intellectual property rights in the data.

SECURITY
- Determination of the minimum level of security to be procured by the market survey firm in order to protect data gathered on the site.
- Description of the security features that are to be used when transferring the data to the client.

TRANSFER OF DATA
- Manner and format in which collected data is to be communicated to the client.
- Obligation of the market survey firm to obtain all necessary authorizations and to give any notices required by applicable law before transferring the data to the client.

TERMINATION
- Right of the client to unilaterally terminate the agreement without notice if the rate of response as measured by the site access logs is insufficient or if a minimum number of responses is not obtained within a certain delay.

EVIDENCE
- Computer records stored in reasonably secure conditions on the computer system of either party shall be accepted as evidence of communications, contracts and payments made between the parties.
- Records shall be presumed to have been stored in reasonably secure conditions if the documents are systematically recorded on a durable and inalterable medium.

FORCE MAJEURE

CHOICE OF APPLICABLE LAW AND JURISDICTION

11. ONLINE DISTRIBUTION AGREEMENT

Many businesses are setting up virtual storefronts on the Internet to sell their products, be they tangible goods or intangible goods such as software. If a business does not wish to make the investment of time and money required by such a venture, it may prefer to use an Internet distributor, who would handle all or part of the operations required to bring the product to the customer. The role of the distributor may be merely that of a broker, and it may thus simply transmit orders to the manufacturer, or it may administrate inventory and possibly even keep goods in stock.

If the product is to be «shipped» via the Internet itself, the manufacturer should insist on the stipulation of specific controls and safeguards permitting precise tracking of the number of units sold and shipped.

SERVICES
- Description of the scope of the activities to be carried out by the distributor (display of product photographs, order processing, order fulfillment and billing).
- Description of the online storefront to be used, including the trademark or tradename to appear there, for example.
- Description of the product to be distributed.
- The parties will specify whether or not they intend to grant exclusivity of distribution. In the absence of exclusivity, they will disclose all other distribution agreements concerning the product.

INTELLECTUAL PROPERTY
- In the case of an intangible product, the agreement stipulates the granting of license to reproduce, distribute and transmit the product in electronic form on the Internet.
- The agreement also stipulates the granting of license to use the manufacturer's trademark and other intellectual property rights in the storefront and in the online catalogue.

ORDERS AND SHIPMENT
- Determination of the manner in which orders are to be placed and conditions for placing orders.
- Minimum allowable quantity of each order and of each shipment.

- Shipment dates and the possibility of additional shipments.
- Incoterms applicable to these sales contracts and other conditions of sale.
- Place from which goods are to be shipped and where goods are to be tendered.

PRICE AND PAYMENT

- Advance paid upon signature of the agreement, possibly taking into consideration any exclusivity granted to the distributor.
- The agreement stipulates the commission per unit sold due by the manufacturer to the distributor, either as a fixed percentage of the customer sale price or as a fixed amount.

RECORDS AND AUDITING

- Obligation of the distributor to keep adequate records, on a durable and inalterable medium, of all transactions with customers.
- Content of sales reports and frequency of their communication to the manufacturers.
- Right of the manufacturer to access or inspect the distributor's records, or to have the records audited.

ADVERTISING

- Obligation of the manufacturer to provide the information and the «documents» required for setting up the storefront.
- Obligation of the distributor to ensure the promotion of the product on the Internet, notably by providing a link from the virtual storefront to the manufacturer's home page.
- Possible obligation of the distributor to create and administrate a message base or a discussion area on the Internet for actual and potential users of the product. The distributor would then be obligated to participate in discussions concerning the product or in discussions specified in the agreement.
- The manufacturer has a right of prior approval of all promotional material concerning the product.

SALES CONTRACTS AND EVIDENCE

- Obligation of the distributor to include standard terms and conditions (including disclaimers) in its contracts with customers, with particular attention to consumer contracts.
- The distributor must take the necessary measures to ensure the enforceability of contracts concluded with customers on the Internet (as concerns rules of evidence, consumer protection laws, etc.).

SECURITY

The distributor must:
- Protect confidential information transmitted to the distributor and stored in the distributor's system.
- Respect the conditions which establish a certain degree of security during transactions with customers.
- Take the technical measures necessary to prevent illegal distribution of the product and to prevent the illegal copying of an intangible product.

CUSTOMER INFORMATION

- The distributor must:
  a) keep a record, on a durable and inalterable medium and compliant with applicable law, of data concerning purchases and of all other customer information.
  b) transmit the customer list and its updates, in accordance with applicable law, (having advised the customer of any use to be made of information concerning him or her, and having obtained the customer's consent where necessary).
- This clause should also stipulate that the Internet customer list is confidential, and it should determine ownership of copyright on this list.

CUSTOMER SUPPORT

The distributor must:
- Create, update and distribute online a list of frequently asked questions (FAQ) concerning the business, its products, prices, conditions and payment.
- Provide a customer support e-mail address and customer telephone support line in order to ensure follow-up service.

WARRANTY AND DISCLAIMER

- Standard distribution agreement warranty and disclaimer provisions.

NATURE OF RELATIONSHIP BETWEEN THE PARTIES

- No partnership between the distributor and the manufacturer.

TERM AND TERMINATION

- Duration of agreement and renewal. No tacit renewal.
- Procedure for obtaining termination in case of nonperformance of contract.
- Definition of minimal sales requirements per year and right of the manufacturer to unilaterally terminate the agreement at the end of the year if such requirements are not met.

EVIDENCE

- Computer records stored in reasonably secure conditions on the computer system of either party shall be accepted as evidence of communications, contracts and payments made between the parties.
- Records shall be presumed to have been stored in reasonably secure conditions if the documents are systematically recorded on a durable and inalterable medium.

FORCE MAJEURE

CHOICE OF APPLICABLE LAW AND JURISDICTION

12. WEB PAGE DEVELOPMENT AND MAINTENANCE AGREEMENT

Most businesses wishing to create a presence on the World Wide Web do not have «hypertext» programming experts or even computer experts within their ranks. They will therefore engage specialized firms to design and produce the pages of their Web site. They will conclude a Web page development and maintenance agreement. The parties will agree on a set of site specifications consecrated as precisely as possible in a technical document incorporated into the agreement as a schedule.

It is particularly important for the parties to define the extent of any intellectual property rights to be acquired by the client as a result of this production. Software provided by the developer will usually be standard and the developer or the software creator will normally retain the rights. If custom software is developed for the client, however, the client can normally obtain the intellectual property rights.

SERVICES
- Description of the elements to be developed (content and number of pages, graphic interface, photographs, animation, sound, text, logos, etc.).
- Description of the computer programs to be provided by the developer (order taking modules, module for the automatic generation of additional pages or updates, usage report generation module, etc.).
- Assistance in selecting an Internet access provider.

TIMETABLE
- Obligation of the client to provide the necessary information and elements within a specified time after the signature of the contract.
- Deadlines upon which a preliminary (BETA) version of the site and the final version of the site must be accessible via the Internet. Determination of the method of final approval by the client, and the respective rights of the parties in the event that the software provided by the developer does not work.

PAYMENT
- Description of development and maintenance fees.
- Timetable for the payment of fees.

INTERNET ACCESS
- The developer is not liable for any interruption of service or loss of data caused by the Internet access provider.

INTELLECTUAL PROPERTY
- The developer of the Web page assigns copyright in the elements created for its Web site to the client, and possibly grants license to use on the Web site the computer programs for which the developer owns intellectual property rights.

ADVERTISING ON THE SITE
- Obligation of the Web page developer to ensure the promotion of the page created, by notifying Internet search and indexing engines of the inauguration of the client's site.
- Description of any additional advertising services to be provided by the developer.

UPDATES
- Schedule of updates to be accomplished by the developer, including software updates.

MAINTENANCE AND CONSULTATION
The developer must:
- Maintain the site for a determined period of time.
- Provide consultation services at a fixed price.

WARRANTIES AND LIABILITY
- The client guarantees the developer that material supplied is not illegal and does not infringe the rights of third parties.
- The developer warrants that software and elements created and supplied to the client do not infringe the rights of third parties and are not illegal.
- Indemnification of the other party by the warrantor for any claims by third parties.
- The developer is not liable for damages suffered by a client as a result of site modification effected by the client or by an Internet user.

TERM AND TERMINATION
- Duration of agreement and renewal.
- Right of either party, having given notice and term of prior notice, to terminate the agreement upon accomplishment of the Web page.
- Immediate termination in case of nonperformance of contract.

EVIDENCE
- Computer records stored in reasonably secure conditions on the computer system of either party shall be accepted as evidence of communications, contracts and payments made between the parties.
- Records shall be presumed to have been stored in reasonably secure conditions if the documents are systematically recorded on a durable and inalterable medium.

FORCE MAJEURE

CHOICE OF APPLICABLE LAW AND JURISDICTION

13. ONLINE RESEARCH AGREEMENT

A wealth of information is available on the Internet. Information searches can, however, be long and tedious. An agreement may be concluded with a firm specializing in netsurfing and in researching specific information. In order to protect the parties, it is important to precisely define the nature of the documents sought by the client or his or her field of interest.

If the client wishes to find documents that may be reproduced free of charge, this should be specified in the agreement. This provision should be stated in the form of a warranty stipulating indemnification in case of a claim by the owner of copyright on the document reproduced.

SERVICES
- Research of a specified field of interest, of a general subject area or of specific information.
- Types of servers to be researched (Web pages, F.T.P. servers, Gopher servers, forums, discussion list archives).

PERFORMANCE
- Term within which the research must be accomplished.
- Form of presentation of search results, and the obligation to indicate the exact Internet location of the information.
- The agreement may specify a minimum number of documents or pages to be gathered by the netsurfers.

COPYRIGHT
- The netsurfing firm assigns all rights on any compilation of information generated in the course of research.

PAYMENT
- Method of remuneration to be adopted (per page, per kilobyte, per document, flat rate or other method).
- Time and manner of payment.

LEGALITY OF RESEARCH
- The research must be accomplished within the limits of the applicable law, notably as concerns rules regarding unauthorized access, data manipulation, etc.

DISCLAIMER
The netsurfing firm does not guarantee:
- That the information collected is precise or true.
- That the information or documents collected are free of intellectual property rights, unless such information or document contains a provision to the contrary.

EVIDENCE
- Computer records stored in reasonably secure conditions on the computer system of either party shall be accepted as evidence of communications, contracts and payments made between the parties.
- Records shall be presumed to have been stored in reasonably secure conditions if the documents are systematically recorded on a durable and inalterable medium.

TERM AND TERMINATION
- Term of agreement and renewal.
- Right of either party to terminate the agreement upon notice and term of prior notice.
- Immediate termination in case of nonperformance of contract.

FORCE MAJEURE

CHOICE OF APPLICABLE LAW AND JURISDICTION

14. ONLINE LOBBYING AND MARKETING AGREEMENT

Offering the service of making contacts or of promoting a certain cause on the Internet is possible if carried out in an acceptable manner. This may be accomplished by participating in discussion forums or even by creating appropriate discussion forums.

The parties should be aware that legislation requiring the registration of lobbyists applies to the Internet. If there are any specific requirements to be met, the agreement should state that the lobbyist is obliged to respect them.

SERVICES
- Promotion of an opinion or of a specific cause described in the agreement.
- Development of contacts within a specific organization identified in the agreement.

PAYMENT
- Determination of the commission or fees payable to the lobbyist.
- Periodicity and manner of payment.

MINIMUM EFFORTS
The lobbyist is obligated:
- To send a minimum number of electronic messages.
- To attract, within a determined timeframe, a minimum number of participants to the online messages bases created by the lobbyist for the purposes of promoting the cause or interests of the client.
- To ensure the minimal Internet presence stipulated by the client.

RECORDS
- Obligation of the lobbyist to keep records, on a durable and inalterable medium, of the messages sent and of the coordinates of persons contacted.
- Right of the client to examine the records upon prior notice.

DISCLOSURE OF IDENTITY
- Obligation to preserve the confidentiality of client identity. Determination of the precise circumstances in which client identity may be disclosed.
- Disclosure when required by law, upon notice to the client.

NETIQUETTE
- Obligation of the lobbyist to comply with the rules of netiquette, particularly when sending messages or creating an Internet presence.
- Liability for any damages to the reputation or clientele of the client.

SECURITY
- The agreement stipulates security measures to be observed in order to preserve the confidentiality of communications between the client and the lobbyist, and particularly when such communications occur via electronic means.

EVIDENCE
- Computer records stored in reasonably secure conditions on the computer system of either party shall be accepted as evidence of communications, contracts and payments made between the parties.
- Records shall be presumed to have been stored in reasonably secure conditions if the documents are systematically recorded on a durable and inalterable medium.

TERM AND TERMINATION
- Term of agreement and renewal.
- Right of either party to terminate the agreement upon notice and term of prior notice.
- Immediate termination in case of nonperformance of contract.

FORCE MAJEURE

CHOICE OF APPLICABLE LAW AND JURISDICTION

15. ONLINE FORUM PARTICIPANT AGREEMENT

Discussion forums allow Internet users to participate in discussions organized according to specific topics. Only a very few of these forums habitually conclude contracts with participants. Such an agreement may, however, be used as a means of discouraging irresponsible behaviour on the part of participants, for example by charging a fee for accessing the forum. An agreement may also serve to limit the liability of the organizer or moderator of the discussion group.

SERVICES
- Description of the nature and subject matter of the «conference» to which participant is to have access.
- Description of the format of the discussion group, either «moderated» or «unmoderated».
- Time and methods of payment of fees.

PARTICIPATION
- Obligation to respect the subject matter of the discussion group.
- Statement of rules concerning commercial solicitation or advertising in messages.

NETIQUETTE
- Obligation of participants to comply with the rules of netiquette when sending messages or otherwise participating in the forum.
- Description of the specific rules particular to a given forum (possibly including an Acceptable Use Policy incorporated as a schedule).

LIABILITY
- The forum organizer bears no liability for any damages suffered by a participant as a consequence of the conduct of other participants.
- The participant whose conduct provokes a claim or any recourse against the organizer must indemnify the organizer according to the terms and conditions stipulated in the agreement.

TERM AND TERMINATION

- Term of agreement and renewal.
- In the event of nonperformance of contract by the participant, right of the organizer to immediately terminate his or her participation in the forum and to immediately terminate the agreement.

EVIDENCE

- Computer records stored in reasonably secure conditions on the computer system of either party shall be accepted as evidence of communications, contracts and payments made between the parties.
- Records shall be presumed to have been stored in reasonably secure conditions if the documents are systematically recorded on a durable and inalterable medium.

FORCE MAJEURE

CHOICE OF APPLICABLE LAW AND JURISDICTION

16. AGREEMENT FOR ONLINE DATABASE ACCESS

Firms in the business of providing access to information will generally conclude a formal agreement with users of their services. In order to maintain the commercial value of the database, the agreement normally stipulates that users may not copy information other than for personal use. It may also be acceptable in certain countries for the owner of the database to limit his or her liability regarding the information provided. If a user subscribes to the database for professional purposes, he or she may try to obtain stronger guarantees of reliability from the database owner. Database owners tend, however, to be quite inflexible on this point.

SERVICES
- Description of the databases to be made available to the user by the owner.
- Right of the database owner to modify the content of databases.

FEES
- Detailed description of fees to be paid by the user to the owner, including both general subscription rates and specific fees for certain operations or types of operations.
- Periodicity and methods of payment of these various rates and fees.
- Right of the database owner to modify rates and fees upon prior notice, and the right of the user to terminate the contract if he or she does not agree to the modification.

LICENSING
- Scope of the license to reproduce documents granted to the user (personal use, business use, etc.).

INSTRUCTIONS FOR USE OF THE DATABASE
- Obligation of the database owner to provide Internet users with both an online instruction manual for the database and with a version on paper of the instruction manual free of charge.

INTERRUPTION OF SERVICE
- Right of the database owner to interrupt service with or without notice.

  OR (more frequently)
- Determination of a period of time in which the database owner may interrupt service.

RESTRICTION ON USE OF DATABASE
- Description of allowable uses of information obtained from the database.
- Limitation of the right to commercially exploit information obtained.
- Maximum number of users per subscription or per account.

DISCLAIMER AND LIMITATION OF LIABILITY
- The database owner does not guarantee the user that information contained in the database is accurate or true.

  OR
- Limitative description of the degree of care which the owner must exercise in ascertaining the accuracy of the information or in updating the information.
- Limitation of the liability of the database owner for damages or loss of profits suffered by the user in the event that the service is unavailable.

TERM AND TERMINATION
- Duration of the agreement and renewal.
- Right of either party to terminate the agreement upon notice and term of prior notice.
- Immediate termination in case of nonperformance of contract.

EVIDENCE
- Computer records stored in reasonably secure conditions on the computer system of either party shall be accepted as evidence of communications, contracts and payments made between the parties.
- Records shall be presumed to have been stored in reasonably secure conditions if the documents are systematically recorded on a durable and inalterable medium.

FORCE MAJEURE

CHOICE OF APPLICABLE LAW AND JURISDICTION

17. MASTER RETAIL SALES AGREEMENT

In order to avoid the legal uncertainties which can be involved in sales agreements concluded on the Internet, it may be wise to define, in a master retail sales agreement, certain ground rules concerning the conclusion of contracts and the manner in which contracts may be proven (in this sense, this master contract also constitutes an evidentiary agreement). As we have mentioned in our chapter on electronic commerce, this master contract may take the form of standard terms and conditions posted on Web servers, to which a user must consent in order to access a virtual store. Even if it is impossible to access the store without agreeing to the terms and conditions, however, this contract may not have all of the desired legal effects under the evidence laws of certain jurisdictions. For this reason it is preferable to sign a paper version of the agreement, which will increase its chances of being admissible evidence in legal proceedings.

This contract may be used, for example, to indicate to a buyer that the display of merchandise in the virtual storefront does not constitute an offer to contract.

CONCLUSION VIA THE INTERNET OF RETAIL SALES AGREEMENTS
- The information displayed in the virtual storefront does not constitute an offer to contract.
- The message sent by the user to the virtual store shall constitute an offer to purchase the goods according to the terms and conditions displayed.
- The virtual store indicates its intention to conclude the contract by sending a message confirming the sale and signed using technical means of identification, such as a private cryptographic key .
- The contract is formed at the time when the confirmation message reaches the user's electronic mailbox on his or her Internet access provider's server.
- Responsibility of the buyer to verify that his or her electronic mailbox is in proper working order. He or she assumes all consequences of operational failures.

EVIDENCE
- Computer records stored in reasonably secure conditions on the computer system of either party shall be accepted as evidence of communications, contracts and payments made between the parties.
- Records shall be presumed to have been stored in reasonably secure conditions if the documents are systematically recorded on a durable and inalterable medium.

TERM AND TERMINATION
- Duration of the agreement and renewal.
- Right of either party to terminate the agreement upon notice and term of prior notice.
- Immediate termination in case of nonperformance of contract.

FORCE MAJEURE

CHOICE OF APPLICABLE LAW AND JURISDICTION

18. ELECTRONIC COMMERCE AGREEMENT BETWEEN PROFESSIONALS

Parties maintaining a regular commercial relationship with one another may wish to conclude a large part of their contracts via the Internet. In order to avoid problems related to establishing the existence of such contracts or of other related documents, but also in order to establish a broader legal framework as regards the conclusion and performance of these contracts, businesses resort to electronic commerce agreements. These agreements establish the conditions which govern the exchange of electronic documents between the parties, and notably the security measures required in order to protect the information exchanged against possible interception by third parties. If so desired, the parties may specify a mutually acceptable standard (such as the EDIFACT or ANSI) for the format of the documents exchanged.

NATURE OF THE AGREEMENT
- Agreement to facilitate electronic commerce between professional parties.
- The conclusion of this agreement entails no obligation to conclude further contracts.

LEGALITY
- Verification that the law applicable to each party does not compromise the validity of commercial exchanges via the Internet or evidence of such exchanges.
- Obligation of each party to notify the other party of the existence of any applicable rule of law which could limit the possibility of pursuing electronic commerce.
- Indemnification of the party that is not in default for any damages or any losses caused by the failure to notify that party of such a limit.

RECOURSE TO ELECTRONIC COMMUNICATIONS
- The parties must indicate whether or not they wish to limit their exchange of documents to exchange exclusively via the Internet.
- If such an obligation exists, the agreement should stipulate the weight to be accorded to a message received via a means of communication other than the Internet.
- Use of other means of communication if electronic mail via the Internet is unavailable.
- Identification of the types of documents to be exchanged in virtue of this agreement, or stipulation that the agreement applies to all forms of electronic communication between the parties.

EQUIPMENT AND INTERNET ACCESS
- Each party bears the cost and is responsible for obtaining and maintaining any equipment and software needed for communicating via the Internet.
- Each party is responsible for securing adequate access to the Internet, for providing the other party with an Internet electronic mail address, and for notifying the other party of any change of address according to an established procedure, which includes specifying the moment at which such change takes effect.

SECURITY AND CONFIDENTIALITY
- Description of the security features chosen for the purposes of preserving the confidentiality of messages sent and received.
- Obligation to take sufficient precautions for preserving the confidentiality of information in each party's computer system.

VALIDITY OF CONTRACTS
CONCLUDED ELECTRONICALLY
- A valid contract is concluded only when all messages required by its conclusion have full legal effect according to procedures determined in the agreement.
- The parties agree that a message shall have full legal weight if the recipient party does not indicate to the other party within a reasonable delay that the message is illegible.
- A message will be considered received only upon acknowledgment of reception by the recipient party.
- The recipient party is obligated to promptly send an acknowledgment of the receipt of a message.

FORM OF THE MESSAGES
(IN THE CASE OF EDI EXCHANGES)
- Definition of the EDI communications standard that the parties may have chosen.
- Procedure agreed to by the parties for the timely adoption of new versions of such standards.

DIGITAL SIGNATURE
- Agreement to use digital signatures and description of a chosen technology that will ensure the authentication and the integrity of the message.
- The use of an electronic signature shall constitute proof of the existence, the origin, and the integrity of the electronic message sent.
- Obligation of each party to ensure that the access to the means of producing such digital signatures is adequately controlled and restricted.

RECORDS
- Obligation to keep adequate records, on a durable and inalterable medium, of the electronic messages sent and received.
- Period of time during which these records must be kept.

EVIDENCE
While respecting the particular conditions of the agreement:
- The computer records stored in reasonably secure conditions on the computer system of either party shall be accepted as evidence of communications, contracts and payments made between the parties.
- Records shall be presumed to have been stored in reasonably secure conditions if the documents are systematically recorded on a durable and inalterable medium.

TERMINATION
- Procedure for terminating the agreement in the absence of fault on the part of the other party.
- Immediate termination in case of nonperformance of contract.

FORCE MAJEURE

CHOICE OF APPLICABLE LAW AND JURISDICTION

19. CERTIFYING AUTHORITY AGREEMENT

One of the major difficulties of doing business on the Internet is that of determining the identity of the persons with whom one is dealing. This is particularly important when legally binding agreements such as contracts are to be concluded via the Internet. In order to at least provisionally resolve this legal but also psychological impediment, certain firms and governmental authorities offer a service to users wishing to have their identity certified on the Internet.

The service formally certifies to the Internet world that a particular public encryption key is used by a particular person. This is accomplished by issuing a certificate of electronic identity upon presentation to the certifying authority of prescribed documents establishing the identity of the person or company. We propose an agreement which could be concluded between the certifying authority and the user wishing to have his or her identity certified. It is nonetheless to be noted that, since the full implications of such a process have not yet been widely debated, the actual content of this agreement may vary.

SERVICES
- Certification of the user's identity by the issuance and publication of a certificate accessible via the Internet.

DOCUMENTS
- Description of the documents required by the certifying authority in order that it may attest to the identity of the person or business. If the entity wishing to be certified is a corporation, the documents should include the certificate of incorporation and the authorizations necessary to prove the applicant's authority.
- Right of the certifying authority to reject the documents if it has any doubt as regards their validity.

ISSUANCE OF THE CERTIFICATE
- Description of the content of the certificate to be issued and of its duration.
- Delay within which the certificate will be issued following the presentation of the required documents.

TERM
- Time and methods of payment.

SECURITY
- The user is obligated to preserve the confidentiality of the password providing access to his or her private key, and to promptly inform the certifying authority of any breach of security in his or her computer system which could imperil this confidentiality.
- The certifying authority is not liable towards the user for any damages or any losses sustained before reception of such notice of breach of security.
- Obligation of the user to periodically modify his or her public key, and to obtain a new certificate each time.

TERM, TERMINATION AND RENEWAL OF CERTIFICATE
- Duration and renewal of the agreement.
- Right of the certifying authority to remove expired certificates from its server.
- Right of the certifying authority to terminate the agreement if it doubts the validity of the documents presented as attestation of the identity of the person or business.
- Right of either party to terminate the agreement upon notice and term of prior notice.
- mmediate termination in case of nonperformance of contract.

DISCLAIMER AND LIMITATION OF LIABILITY
- Limitation of the certifying authority's liability to a fixed amount or to the fees paid by the user.
- No liability of the certifying authority in the event that its server is not accessible via the Internet, or description of the minimal efforts to be undertaken by the certifying authority in order to maintain the accessibility of its server at all times.

EVIDENCE
- Computer records stored in reasonably secure conditions on the computer system of either party shall be accepted as evidence of communications, contracts and payments made between the parties.
- Records shall be presumed to have been stored in reasonably secure conditions if the documents are systematically recorded on a durable and inalterable medium.

FORCE MAJEURE

CHOICE OF APPLICABLE LAW AND JURISDICTION

20. ACCEPTABLE USE POLICY

Many networks have a document (Acceptable Use Policy or AUP) indicating what types of uses are considered acceptable and unacceptable. This is particularly true of the educational networks that comprise part of the Internet. Such a document may also, however, prove to be useful in educating the users of a private network about policy concerning its use. Internet access providers also sometimes impose this type of AUP upon their users by contract. An AUP governs the conduct of newsgroup users. In general, AUPs constitute the charters of reasonable conduct and of the rights and freedoms of users in a given Internet zone.

If the acceptable use policy is that of a company, it will usually stipulate that the network may only be used for company purposes. An educational network may want to restrict the use of its network to educational, research or other not-for-profit purposes. Other aspects of acceptable use policies are common to both types of networks, and concern not the purpose of communications but rather user conduct.

ACCEPTABLE AND UNACCEPTABLE USES

1. Unacceptable uses on any network:
- unauthorized access to computer systems or networks;
- infringement of third party privacy rights;
- infringement of third party intellectual property rights;
- transmission of threatening, obscene or harassing material;
- illegal transmission of unsolicited advertising;
- corruption or destruction of data or any action which could impede legitimate access to data, including the launching of a virus, of worms or of any other malicious software in any computer system connected to the network;
- interruption of the legitimate use of the network or of A computer system by third parties;
- waste of network resources;
- any use condemned by the acceptable use policies of the network contacted;
- any conduct which is illegal according to the applicable law of any country that may be accessed via the network;
- use of the network for recreational games.

2. Particularities of certain networks:

Regarding an educational network:

a) acceptable uses:
- use for educational or research purposes;
- use by non-profit organizations;
- use for infrastructure administration purposes and for educational and research communications;
- use for accessing libraries;
- use for joint projects by educational institutions or for private sector research projects.

- b) unacceptable uses:
- commercial use of the network;
- use of the network for the transmission of commercial advertising.

Regarding a business network:

a) acceptable uses:
- use for business purposes;
- use for participating in online forums related to the company's business in accordance with company policy;
- use for personal communications with other employees after or before a certain time of the day, insofar as such communication does not interfere with the employee's duties.

- b) unacceptable uses:
- use of the network for purposes not related to the company's activities
- use of the network to conduct personal for-profit activities;
- use of the network to send commercial advertising not related to the company, or advertising related to the company but not approved in accordance with company policy;
- authorizing or permitting a person not connected to the company network to use it illegally.

CONSEQUENCES OF POLICY BREACH
- Description of the disciplinary actions that may be taken against users who violate the acceptable use policy.
- When the AUP is incorporated into a contract as a schedule, the contract shall stipulate contractual penalties for breach of the AUP.

Outlook

This brings us to the end of our tour. A legal tour, admittedly, but a tour nevertheless. And one that cannot be completed. But the future promises us another journey-a journey on the information superhighway. The Internet heralds the arrival of the superhighway, and already gives us some idea of the challenges and debates that it will provoke.

As the Internet experience has shown, the internationalization of the information superhighway will not prevent a legal framework from being created and applied. On the contrary, it will make it imperative to place the new standards adopted in an international framework, and in particular as regards relationships between the European Union and the United States.

The actual application of the principles of the free provision of services within the European Union will, moreover, be a sine qua non for the development in Europe of telematic services on networks which will need international markets in order to be profitable.

As regards private individuals, it is essential that the protection of fundamental rights and values (such as freedom of expression and privacy.) continues to be guaranteed, despite economic and industrial pressures.

Maintaining a balance between these different objectives and other duties in the general interest (protection of law and order, crime prevention), and between fundamental rights and values, will require vigilance and innovation. The future of telematic services is thus linked to the use of cryptography, which must not endanger the legitimate tasks of maintaining law and order and of preventing crime.

Law and policy must give confidence, a legitimate expectation in any fulfilled commercial or personal life, to one and all.

Above and beyond the specific political and economic tasks at hand, however, we all have a part to play in the building of this world of communication. The future is there for the building.

References

Part one

«The Internet in practice and in business»

1 B. LIPS, *Internet en Belgique*, 2nd ed, Brussels, Best Of, 1996, p.452.
2 R. RESNICK and D. TAYLOR, *The Internet Business Guide : Riding the information Superhighway to profit*, Sams Publishing, 1994, p.XXV.
3 B. LIPS, *op. cit.,* pp.103-105.
4 Source: Central Source Yellow Pages, The Internet Index- *http://www.openmarket.com/diversions/internet-index/96-01.html*, Number 12, Inspired by «Harper's Index», Compiled by wintreese, 2 January 1996.
5 R. RESNICK and D. TAYLOR, *op. cit.*, p.114.
6 For a more detailed discussion, however, see Part two, Chapter 5, «The Internet and commercial communication».
7 As an example, see the Web site of the famous GODIVA chocolates (*http://www.godiva*).
8 «Infosight Innovative Ideas & Information-Businesses on the Web», *htpp://www.téléport.com/~speaker/business.htm*
9 «The Best of The Best: Grading the Top 25 - Special Report: cent Best Business Web Sites», CMP Publications Inc, (*http://techweb.cmp.com*).
10 *http://www.commerce.net/information/reference/Web.efsect.html*
11 *http://www.sni.be/fr/index.htm*
12 *http://www.McKinsey.com/*
13 *http://www.euromktg.com/euromktg/eurobus.html*
14 *http://www.londonmall.co.uk/default.htm*
15 *http://www.xxlink.nl/ExxPo/*
16 *http://www.com/ibi/index.htm*
17 *http://www.commerce.net/*
18 *http://www.Industry.Net/IndustryNet.html*
19 *http://www. Industry.Net/guide.html#6*
20 *http : // www. ccc. net/ home. html*
21 *http://www1.usa1.com/~ibnet/icchp.html*
22 *http://www.embassy.org/*
23 http://gatekeeper.unicc.org/wto/
24 *http://www.marktwain.com*
25 *http://www.digicash.com*
26 *http://www.fv.com*. For more detailed information on the *Mark Twain Bank*, *Digicash* and the other electronic payment systems and new commercial intermediaries, see Part two, Chapter 6, on electronic commerce.
2 7 See the *Market Places and Quotations* servers (*http://www.wiso.gwdg.de/ifbg/stock1.html*) and the Web server *http://www.zse.com.hr/exchange.html* which gives all the «hypertext» links of stock exchanges in the world, classified by continent and country.
28 For example, *The Net Investor* (*http://www.pawws.secapl.com/invest.html*).
29 See for example, the *Frankfurt Money Strategist* site (*http://www.henix.net/mns/*) which disseminates information and research reports on the Bundesbank and the Deutschmark, on macroeconomic trends in Germany as well as on European developments regarding issues of currency and policy.
30 *http://www.FinanceNet.gov/*
31 *http://www.corpfinet.com/*
32 See for example, *BankNet Electronic Banking Service* (*http://mkn.co.uk/bank*), *Bank of Canada* (*http://www.royalbank.com/*), *Banque Paribas* (*http://www.paribas.com/*), *Deutsche Bank* (*http://www.deutsche-bank.de/index_e.htm*), *Bank of England* (*http//galaxy.einet.neta/hytelnet/FUL031.html*), *Banca di Credito di Trieste* (*http://www.bctkb.it/bctkb/*), *Liechtensteinische Landesbank* (*http://www.bodan.net/lld/index.html*); *Kredietbank* (*http://www.limbu.nl/linma/adv/h/krediet/index.html*), *CERA Bank* (*http://www.Bank.CERA.be/CERA/*), ...
33 *http://www.worldbank.org/*
34 *gopher://gopher.imf.org*
35 *htpp://www.cox.smu.edu/mis/cases/dec/internet.htmtl*
36 For example, a server such as that of the *National Trade Databank* alone disseminates over 300,000 documents and over 130 information programs on trade and the economy (*http://www.statusa.gov/BEN/Services/ntdbhome.html*).

37 *htpp://www.civl.port.ac.uk/resources/resources.html*
38 *http://www.iso.ch/welcome.html*
39 *http://www.mew.com/index.html_R&D*
40 *Nippon Telegraph and Telephone Corporation - http://www.info.hqs.cae.ntt.jp/RD/RDreport.html*
41 *http://www.Fortis.com/*
42 Quoted by Internet reporter-Le guide du multimédia on-line, issue 5, p.4 (*http://www.imaginet.fr/netreporter*
43 *http://www.occ.com/occ/member/cpprocte.html*
44 *http://www.philips.com/*
45 *http:// www.embassy.org/*
46 Infoseek Guide: International jobs
    (*http://guide-p.infoseek.com/DB?tis=499&tid=427&db=82&sv=NS&ik=noframes&col=WW*)
47 UK Business Park (*http://www.zynet.co.uk/ppark/pprecep*).pour un nouveau droit du marché intérieur», *Revue du Marché Unique Européen*, 1995, 1, pp.54 ff.

Part two

Introduction

1 Austria, Belgium, Denmark, Finland, France, Germany, Greece, Ireland, Italy, Luxembourg, Netherlands, Portugal, Spain, Sweden, United Kingdom.
2 Albania, Andorra, Bulgaria, Cyprus, the Czech Republic, Estonia, Hungary, Iceland, Latvia, Liechtenstein, Lithuania, Macedonia, Moldavia, Norway, Romania, Saint-Marino, Slovakia, Slovenia, Switzerland, Russia, Turkey, Ukraine.
3 C.J.E.C., 14 May 1984 (NOLD, KOHLEN - UND BAUSTOFFGROBHANDLUNG v. COMMISSION OF THE EUROPEAN COMMUNITIES), 4/73, Rec. *C.J.E.C.*, p. 3727.
4 C.J.E.C., 26 JUNE 1980 (NATIONAL PANASONIC (U.K.) LIMITED v. COMMISSION OF THE EUROPEAN COMMUNITIES), 136/79, Rec. *C.J.E.C.*, p. 2033.

Chapter one

«Your first steps on the Internet and the law»

1 Sources for European national law: *http://www.eto.dk*
2 Finally, as regards the establishment of a Community Internet access provider in another state in the European Union, the principle is that of freedom of establishment. European law does, however, allow member states the possibility of restricting this establishment (for example by means of licensing regimes), either by discriminatory means (when this restriction is justified by reasons of public policy, public health or public security and is proportionate) or by non-discriminatory means (when the restriction is based on the protection of the general interest and is proportionate). As regards the concepts of restriction, discrimination, general interest and public policy, see below: the free provision of services within the European Union.
3 The declaration must be made, under the terms of Article 89 of the law of 21 March 1991 on telecommunications, to the *Institut Belge des Services Postaux et des Télécommunications.*
4 That is, a simple data transport service, the purpose of which is either to transmit or to transmit and forward signals between the terminals of a telecommunications network, without processing these signals in a manner other than is necessary for a transmission, for their routing and for the monitoring of these functions (Art. L.32-9 of law n°90-1170 of 29 December 1990 on the regulation of telecommunications).
5 See Article 2 of the decree of 30 December 1992 on support services and amending the second part of the Post and Telecommunications Code.
6 See the Deeds of Constitution of the postal and telecommunication services (FernmeldeAnlagenGesetz),
7 Proposal for a European Parliament and Council directive on a common framework for general authorizations and individual licences in the telecommunications services sector, Brussels, 14 November Com(95) 545.
8 This limitation may only be justified by the need to guarantee an efficient allocation of radio frequencies.

9   The signatory states of this agreement are Belgium, Denmark, Finland, France, Germany, Hungary, Ireland, Italy, Luxembourg, the Netherlands, Norway, Spain, Sweden, Switzerland and the United Kingdom.

10 *North American Free Trade Agreement* (hereinafter referred to as the NAFTA), 1992, art. 1310.

11 See Steven B. BARNETT, «Law of International Communications in the United States», in *Law and Economics of International Telecommunications*, Baden-Baden, Ed. Auflage, 1988, vol.4, p.25.

12 Amendment of Section 64.702 of the Commission's rules and regulations (Second Computer Inquiry), 77 *F.C.C.*, 419-420 (1980), quoted by I. K. Gotts and A. D. Rutenberg *in* «Navigating the Global Superhighway: A Bumpy Road Lies Ahead», *Harvard Journal Of Law and Technology*, vol.8, n°2, Spring 1995, p.284.

13 *Federal Communications Act of 1934*, ch. 652, 48 stat. 1064 (1934), amended at 47 *USC.* § 151-613 (1988).

14 *Loi sur les Télécommunications*, L.C. 1993, c.38. According to the definitions contained in Article 2 of the law, appliances capturing, receiving, storing, classifying, modifying, retrieving or otherwise processing information are excluded from the field of application of the law.

15 CANADA, Industrie Canada, *L'autoroute canadienne de l'information - une nouvelle infrastructure de l'information*, Approvisionnements et Services Canada, April 1994, pp.15-16.

16 Hank Intven, «Traffic rules on Canada's information highway: the regulatory framework for new cable and telephone services», *Developping Multimedia Products*, Insight Press, Toronto, 1994, p.35.

17 As may be imagined, the objectives guiding this exception are those of healthy competition and of the fight against monopolies.

18 See. articles 59 and 60 of the Treaty on European Union.

19 Article 1303 of the NAFTA.

20 Articles 59 and 60 of the treaty forbid all forms of discrimination. They apply not only to unequal treatment clearly based on the nationality of the service provider and the origin of the service, but also to those who conceal this purpose by invoking criteria which are apparently neutral and which in fact achieve the same result (C.J.E.C., 17 December 1981(CRIMINAL PROCEEDINGS AGAINST JOHN WEBB), 279/80, *Rec. C.J.E.C.*, p.3305, point 14 of the reasons; 4 December 1986 (COMMISSION OF THE COMMUNITIES V. THE FEDERAL REPUBLIC OF GERMANY), 205/84, *Rec. C.J.E.C.*, p.3755, point 25 of the reasons and more recently the three «tourist guide» rulings of 26 February 1991 (COMMISSION OF THE EUROPEAN COMMUNITIES V. THE FRENCH REPUBLIC), *154/89, Rec. C.J.E.C. , p.659*, point 12 of the reasons; (COMMISSION OF THE EUROPEAN COMMUNITIES V. THE ITALIAN REPUBLIC), *189/89, Rec. C.J.E.C., p.709,*. point 15 of the reasons and (COMMISSION OF THE EUROPEAN COMMUNITIES V. THE HELLENIC REPUBLIC), *198/89, Rec. C.J.E.C. ,* p.666, point 16 of the reasons. The aim of articles 58, 59 and 65 is to eliminate measures subjecting the national of a member state to more stringent rules or placing him or her, in fact or in law, in a less favourable position than a national of the member state imposing these measures (C.J.C.E., 13 December 1984(EBERHARD HAUG-ADRION C. FRANKFURTER VERSICHERUNGS AG), 251/83, *Rec. C.J.E.C.*, p.4277.

21 C.J.E.C., 16 December 1992 (COMMISSION v. KINGDOM of BELGIUM), 211/91, *Rec. C.J.E.C.*, p.6757.

22 If the conditions required by Community law are fulfilled and in particular if the activity of the user as presented in his *Home Page* or exercised via the Internet can be described an an economic activity. This criterion, which is not strict, would enable the user to benefit for this dissemination from the protection of the free provision of services.

23 The application of the principle of national treatment to authorizations required in the various countries of the Union in order to exercise telecommunications activities implies that these authorizations may not result in preventing the provision of the service by Community providers. In addition, Directive 90/338/EC requires, when the services it liberalizes are subject to an authorization or declaration procedure in the member states, that such authorizations be accorded for objective, transparent criteria which have no discriminatory effect. Where these regimes are nonetheless justified for reasons of protection of public order or other imperative reasons in the general interest, the application of the necessity criterion requires that when a member state subjects an activity to authorization, it must take into account the justifications and guarantees already presented by the service provider in relation to its activity in the member State in which it is established.

24 C.J.E.C., 25 July 1991, *op. cit.* note 20.

25 C.J.E.C., 24 March 1994 (HER MAJESTY'S CUSTOMS AND EXCISE C. GERHARD SCHINDLER ET JÖRG SCHINDLER) 275/92, *Rec. C.J.E.C.*, p.1078.

26 Interpretative commmunication from the Commission concerning the free cross-border movement of services, O.J.E.C., C 334 of 9 December 1993, p.5.

27 C.J.E.C., 18 June 1991 (ELLENIKI RADIOPHONIA TILEORASSI AE C. DIMOTOKI ETAIRIA PLIROFORISSIS ET SOTIROS KOUVELEAS),260/89, *Rec.C.J.E.C.*, p.2951.

28 C.J.E.C, 27 October 1977 (REGINA C. PIERRE BOUCHERAU), *30/77 , Rec. C.J.E.C.*, p.1999.

29 C.J.E.C., 4 December 1986 (COMMISSION OF THE EUROPEAN COMMUNITIES V. THE
    FEDERAL REPUBLIC OF GERMANY), *op. cit.*, 3755, point 27 of the reasons and the references
    it contains to previous jurisprudence.
30 C.J.E.C., 26 April 1988 (ASSOCIATION OF ADVERTISERS AND OTHERS V. THE DUTCH
    STATE), *352/82, Rec. C.J.C.E.,* p.2135.
31 Interpretative communication from the Commission concerning the free cross-border movement of
    service, O.J.E.C., C 334 of 9 December 1993, *op. cit.*
32 C.J.E.C, 25 July 1991(MANFRED SÄGER C. DENNEMEYER & CO. LTD),76/90,
    Rec.C.J.C.E. p.4239.
33 Art. 1202 to 1205 of the NAFTA.

Chapter two

«Copyright on the Internet»

1   Trotter HARDY, «The Proper Legal Regime for 'Cyberspace'», (1993) 55 *University of Pittsburgh
    Law Review* , 1993, p.999.
2   Copyright Act of 1947, 17 U.S.C. s.102(a) (American); Loi sur le droit d'auteur (canadienne)
    L.R.C. 1985, ch C-42, artt. 2 and 3.
3   T. K. DREIER, «La qualité d'auteur et les nouvelles technologies du point de vue des traditions de
    droit civil», *Symposium de l'OMPI*, Paris, 1994.
4   Copyright Act of 1947, art.101.
5   D. LOUNDY, «E-Law 2,0: Computer Information Systems Law and Operator Liability Revisited»,
    http.//www.eff.org/pub/Legal/e-law.papaer,25; the Working Group On Intellectual Property
    (U.S.),*Preliminary Draft*, *gopher:/iitf.doc.gov.*, n°I, A, 1, a.
6   T. HARDY, *op.cit.*, p.1030.
7   Copyright Act of 1947, art. 102(b);D. LOUNDY, *op.cit.*, 27; A. LUCAS and H. LUCAS, *Traité de
    la propriété littéraire et artistique*, Paris, Litec, 1994, p. 222.
8   *Copyright Act of 1947*, 17 U.S.C., art. 412.
9   L. ROSE, *Netlaw: Your rights in the online world*, Osborne McGraw-Hill, 1995, p.84.
10 IBIDEM, p.99.
11 Copyright Act of 1947, art. 102(a); Loi sur le droit d'auteur (canadienne), L.R.C. 1985 artt. 2 and 5.
12 Copyright Act of 1947, art.101.; Loi sur le droit d'auteur (canadienne), art. 3.
13 D. LOUNDY, *op. cit.*, 23; Loi sur le droit d'auteur (canadienne) art. 3.
14 See *Burrow-Giles Lithographic Co. v. Sarony*, 111 U.S. 53 (1984); D. LOUNDY, *Ibid.*
15 Loi sur le droit d'auteur (canadienne), art. 2.
16 Copyright Act of 1947, art. 102(a).
17 *Lotus Development Corporation v. Borland International Inc.*, 831 F. Supp. 223 (D. Mass. 1993), 232.
18 *Apple Computer Inc. v. Microsoft Corp.*, n°93-16833 (9th Cir. 19 Sept. 1994).
19 Council Directive 91/250/EEC of 14 May 1991 on the legal protection of computer programs,
    O.J.E.C., 15 May 1991, n°L 122/42.
20 Quote C. VOSS, «The legal protection of computer programs in the European Economic
    Community», *Computer Law Journal*, 1992, p.448.
21 P. SIM, «Copyright and Electronic Media Part 2: The Challenge of the New Multimedia»,
    http://www.mbnet.mb.ca/~ P. Sim/copyrt.html, 1; L. ROSE, *op. cit.*, p.113.
22 Common position (EC) n°20/95 adopted by the Council on 10 July 1995 with a view to adopting
    the directive on the legal protection of databases, O.J.E.C., 30 Oct. 1995, C 288/14.
23 *Feist Publications Inc. v. Rural Tel. Serv. Co. Inc.*, 111 S. Ct; 1281 (1991).
24 Common position 20/95.
25 Common position 20/95, art. 1-2.
26 Common position 20/95, art. 3-1.
27 M. PATTISON, «The European Commission's proposal on the protection of Computer Databases»,
    EIPR, 1992, p.116; J. P. TRIAILLE, «La protection juridique des bases de données» in *Droit de l'in-
    formatique: Enjeux - nouvelles responsabilités*, Ed. Jeune Barreau de Bruxelles, 1993, p.169;
    Contra: L. ROSE, *op. cit.*, p. 110.
28 Common position 20/95, art 7 to 11.
29 P.J. BENEDICT O'MAHONEY, «Web Issues», Copyright Website, *http:/www. benedict-
    com/webiss.htm# webiss*, 2; *Feist Publications, Inc. v. Rural Tel. Serv. Co., Inc.*, *op. cit.*
30 Directive 91/250/EEC, artt. 2 and 3.

31   In France, art. L 132-24 of the Intellectual Property Code; in Belgium, art. 18 of the 1994 copyright and related rights act.

32   Council Directive 93/98/EEC of 29 October 1993 harmonizing the term of protection of copyright and certain related rights, O.J.E.C., 24 Nov 1993, n°L 290/9, art. 1.

33   *Gillian v. American Broadcasting Cos.*, 538 F.2d 14, 23, C.O. Bull.40, 541 (2d Cir. 1976); A. STROWEL, *Droit d'auteur et Copyright : divergences et convergences : étude de droit comparé*, Brussels, Bruylant, 1993, p.551.

34   Loi sur le droit d'auteur (canadienne), art. 14. 1(1).

35   G. LEA, «Program copyright and moral rights: a culture clash?», *Computer Law and Security report*, 1994, p.304; Contra A. LUCAS, «Résumé des débats du colloque», *Symposium de l'OMPI*, Paris, 1994.

36   A. LUCAS and H. LUCAS, *op. cit*, p.219; Commission of the European Communities, Green Paper: Copyright and related rights in the information society, COM(95) 382 final, p.51.

37   P. B. HUGENHOLTZ, Copyright problems of electronic document delivery in *Copyright on electronic delivery services and multimedia products*, European Commission, DG XIII, EUR 16056 EN; The Working Group On Intellectual Property Rights (U.S.), *op. cit.*, n°I,A,4,a.

38   A. N. DIXON and L. C. SELF, «Copyright protection for the Information Superhighway», *EIPR*, 1994, P.468; A. LUCAS and H. LUCAS, *op. cit.* p.219; T. HOEREN, An assessment of long-term solutions in the context of copyright and electronic delivery services and multimedia products, in *Copyright on electronic delivery services and multimedia products*, European Commission, DG XIII, EUR 16056 EN, p. 28; S. SAXBY, *Encyclopedia of Information Technology Law*, V.I, London, Sweet and Maxwell, 1992.

39   Council Directive 92/100/EEC of 19 November 1992 on rental right and lending right and on certain rights related to copyright in the field of intellectual property. O.J.E.C. 27 Nov. 1992, L 346/61.

40   Council Directive 93/83/EEC of 27 September 1993 on the coordination of certain rules concerning copyright and rights related to copyright applicable to satellite broadcasting and cable retransmission, O.J.E.C. 6 Oct. 1993, L 248/15.

41   T. HOEREN, op.cit. p.30; P. HUGENHOLTZ, op. cit., p.57; GOEBEL, in *Legal Advisory Board, Discussion of Commission Green Paper on Copyright*, Luxembourg, 21 September 1995, *http://www.echo.Iu/legal/eu/ipr/950921/minutes.html*

42   Green Paper: copyright and related rights in the information society *op. cit.*, p.59.

43   *Lamy informatique*, 1992, n°519.

44   Copyright Act of 1947, art. 107.

45   D. LOUNDY, op. cit., p. 27.

46   See *Screen-Gems-Columbia Music Inc. v. Mark-Fi Records Inc.*, 256 F. Supp. 399 (S.D.N.Y. 1966), 523; D. LOUNDY, *op. cit.*, p.27.

47   For example, Belgium: A. BERENBOOM, *Le nouveau droit d'auteur et les droits voisins*, Brussels, Larcier, 1995, p.122; this is also the solution proposed by the OMPI standard bill, see *Dr. auteur*, 1990, p.285 .

48   For example, France, cf. A. LUCAS and H. LUCAS, *op. cit.*, p.253.

49   For example, in Belgium: art. 55 to 61 of the law of 30 June 1994 on copyright and related rights.

50   Directive 91/250/EEC, Arts 5 and 6.

51   Common position 90/25, Explanatory Memorandum from the Council, n°13.

52   T. HOEREN, *op. cit.*, p.19; P. HUGENHOLTZ, *op. cit.*, p.59; P. GOLDSTEIN, «Copyright et droit d'auteur au XXIe Siècle», *Symposium de l'OMPI*, Paris, 1994.

53   Directive 91/250/EEC, arts 5 and 6.

54   Copyright Act of 1947, art. 117(1); Loi sur le droit d'auteur (canadienne), art. 3(2)(1).

55   Copyright Act of 1947, art. 117(2); Loi sur le droit d'auteur (canadienne), art. 3(2)(1)(iii).

56   *Sega enterprise Ltd, v. Accolade Inc*, 975F. 2d832 (Fed. Circ. 1992), quoted in M. F. MORGAN, «Trash talking: the protection of intellectual property rights in computer software», *Revue de droit d'Ottawa*, 1994, p.437.

57   D. LOUDY, *op. cit.*, p.29.

58   *Legal Advisory Board, Discussion of Commission Green Paper on Copyright*, Luxembourg, 21 September 1995, *op. cit.*

59   P. SIM, *op. cit.*, p.3.

60   P. HUGENHOLTZ, in *Legal Advisory Board, Discussion of Commission Green Paper on Copyright*, Luxembourg, 21 September 1995, *op. cit.*

61 *Whitfield v. Lear,* 751 f. 2d 90, 93 (2d Cir. 1984), quoted by T. HARDY, *op. cit.,* 1010; P.J. BENE-DICT O'MAHONEY, «Newsgroups», Copyright Website *http://www. benedict.com/newsgrp.htm# newsgroup,* 2.; Edward A. CAVAZOS; G. MORIN, *Cyberspace and the Law: Your Rights and Duties in the On-Line World,* MIT Press, Cambridge, 1994.

62 P. J. BENEDICT O'MAHONEY, *op. cit.,* p.2.

63 H. TILLIET, «L'édition à l'ère numérique: acquisition et cession des droits électroniques», *Symposium de l'OMPI,* Paris, 1994. For multimedia: see G. VERCKEN, *Guide pratique du droit d'auteur et des sociétés d'auteurs à l'usage des producteurs de multimédias,* European Commission DG XIII, EUR, p.16128, 1995.

64 See for example Loi canadienne sur le droit d'auteur, art. 14 1 (3).

65 Such as in France; Contra: USA where moral rights are transferable, even implicitly, see *Preminger v. Columbia Pictures,* 148 U.S.P.Q. p.398, C.O. Bull., 35, 570 (N.Y. Sup. Ct. 1966).

66 Which will often be the case on the Internet, see *IT Law today,* September 1995, p.2.

67 D. LOUNDY, *op. cit.,* p.29; L. ROSE, *op. cit.,* p.100.

68 L. ROSE, *op. cit.,* p.86.

69 P. J. BENEDICT O'MAHONEY, *op. cit.;* p.1-3.

70 *IDEM,* p.4.

71 *De Acosta v. Brown,* 146 F. 2d 408 (2d Cir. 1994); D. LOUNDY, *op. cit.,* 26; Loi canadienne sur le droit d'auteur, s. 27(1); *Compo Co v. Blue Crest Music Inc.,* (1980) 1 R.C.S. P.357.

Chapter three

«Freedom of expression»

1 See in particular for the countries of the European Convention on Human Rights: C.E.D.H., Sunday Times judgement of 26 April 1979, *Publ. Sér. A,* n°30.

2 *Charte canadienne des droits et libertés,* Part 1 of the *Loi constitutionnelle de 1982* [Annex B of the *Loi de 1982 sur le Canada* (1982, R.-U., c.11)]; hereinafter referred to as *Charte canadienne*), art. 2(b); U.S. CONST. amend. I.

3 *Charte canadienne,* aforementioned, note 2, arts. 1 and 33; U.S. CONST.amend. I; J. E. NOWAK, R. D. ROTUNDA, J. N. YOUNG, *Constitutional Law,* 2nd ed., St. Paul, West Publishing, 1991, p.791; *Perry Education Association v. Perry Local Educators Association,* (1983) 460 U.S. 37, 45; *First National Bank of Boston v. Bellotti,* (1978) 435 U.S. 765.

4 D. L. Appleman, «The Law and the Internet», *http://inet.nttam.com,* 12 May 1995, 6; It is, however-er, important to note the existence of legal regimes of civil liability, which may vary from one juris-diction to another, and of criminal offenses stipulated by the Canadian *Criminal Code* (R.S.C., 1985, c. C-46, art. 300; Id., art. 301).

5 RESTATEMENT (SECOND) OF TORTS, s. 568 cmt. b.(1989); David LOUNDY, «E-Law 2.0: Computer Information Systems Law and Operator Liablity Revisited», *http://www.eff.org/pub/Legal/e-law.paper,* p.7.

6 D. LOUNDY, *Ibid.*

7 RESTATEMENT (SECOND) OF TORTS, art.559;*Id.,* p.8.

8 IBIDEM.

9 *Ben-Oliel v. Press Publishing Co.,* 167 N.E. 432 (N.Y. 1929); D. LOUNDY, *op. cit.*

10 D. LOUNDY, *Ibidem.*

11 On the application of these principles in Australian law, see the decision of the Supreme Court of Western Australia in the case of *Rindos v. Hardwick,* 31 March 1994, 1994/1993, SCLN #940164 (Supreme Court of Western Australia).

12 See the discussion of Rindos v. Hardwick in Frances Auburn,*Usenet News and the law,* 1 Web J.C.L.I, pp.4-5.

13 *Id.,* p.5.

14 *Id.,* 340; T. D. BROOKS, «Catching Jellyfish in the Internet: The Public-Figure Doctrine and Defamation on Computer Bulletin Boards», *Rutgers Computer & Law Technology Journal,* vol.21 n°2, 1995, pp.461-471; RESTATEMENT OF TORTS § 582 (1938); R. A. SMOLLA, *Law of Defamation,* §1.03(2), pp.1-8 (1994).

15 T. D. BROOKS, *op. cit.,* note 14, p. 472; Michael J. BRYANT, «Section 2(b) and libel law defam-atory statements about Public Officials», 2 *M.C.L.R.,* pp.336-340.

16 Michael J. BRYANT, *op. cit.,* p.341;

17 T. D. BROOKS, *op. cit.,* p. 472; RESTATEMENT OF TORTS § 606 (1938).

18 Michael J. BRYANT, *op. cit.,* p.340.

19   *IDEM*, p.342.

20   18 U.S.C, s. 871 ff.

21   18 U.S.C. s. 2252.

22   *United States* v. *Lumbey*, 949 F. 2d 133 (1991); *United States* v. *Depew*, 751 F. Supp. 1195 (E.D. Va. 1990).

23   *Miller* v. *California*, 413 U.S. 15 (1973), n°2, reh'g denied, 414 U.S. 881 (1973).

24   *Criminal Code* (canadien), R.S.C. (1985), ch. C-46, art. 163.1; *Child Pornography Statute*, 18 U.S.C. 2252 (1991); *Stanley* v. *Georgia*, 394 U.S. 557 (1969); *U.S.* v. *Orito*, 413 U.S. 139 (1973) to 143.

25   D. LOUNDY, «E-Law 3.01: Computer Information Systems Law and System Operator Liability in 1995», *http://www.leepfrong.com/E-Law/E-Law/Part_VI.htm*, 1.

26   Case before the U.S. District Court of Western District of Tennessee, 1994, now in appeal n°94-6648 and 94-6649 before the U.S. Court of Appeals for the Sixth Circuit.

27   18 U.S.C. §1462, 1465.

28   D. LOUNDY, *op. cit.*, p.4.

29   Decision of the Sixth Circuit Court of Appeals, 19 January 1996, available on *http://www.callaw.com/edtl30b.html*

30   *Communications Decency Act*, art. 223(d)(1)(b), 47 *U.S.C.*

31   «Your Constitutional Rights have been Sacrificed for Political Expediency», Electronic Frontier Foundation Statement on 1996 Telecommunications Regulation Bill, *http://www.eff.org/pub/-Alerts/Cda_020296_eff.statement*

32   F. RIGAUX, La protection de la vie privée et des autres biens de la personnalité, Bruxelles - Paris, Bruylant - L.G.D.J., 1990, p.217 e.v.

33   For example, C.J.E.C., 28 October 1992, (PROCEDURE PENALE AGAINST JOHANNES STEPHANUS WILHELMUS TER VOORT) C-219/91, Rec. C.J.E.C., p.5483.

34   See, however, the nuancing of this principle found in the judgement of the European Court of Human Rights of 20 September 1994 «Otto-Reminger-Institut c. Autriche» (Case n°11/1993/406/485) and the comments of Messrs Crabit and Bergevin; E. Crabit and J. Bergevin, «Le cadre réglementaire des services de la sûreté de l'Information: laboratoire pour un nouveau droit du marché intérieur», Revue du Marché Unique Européen, 1995/1, pp.54 ff.

35   On 29 April 1982 The Committee of Ministers of the Council of Europe adopted a «Declaration on freedom of expression and information» stating in particular that the Member States will intensify their cooperation in order to «ensure that new information and communication services and techniques, when available, are actually used to extend the scope of freedom of expression and information».

3   6F. RIGAUX, «La liberté d'expression et ses limites», *Rev. Trim. Dr. H.*, 1995, p.401.

37   D. VOORHOOF, «Defamation and libel laws in Europe - the framework of Article 10 of the European Convention on Human Rights (ECHR)», *Media Law and Practice*, 1992, p.254.

38   Lingens judgement of 8 July 1986, Publ. Sér. A, n°103

39   IBIDEM.

40   Report of the European Commission for Human Rights, 14 January 1993 in Scherer v. Switzerland, § 65.

Chapter four

«Protection of privacy on the Internet»

1   Council of Europe, *Les nouvelles technologies: un défi pour la protection de la vie privée?*, Strasbourg, 1989.

2   See note V. SEDALLIAN and Ph. LANGLOIS, «Le grand secret,... le plus partagé du monde», *Planète Internet*, 1996, March 28-29.

3   U.S Constitution;*Griswold* v. *Connecticut*, (1965) 381 U.S. 479, Roe v. Wade, 93 S. Ct. 705 (1973) (recognition of a certain protected area of confidentiality); *Katz* v. *United States*, (1967) 389 U.S. 347, 351 (electronic monitoring constitutes an attack on the reasonable expectation of confidentiality, which is equivalent to an abusive search of one's person or property), *Canadian Charter of Rights and Freedoms*, Part 1 of the *Constitution Act, 1982* , being Schedule B to the *Canada Act, 1982* (U.K.), 1982, c.11)] (hereinafter *Canadian Charter*), s. 8; *Hunter* c. *Southam*, [1984] 2 S.C.R. 145, *R.* c. *Dyment*, [1988] 2 R.C.S. 417, 427-428 (that the guarantee against abusive searches of one's person or property constitutes a right to privacy); *R.* c. *Duarte*, [1990] 1 S.C.R. 30 (that the right to privacy applies to electronic surveillance in cases where there is a reasonable expectation of confidentiality).

4   *Electronic Communications Privacy Act of 1986*, 18 U.S.C. (1968) (quoted below *ECPA*).

5   *Criminal Code* (Canadian), R.S.C., 1985, c. C-46.

6   *ECPA.*, aforementioned, note 5, s..2510; *Criminal Code, Id.*, ss. 185, 186.

7   *ECPA, Id.*, s..2511(2)(h)(i).

8   *Id.*, ss. 2701, 2703.

9   *Privacy Protection Act of 1980*, 42 U.S.C. s. 2000aa (1980); D. LOUNDY, «E-Law 2.0: Computer Information Systems Law and Operator Liability Revisited», *http://www.eff.org/pub/Legal/e-law.paper*, 22; In the case of *Steve Jackson Games*, the Court decided that the *Privacy Protection Act* had been infringed, but did not specify which article or articles formed the basis for the conclusion that the seizure had led to an infringement. The infringement may have resulted from the seizure of paper documents, of computers used for word processing, or of the BBS. Consequently, the question remains unanswered as to whether the seizure of the BBS, which was being used to generate work product for the publisher, would have constituted an infringement of the law. Other users of the BBS, who had displayed public comments on it, were also plaintiffs in this case, but were not allowed recovery based on the *Act*. Thus either they were not considered to be publishers themselves, or their messages were not considered to be work product subject to protection.

10 «Work product materials possessed by a person reasonably believed to have a purpose to disseminate to the public a newspaper, book, broadcast, or other similar form of public communication, in or affecting interstate commerce». *Privacy Protection Act of 1980, Id.*, s..2000aa(a).

11 *Id.*, s..2000aa(a)(1).

12 *Id.*, s..2000aa(a)(2).

13 The secrecy of correspondence, which is very similiar to the protection of privacy, is protected under various European constitutions, see S. GILCART, *Douze constitutions pour une Europe ...*, Kluwer, Diegem, 1994.

14 For the Court's detailed interpretation of the material scope of the *Convention*, see C.E.D.H., Aff. Clays of September 6 1978.

15 Moreover, it is directly applicable and involves public order.

16 The notion of 'prescribed by law' comprises the common law in particular in the eyes of the Court.

17 G. COHEN JONATHAN, «Les écoutes téléphoniques», in F. MATSCHER and H. PETZOLD, (ed.), *Protection des droits de l'homme: la dimension européenne. Mélanges en l'honneur de Gérard J. Wiarda*, Carl Heymans Verlag, Köln, 1988, p.97-105.

18 C.E.D.H., Klass judgment of 6 September 1978, *Publ. Sér. A*, No 28. This judgment in principle was subsequently confirmed on many occasions: Kruslin and Hüvig of April 24 1990 (Publ. Sér. A, No 176-A et 176-B).

19 O.J. of July 13 1991.

20 See Mémento-Guide, A. Bensoussan, *Les fichiers de personnes et le droit*, Pariséd. Hermes 1991, p.35 ff.

21 Lamy informatique 1995 n°490.

22 Encyclopedia of information and technology law: Sweet and Maxwell, UK, 1994 page e1.11.

23 «...whoever (1) intentionally accesses without authorization a facility through which an electronic communication service is provided; or (2) intentionally exceeds an authorization to access that facility; and thereby obtains, alters, or prevents authorized access to a wire or electronic communication while it is in electronic storage in such system shall be subject to fines and/or imprisonment».

24 See. M. RIDDLE, «Sysop Liability for Enroute (and/or Encrypted) Mail», *FIDO NEWS*, vol.10 n°45, 7 November 1993, 3.

25 *ECPA*, aformentioned, note 5, s..2511(4).

26 *Id.* , s. 2511(1)(c).

27 *Criminal Code*, aforementioned, note 6, ss. 183-184.

28 «*Electronic communication system* any wire, radio, electromagnetic, photooptical or photoelectronic facilities for the transmission of electronic communications, and any computer facilities of related electronic equipment for the electronic storage of such communications». (*ECPA*, s. 2510(14). «*System operator*»: the operator of a switchboard, or an officer, employee, or agent of a provider of wire or electronic communication service, whose facilities are used in the transmission of a wire communication...(*ECPA*, s.2511(2)(a)(i), cité dans David Loundy, «E-Law 2.0: Computer Information Systems Law and System Operator Liability Revisited», *http://www.eff.org/-pub/Legal/e-law.paper*, 20.),

29 M. RIDDLE, «Sysop Liability for Enroute (and/or Encrypted) Mail», *FIDO NEWS*, vol.10, n°45, November 7 1993, *http://www.eff.org/pub/Privacy/Crypto_mail_liability.article*, 3.

30 T. R. GREENBERG, «E-mail and Voice Mail: Employee Privacy and the Federal Wiretap Statute (Comment)», The American University Law Review vol.44, n°1, 1994, 248.

31 *ECPA,,* aforementioned, note 5, s. 2511(2)(a)(i); *Criminal Code*, aforementioned, note 5, s. 184(2)(c).

32 Larry O. Natt GANTT, «An Affront to Human Dignity: Electronic Monitoring in the Private Sector Workplace», *Harvard Journal of Law and Technology*, vol.2, Spring 1995, p. 360.

33 *ECPA*, aforementioned, note 5, s..2511(3)(b)(iii); *Criminal Code*, aforementioned, note 6, s. 184(2)(b).

34 *ECPA, Id.* s. 2511(3)(b)(iv).

35 *Id.* s..2511(3)(b)(iv).

36 *Id.* s..2511(3)(b)(i).

37 *Id.*, s..2511(3)(b)(ii), *Criminal Code*, aforementioned, note 6, s. 184(2)(a).

38 On the common law privacy right, see the famous Brandeis and Warren article of 1890 which announced it. Karim BENYEKHLEF, *La protection de la vie privée dans les échanges internationaux d'informations*, Thémis, Montréal, 1992, p.16.

39 «One who intentionally intrudes, physically or otherwise, upon the solitude or seclusion of another or his private affairs or concerns, is subject to liability to the other for invasion of his privacy, if the intrusion would be highly offensive to a reasonable person» (Restatement Second of Torts §625B (1977); *Leggett* c. *First Interstate Bank, N.A.* 739 P.2d 1083, 1086 (Or. Ct. App. 1987).

40 *Nader* v. *General Motors Corp*, 255 N.E.2d 765 (N.Y. 1970); *Billings* v. *Atkinson*, 489 S.W. 2d 858 (Tex. 1973)

41 *Sistok* v. *Northwest Tel. Sys., Inc.* 615 P.2d 176, 182 (Mont. 1980).

42 *Vermars* v. *Young*, 539 F.2d 966, 969 (3d Cir. 1976).

43 Larry O. Natt GANTT, *loc. cit.*, note 26, 376.

44 T. R. GREENBERG, *loc. cit.*, note 24, 250.

45 As we have seen, there is no doubt that this protection can cover the various types of interpersonal communication on the Internet (e-mail, chat, telnet).

46 E. A. ALKEMA, «The third-party applicability or «Drittwirkung» of the European Convention on Human Rights», in F. MATSCHER, F. and H. PETZOLD (ed.), *Protection des droits de l'homme: la dimension européenne. Mélanges en l'honneur de Gérard J. Wiarda*, ,Köln, Carl Heymans Verlag, 1988, p.33-45.

47 F. RIGAUX, *La protection de la vie privée et des autres biens de la personnalité*, Brussels - Paris, Bruylant - L.G.D.J, 1990, p.205.

48 Niemitz v. Germany, judgment of December 16 1992, *Rev. Trim. Dr. H.*, 1993, 467 and A. v. France judgment of November 23 1993, *Rev. Trim. Dr. H.*, 1994, 575.

49 See section 186-1 NCP.

50 A. *Bensoussan*, les fichiers des personnes et le droit, Paris, Hermès, 1991, p.35 ff.

51 Encyclopedia of information and technology law; Sweet and Maxwell, UK, 1994 page e1.11

52 D. ROSE, *op. cit.*, note 109, p.24.

53 *Id.*, p.145.

54 *Id.*, p.147.

55 Guidelines on the protection of privacy and transborder flows of personal data. Annex to the Council Recommendation of September 23 1980 on the protection of data and privacy: problems and challenges, O.E.C.D. documents, Paris, 1994.

56 See Convention No 108 of the Council of Europe for the protection of individuals with regard to computerized processing of personal data of January 28 1981.

57 R.S.C.. 1985, c. P-21.

58 Unlike the federal government and most of the other Canadian provinces, Quebec has also enacted a law protecting personal data in both the public and private sectors. *(Loi sur l'accès aux documents des organismes publics et sur la protection des renseignements personnels*, L.R.Q., c. A-2.1; K. BENYEKHLEF, «Les transactions dématérialisées.sur les voies électroniques: panorama des questions juridiques», Public law research centre, Montreal University, *http://www.droit.umontreal.ca/-CRDP/ Conferences/AE/Benyekhlef.html*, 9; Industry Canada, *loc. cit.*, note 100, 8.). In addition, the *Civil Code of Québec* includes a privacy right which applies to both the private and public sectors (*Civil Code of Québec*, s..35 ff.), and the *Charte des droits et libertés de la personne* of Quebec, which grants the right to privacy, applies not only to state actions but also to private parties. Finally, since 1994, Quebec has also had a law protecting the processing of personal data in the private sector only. (*Loi sur la protection des renseignements personnels dans le secteur privé*), L.Q. 1993 chap. 17 (completes ss.35-40 *CCQ*); see on all these issues: K. BENYEKHLEF, *loc. cit.*, note 169, 9.

59 Section 32 of the privacy directive.

60 JO L, 281/31 of November 23 1995.

61 J. M. A. BERKVENS, «Gemeenschappelijk standpunt privacy-richtlijn», *Computerrecht*, 1995, 103.

62 Considering section 47 of the privacy directive.

63 Section 17 of the privacy directive.

64 K. BENYEKHLEF, *op. cit.*, note 116, p.343.

Chapter five

«The Internet and commercial communication»

1 J. MOGG, Communiquer avec les communicateurs, *Communications Commerciales* , ed. asi, Brighton, July 1995, n°1, p.1.

2 In addition, the rights of others are protected as regards both advertising and marketing. This also applies to any intellectual property rights violated by an advertisement, or to a person's right to protect his or her image from unwanted commercial exploitation. On this issue in American and Canadian law, see *Motschenbacher* v. *R.J. Reynolds Tobacco Co.*, 498 F.2d 821 (9th Cir. 1974); *Midler* v. *Ford Motor Co.*, 849 F.2d 460 (9th Cir. 1988); P. TRUDEL, «La protection de la vie privée et le droit à l'image aux États-Unis», in *Liberté de la Presse, Respect de la vie privée et de l'image en droit comparé*, Actes de Colloques de l'I.F.C., 22-23 March 199116; L.O. GANTT, «An Affront to Human Dignity: Electronic Monitoring in the Private Sector Workplace», *Harvard Journal of Law and Technology*, n°2, Spring 1995, p.374. See. L., POTVIN, *La personne et la protection de son image Etude comparée des droits québecois, français et de la common law anglaise*, Yvon Blais, Cowansville, 1991, p.110: *Charte des droits et libertés de la personne*, L.R.Q., c.C-12 (quoted hereafter *Charte québecoise*] art.5; *Code Civil du Québec* arts. 3 and 35.
On exploiting a person's image for advertising purposes in Europe, see F. RIGAUX, *La protection de la vie privée et des autres biens de la personnalité*, Brussels-Paris, Bruylant-L.G.D.J., pp.278-285.

3 *Canadian Charter of Rights and Freedoms*, Part 1 of the *Constitution Act, 1982* [Schedule B to the *Canada Act 1982* (U.K.), 1982, c.11 (hereinafter *Canadian Charter*), art.8; *Ford* v. *Québec*, [1988] 2 S.C.R. 712;*Virginia State Bd. of Pharmacy* v. *Virginia Citizens Consumer Council*, (1976) 425 U.S.; L.H. TRIBE, *American Constitutional Law*, 2nd ed., Mineola, Foundation Press, 1988, p.933.

4 Various decisions and rulings by the Commission and the European Court of Human Rights establish this freedom of commercial expression: *X. and Church of scientology v. Sweden* of May 5 1979; *Liljenberg et al. v. Sweden* of March 1 1983; *Markt Intern Verlag Gmbh et Klaus Beerman v. FRG* ruling of November 20 1989. Under European law, the conformity of these restrictions can be assessed at two levels. Firstly, as regards freedom of commercial expression, the European Court of Human Rights guarantees the freedom of commercial expression. Secondly, the Court of Justice of the European Communities ensures that restrictions on the free provision of advertising services, even when these prove necessary, do not constitute obstacles and are proportionate. (On these principles, see Chapter 1 on the free provision of services).

5 J. LAFFINEUR, *La Télématique grand public en Belgique*, Brussels, ed. Story Scientia, 1989, pp.42-43.

6 *The Federal Tobacco Products Control Act* in Revised Statutes of Canada, 1985.

7 *R.J.R. MacDonald Inc.* v. *P.G. Canada*, 127 D.L.R., (1995) R.J.Q. 375 (C.A.).

8 E. W. GROSS, S. VOGT, *Advertising Law in Europe and North America*, Boston, ed. Kluwer Law and Taxation Pubisher, 1992, p.55;*United States Code* (15 U.S. C.), § 1333.

9 J. R. MAXEINER, *Advertising Law in Europe and North America* , *op. cit.*, p.334.

10 E. W. GROSS, Vogt, S., *op. cit.*, p.53.

11 J. R. MAXEIMER, *op. cit.*, p.332.

12 K. PRESLMAYER, G-J. RIBBINK, G. JENNES, regarding the prohibition on psychological pressure. As regards Germany, Austria and the Netherlands, see *Advertising law in North America, op. cit.*

13 In the United States the Federal Trade Commission. (FTC), which regulates advertising and marketing, has frequently taken legal action against those whose advertising could entail a risk of bodily injury to children, or who incite children to become involved in dangerous activities. In Canada the self-regulatory *Canadian Code of Advertising Standards* of the *Canadian Advertising Foundation* (1991) stipulates that advertising intended for children should not exploit their credulity, their lack of experience, or their sense of loyalty, and should not contain information or illustrations likely to injure children physically, emotionally or morally. Furthermore, as regards products which cannot legally be sold to minors, such as cigarettes, advertising likely to attract minors is forbidden. In Europe, children are especially protected from the various advertising targetting them. An advertisement intended for children cannot aim to incite them to pester their parents to buy the advertised product. Some national laws go even further. In the United Kingdom, for example, advertisements aimed at a wide audience of children may not incite them to bulimia (S. GROOM, A. EVANS, K. SMITH, *Advertising Law in Europe and North America, op. cit.*, p.304).

14 *Federal Trade Commission Act* , 15 U.S.C. 41-58 (1988 & Supp. V 1993).

15 15 *USC* 45(a)(1) (1988).

16 *Federal Trade Commission Deception Policy Statement*, October 14, 1983, *http://www.web.com/- ~lewrose/deceptionpol.html*, 4.

17 *Id.*, pp.7-8.

18 *Federal Trade Commission Deception Policy Statement*, October 14, 1983, *http://www.web.com/~-lewrose/deceptionpol.html*, 13. The FTC makes a distinction between statements accompanied by facts or studies and personal opinions. The former are subject to the control described above, while the latter are rarely likely to involve the liability of the seller, as a reasonable consumer is presumed to be aware of the limited nature of a personal opinion. However, statements presented as personal opinions are likely to be considered misleading if they are not honest, if they misrepresent either the qualifications of the person making the statement or the premises of his or her opinion, or if the consumer may reasonably interpret them as an implicit statement of facts.

19 *Trade-marks Act*, R.S.C. 1985, c. T-13.

20 J. HOLMES, «Meeting your competitor in court», in *Absolutely the Best Conference you will ever Attend on Advertising Claims*, Insight Press, 1992, 5.

21 *Competition Act*, R.S. (1985), c. C-34, art. 1; R.S. (1985), c. 19 (2nd supp.), art. 19.

22 J. GROIA and S. LEDERMAN, «Advertising Prosecutions: You Can Run But You Can't Hide», in *Absolutely the Best Conference you will ever Attend on Advertising Claims*, Insight Press, 1992, pp.4-6.

23 Directive 84/450/EEC of 10 September 1984 on the reconcilation of the legislative, regulatory and adminsitrative provisions of the member states as regards misleading advertising, *O.J.E.C.*, L, 250 of 19 September 1984, p.17.

24 H. L. NELSON, D. L. TEETER, D. R. LE DUC, *Law of Mass Communications: Freedom and Control of Print and Broadcast Media*, 6th ed., The Foundation Press Inc., Westbury, 1989, p.692.

25 *Competition Act*, R.S. (1985), c. C-34, art. 1; R.S. (1985), c. 19 (2nd supp.), art. 52 (1); D. M. YOUNG, B. R. FRASER, *Canadian Advertising and Marketing Law*, vol.1, Rel. n°4, Carswell, Scarborough, 1995, pp.21-106.

26 D. M. YOUNG and B. R. FRASER, *op. cit.*, pp.21-109.

27 Amended proposal for a directive on the harmonization of the legal systems of the member states as regards comparative advertising, amending Directive 84/450/EEC, *O.J.E.C.*, C., 136 of 19 May 1995, pp.4-10.

28 Thus advertisers who would like their advertising to reach both an Italian and an English public must abide by the requirements of the Italian *Civil Code*, which provides a very strict framework for comparative advertising, while the United Kingdom does not have a specific text regulating this kind of advertising, which is considered a stimulus to free competition. On this subject, see F. HOFER, M. LÖSCH, A. TORICELLI, and S. GROOM, A. EVANS, K. SMITH in *Advertising law in Europe and North América*, *op. cit.*, pp.218 and 298.

29 C.J.E.C., ruling of December 3 1974, «johannes maria Van Binsbergen c. bestuur Van de bedrijfsvereniging voor de metaalnijverhein», aff. C-33/74, *Rec. C.J.E.C.*, p.1299.

30 P. WATERSCHOOT, Les communications commerciales européennes et la société de l'information, Communications Commerciales, *op. cit.*, p.15.

31 A. TEBOUL, Publicité et Télécommunication in Juris PTT n°25, 1991, p.36.

32 Because the cost of an e-mail message to an address anywhere in the world is usually equal to the cost of a local telephone call, which will be added to the cost of subscription to the local provider.

33 These regulations on advertising by fax are more strict. The situation varies, however, from one country to another. Advertising by fax is permitted in France, but it is regulated by the law of December 31 1989. Germany, on the other hand, adopts a more restrictive attitude in that it prohibits advertising by fax, unless the recipient has shown a particular interest in the advertisement in question, because it entails expenditure on the part of the recipient. Advertising by fax is not regulated in Canada. In the United States, the State of New-York regulates advertising by fax. See on these issues Advertising law in Europe and North América, *ibidem*.

34 For example, the code elaborated by the Canadian Direct Marketing Association stipulates that any consumer may request that his or her name be withdrawn from a mailing list or that his or her name not be sold to other companies. This also applies in France as regards the code of ethics of direct marketing professionals, which foresees an opposition list, known as the «Robinson» list, which contains the names and addresses of persons wishing to receive less advertising mail in their mailboxes.

35 See *CICNet Acceptable Use Policy*, <NIC.MERIT.EDU>/nsfnet/acceptable.use. policies/cicnet.txt (December 1991), 2; *JVNCnet Acceptable Use Policy*, <NIC.MERIT.EDU>/jvncnet/-acceptable.use.policies/ jvncnet.txt, 1; *NORTHWESTNET Acceptable Use Policy*, <NIC.-MERIT.EDU>/northwestnet/acceptable. use.policies/northwestnet.txt, 2, *MichNet Acceptable Use Policy*, <NIC.MERIT.EDU>/michnet/ acceptable.use.policies/michnet.txt,1-2; *CA*net Mandate, Acceptable Use Policy, and Statement of Regional Responsiblity* (November 1990) (Canada), quoted in J. CARROLL et R. BROADHEAD, *Canadian Internet Handbook*, Prentice Hall, Scarborough, 1995, p.56.

36 R. RESNICK and D. TAYLOR, *The Internet Business Guide*, Indianapolis, Sams Publishing, 1994, p.12.

37 R. RESNICK and D. TAYLOR, *op. cit.*, pp.148-152.

38 D. ROSE, *Minding your Cybermanners on the Internet*, Indianapolis, Alpha Books, 1994, pp.152-157.

39 The survey undertaken by the Directorate General of the Single Market and of Financial Services on commercial communications in Europe and the information society should lead to the preparation of a Green Paper on commercial communications in Europe, which will contain proposals from the Community authorities on this matter.

Chapter six

«Electronic commerce»

1 See the chapter on evidence on the Internet.

2 F. M. GREGURAS, T. A. GOLOBIC, R. A. MESA and R. DUNCAN, «Electronic Commerce: On-line Contract Issues», *http://www.batnet.com?oikoumene?ec-contraqcts.html,* p.2.

3 *Ibidem,* p.3.

4 See sections 1101 ff of the civil code. Under English law, no law or judgment precisely defines the concept of the contract. Several doctrinal definitions contradict one another (A.G.GUEST, *Chitty on contracts* , London, SWEET & MAXWELL, 1983; G. H. TREITLE, *The law of the contracts,* London, Stevens & Sons, 1987; J. C. SMITH, *The law of the contracts* , SWEET & MAXWELL, London, 1993).

5 See J. CALAMARI and J. PERILLO, *The Law of Contracts* 25 (3d ed. 1987), cited in Fred M. GREGURAS, *loc. cit.,* note 3, p.16.

6 *Ibidem,* p.564; S.M. Waddams, *The Law of Contracts,* pp.18 and 97, 3rd ed., Toronto, Canada, Law Book Inc., 1993.

7 R. DAVID, and D. PUGSLEY, *Les contrats en Droit anglais,* Paris, ed. L.J.D.J., 1989.

8 Cass.Civ. I, 13.06.1972, *Bull.Civ.,* III, n°392; Cass.Civ. I, 23.05.1979, *D.S.,* 1979, inf.rap.488.

9 MOUSSERON, *Technique contractuelle* , n°203, Paris, ed. Francis Lefebvre.

10 J. Ghestin, Traité de droit civil. Les obligations: le contrat, Paris, L.G.D.J., 1980, n°201; Cass.civ.I, 18.07.1967, *Bull.civ.,* I, n°268; *idem, Rev.Trim.Dr.Civ.,* 1968, 355, obs CHEVALIER.

11 GHESTIN, *Traité de droit civil. Les obligations. Le contrat: formation,* 2 ed., L.G.D.J., n°198 ff.

12 *Manchester Diocesan Council for Education* v. *Commercial and General Investments Ltd.,* 19.

13 Since a contract is concluded upon acceptance of an offer.

14 *Stevenson* v. *McLean,* 1880, 5, see also *Uniform Laws on International Sales Act,* 1967.

15 However, English law allows the acceptor to add terms to the initial offer, and that these terms may be considered to be tactily understood by the offeror.

16 *Felthouse* v *Bindley* (1862) 11 CBNS 869, (1863) 1 New Rep 401; CA Paris, 5e Ch. B, February 7 1986, *Caisse de retaite des notaires* v. *Société Map informatique,* juris-data, n°20411.

17 J. PINEAU and D. BURMAN, *Théorie des Obligations,* 2nd edition, Montréal, Thémis, 1988, p.70; B. WRIGHT, *op. cit.,* note 2, p.5-6; exs. art. 1386 *Civil Code of Québec* (hereinafter *CcQ).,* UCC 2-204.

18 *Hobbs* v. *Massasoit Whip Co.,* 33 N.E. 495 (Mass. 1893); *American Bronze Corp.* v. *Streamway Products,* 456 N.E. 2d 1295 (Ohio App. 1982); CHITTY, *Law of contracts,* No2-047to2-051; Civ. 1st Ch. 1 Dec. 1969, *JCP,* 1970, II, 16445, note AUBERT.

19 See P. Diener, Le silence et le droit. Thése bordeaux 1975.

20 PLANIOL, RIPERT and ESMEIN, *Traité pratique de droit civil français,* 2nd ed., t.VI, Obligations, First Part, ed. L.G.D.J., n°94 ff.

21 See Code V.I.A. which stipulates that in principle the information circulated constitutes «invitations to treat», Code V.I.A., Section 2 (Advertising), §27.

22 J. LAFFINEUR and M. GOYENS, *La télématique grand public en Belgique,* pp.93-95; *Grainger and son* v. *Gough* (1896) A.C. 325.

23 Subject to being able to admit these computer documents into evidence before a court of law; see Chapter 9 on evidence.

24 In France, the Court of Cassation, in its judgment of January 7 1981 (Cass.Com., 07.01.1981, *Rev.Trim.Dr.Civ.,* 1981, p.349, n°1, obs. F., CHABAS), established the expedition theory regarding certain forms of communication and in the absence of any stipulation to the contrary. In the United Kingdom, the *transmission* theory continues to be taken into consideration as regards contracts concluded via the post (*Brinkibon Ltd.* v. *Stahag Stahl,* 1983, 2 A.C. 34 at p.42; S. & t.63). For all other forms of communication, English law prefers the information theory (*Entores Ltd.* v. *Miles Far East Corporation,* 1955, 2, Q.B. 327,C.A.; S. & T. 60). Québec law, for its part, affirms the reception theory (*Civil Code of Québec,* s. 1387).

25 *Section 23 of the Convention on international sales of goods of April 11 1980.* It should, however, be noted that this section deals exclusively with the moment of contract formation.

26 However, it should be noted that Anglo-Saxon law does not take into account the concept of cause. Courts assess the legality of the contract as a whole.

27 See s. 1108 of the French civil code.

28 See s. 1156 of the French civil code.

29 See *Corinthian Pharmaceutical* v. *Lederle Laboratories*, 724 F.Supp. 605, 610 (S.D. Ind. 1989), *in* Fred M. GREGURAS and al., *ibidem*; B. WRIGHT, *The Law of Electronic Commerce* (1991 §Supp. 1994).

30 See s. 1110 of the French civil code.

31 Under English law, see the system of «fraudulent misrepresentation» actionable under the tort of deceit, as well as the system of *innocent misrepresentation*, comprehensively amended by the *Misrepresentation Act, 1967*; in North American law, see J. GRILLIOT, F. A. SCHUBERT, *Introduction to Law and the Legal System*, 4th ed., Boston, Houghton Mifflin Company, 1989, p.575, n°1.

32 F. CHABAS, *Les obligations, théorie générale*, 7th ed, Paris, ed. Montchrestien, n°128 s.

33 J. C.SMITH, *The law of the contract*, London, Sweet & Maxwell, 1993.

34 Minors are not the only people who are legally disqualified. Since minors are the most frequent case on the Internet, however, our discussion will be limited to them.

35 Under English law, see the *Minors' Contracts Act* 1987; in French law, s. 389 of the French civil code; under American law, H. J. GRILLIOT, F. A. SCHUBERT, *Introduction to law and the legal system*, 4th ed., Boston, Houghton Mifflin Company, 1989, pp.563-564.

36 See for an analysis of French law: «Les actes de la vie courante», *JCP*, 1982, ed. G.I.3076; G.M.A.C. v. Stotsky, 60 Misc2d 451, 303 N.Y.S.2d 463 (Sup.Ct.1969); E. A. FARNSWORTH, W. F. YOUNG, *Contracts: case and Materials*, 5th ed., Westbury, The Foundation Press Inc., 1995, p.326.

37 Cass.Civ.fr., 21 June 1977, *Bull.Civ.*, I, n°285.

38 J. D. CALAMARI and J. M. PERILLO, *Contracts*, 3rd ed., St Paul, West Publishing Co, 1987, p.317.

39 Moreover, it is important to note that the question of the time and place of contract formation may, in certain cases, be clearly separated from provision concerning the choice of applicable law, if the legal system chosen does not provide for the approach required by the parties (S. EISELEN, *op. cit.*, pp.12-13); B. AUDIT, *Droit international privé*, Paris, ed. Economica, 1991; H. BATTIFOL and P. LAGARDE, *Droit international privé*, Paris, ed. L.G.D.J., t.I, 8th ed. (1993) and t.2, 7th ed. (1983).

40 Restatement, Second, Conflict of Laws; §187; *UCC* §1-105 (U.S.A.).

41 E. F. SCOLES, Peter HAY, *Conflict of Laws*, 2nd ed., St. Paul, West Publishing Co., 1988, p.661.

42 B. WRIGHT, *op. cit.*, p.14.9, n°2.

43 S. EISELEN, *op. cit.*, pp.16-17, n°35.

44 For this section, see B. WRIGHT, *op. cit.*, pp.14.6-14.7, n°2.

45 Particularly as regards evidence. See Chapter 10.

46 The scope of application of the different laws obviously varies from one legal system to another.

47 In Europe, within the European Union, see Council Directive n°93-13-EEC of April 5 1993 on abusive clauses in contracts concluded with consumers, *O.J.E.C.*, 21.04.1993, n°L95/29. At the national level, *under Belgian law*, see the law of July 14 1991 on commercial practices, information and consumer protection; *under French law*, see the law of January 10 1978 on consumer protection and the provision of consumer products and services information, the law of January 18 1992 and the various complementary texts which complete it, ss. 1603, 1610, 1611, 1641 to 1645 of the civil code, s. R. 635 of the N.C.P., s. 26 of the law of Janaury 6 1978 on information technology and freedom, and law n°89-421 on consumer information and protection and on various commercial practices, and the law of February 1 1995; *under English law*, see the *Sale of Goods Act* 1979 and the *Consumer Protection Act* 1987; *under American law*, see the *Consumer Credit Protection Act, Fair Credit Billing Act*, 15 *USC* 1666 (1988), *Magnuson-Moss Warranty Federal Trade Commission Improvement Act*, 15 *USC*. §45 (amendment to the *Federal Trade Commission Act of 1914*), the *Truth-in-Lending Act*, 15 *USC* 1601 ff (1988), the *Uniform Laws on International Sales Act*,1967, and the *Uniform Commercial Code*; *under Canadian law*, there is no federal consumer protection law but only provincial laws. Under Québec law, for example, the *Loi sur la Protection du consommateur* applies to all contracts concluded between a consumer and a trader in the context of his or her commercial activity, the object of which is the provision of a good or a service. (*Loi sur la protection de la consommateur*, L.R.Q. chap. P-40.1, 1978, art.2.). See also sectione 5 of the *Rome Convention* of June 19 1980 on the law applicable to contractual obligations, the signatory states of which are Belgium, Denmark, France, Germany, Greece, Ireland, Italy, Luxembourg, the Netherlands and the United Kingdom.

48 See in Europe the joint position (EC) n°19/95 of 29 June 1995, adopted by the Council with a view to the adoption of a European Parliament and Council directive on consumer protection, as regards contracts between absents. *O.J.E.C.*, 30.10.1995, n°C 288/1 in which the terms of section 2 are broad enough to encompass all contracts currently concluded via the Internet: «*all contracts concerning goods and services* concluded between a supplier and a consumer in the framework of a system of sales or the provision of services, at a distance, organized by the supplier who, for this contract, *uses exclusively one or more remote communication techniques* until a contract is concluded, including the conclusion of the contract itself». See at a national level: in Denmark, the law of December 23 1987 on certain consumer contracts; in Spain, the general law n°26/84 on the pro-

tection of consumers and users; the Code of Ethics of the mail order selling sector in Spain as well as certain specific provisions on distance selling taken at regional level; in France, law n°88.21 of January 6 1988 governing the profession of the distance seller and the law of June 23 1989 amending the law of 1972; in Greece, section 31 of law n°1961/91 of September 3 1991; in Luxembourg, the law of August 25 1983 on the legal protection of the consumer and the Grand Ducal regulation n°01/91; in Portugal, decree-law n°272/87 of July 3 1987; in the United Kingdom, provisions 71/75 on forced dispatches and more precisely in English law the *Mail Order Transaction Order* 1976.

49 As regards tourism services, for example, see in European law the Council Directive of June 13 1990 on voyages, holidays and all-inclusive tours *O.J.E.C.*, 23.06.1990, n°L 158/59.

50 In Europe, the proposal for a directive of June 29 1995, *O.J.E.C.*, 30.10.1995, n°C 288/1, harmonizes the period allowed for a consumer to change his or her mind at 7 days, but currently this period varies between 7 and 15 days, depending on the various national laws.

51 See s. 1437 of the *Civil Code of Québec*. In the European Union, see Council Directive n°93-13-EEC of April 5 1993, *O.J.E.C.*, 21.04.1993, n°L 95/29 protecting consumers from abusive clauses. These clauses will no longer bind the consumer, although the validity of the contract will not be affected. This directive applies to abusive clauses concluded between a professional and a consumer. However, all the clauses resulting from mandatory legislative or regulatory provisions are not subject to it. Section 3 of the directive states that «a clause in a contract which has not been individually negotiated is considered abusive when, despite the good faith requirement, it creates a significant imbalance to the detriment of the consumer between the rights and obligations of the parties resulting from the contract».

52 See in American law, the *Magnuson-Moss Warranty Act*, 15 *USC* &sect.2301 ff.

53 In Québec law, see the *Loi sur la protection du consommateur*, n°50, ss. 29 and 33.

54 At the international level, section 5 of the *Rome Convention* of June 19 1980 on the law applicable to obligations states that, as regards consumer contracts, the place of contract formation will be determined by the law of the consumer's usual place of residence (See H. GAUDEMET-TALLON, *Rome Convention* of June 19 1980 on the law applicable to contractual obligations, *R.T.D. eur.*, 28 (3) July-Sept. 1992).

55 *In Québec law,* see*CcQ.*, s. 3149.

56 In Québec law, the *Loi sur la protection du consommateur*, n°50, s.17; in Europe, s.5 of the Council Directive of April 5 1993, *O.J.E.C.*, 21.04.1993, n°L 95/29.

57 Moreover, it should be noted that in the case of international sales, section 2.a. of the *Vienna Convention* refers to national consumer protection legislation (*Vienna Convention on international sales of goods* of April 11 1980, *Code de commerce*, Paris, ed. Dalloz, 1994-1995, p.18160). See below for a brief analysis of this international convention.

58 Restatement (Second) of Contracts & sect.211 (1981), *in* F. M. GREGURAS and al., *op. cit.*, p.8, n°3.

59 *Ibidem*, p.17, n°3.

60 F. M. GREGURAS and al., *op cit.*, pp.5-8, n°3.

61 *Ibidem.*, 8.

62 *CcQ*, s.1436.

63 *CcQ.*, s.1437.

64 *CcQ.*, s.1432.

65 Paris, 12.12.1989, *Expertises*, n°133, p.409; Paris, 20.11.1990, *Jurisdata*, n°025912.

66 Law n°95-96, 1er.02.1995, *J.C.P.*, 1995, ed.G., III, 67286.

67 Section 1 of the law of February 1 1995.

68 Section 3 al. 2 of the law of February 1 1995.

69 Section 6 of the law of February 1 1995.

70 *Vienna Convention on international sales of goods* of April 11 1980, *Code de commerce*, Paris, ed. Dalloz, 1994-1995, p.18160; since December 30 1994 the signatory States have been: Argentina, Australia, Belarus, Bosnia-Herzegovina, Bulgaria, Canada, Chile, Croatia, Czechoslovakia, the Czech Republic, Denmark, Ecuador, Egypt, Estonia, the Federal Republic of Germany, Finland, France, Georgia, the German Democratic Republic, Guinea, Hungary, Iraq, Italy, Lesotho, Mexico, Moldavia, the Netherlands, New Zealand, Norway, the People's Republic of China, Rumania, Russia, Slovakia, Slovenia, Spain, Sweden, Switzerland, Syria, Uganda, Ukraine, the United States, Russia, Yugoslavia, and Zambia, or 45 States.

71 Cl. WITZ, *Les premières applications jurisprudentielles du droit uniforme de la vente internationale*, Paris, ed. L.J.D.J., 1995.

72 It should be noted that only an acceptance identical to the offer can form the contract,since any modification of the offer constitutes a counter-offer (ss. 19.2 and 3 of the *Vienna Convention*).

73 B. AUDIT, *La vente internationale des marchandises*, Paris, L.J.D.J., 1990.

74 Z. MILOSEVIC, A. BOND, «Electronic Commerce on the Internet: What is still Missing?», 28 April 1995, *http://inet.nttam;com*, p.3.

75 See the text of the rules of uniform conduct for the exchange of commercial data by teletransmission (U.N.C.I.D.) as adopted by the Steering Committee of the C.C.I. during the 50th session (Paris, 22 September 1987), *in* L. ELIAS, J. GERARD and GIEN KUO WANG, *Le droit des obligations face aux échanges de données informatisées*, Namur, ed. Story Scientia, 1992; as well as the model EDI contract adopted in May 1991 by the Commission of the European Communities known as a Community agreement: Tedis programme: The European model EDI agreement (E.E.C. Commission -May 1991 DG XIII-D-5).

76 For an examination of payment cards, cf. X. THUNIS and M. SCHAUSS, *Aspects juridiques du paiement par carte*, Cahiers du C.R.I.D. n°1, Namur, ed. Story-Scientia, 1988.

77 CNUDCI, *Draft legal guide on Electronic Fund Transfers*, April 30 1985, A/CN9/266/Add.1.

78 J. ALLIX, «Consommateurs et paiements électroniques transfrontières», *Banque*, n°536, March-April 1993, p.60. One may imagine, in particular, a situation in which a person collects the duplicates of the «stubs» of customers' cards in a waste paper basket in a restaurant, a situation which has already arisen in Great Britain. Another case of fraud cited by G. ARIRA, «Banques et commerce électronique», *Banque*, n°560, June 1995, p.80, is that involving pseudo-traders offering access to an enticing shop window with a view to obtaining the card numbers of customers placing orders.

79 A. BERTRAND and P. LE CLECH, *op. cit.*, p.44 and p.72.

80 See Section 3.3 of the Carte Bleue subscriber's agreement in France, and F. GREDOT, «Le contrat porteur et la loi», *Banque*, n°563, Oct. 1995, pp.36-38.

81 Clause on the groupings of Bank Cards in France, see F. GRUA, *Contrats bancaires*, t.1, Paris, ed. Economica, 1990, p.186.

82 Recommendation for the second reading on the joint position adopted by the Council with a view to adopting the European Parliament and Council directive on consumer protection as regards contracts between absents, Nov. 23 1995.

83 See *Guide du consommateur européen dans le marché unique*, Commission européenne, *http://www.cec.lu/en/comm/spc.cg/index.htm*

84 J. HUET, *D.I.T.*, 1988/1, pp.87-88.

85 *Consumer Protection Act* 1987.

86 S. A. JONES, *The law relating to credit cards*, Oxford, BSP Professional Books, 1989, pp.12-16.

87 Y. W. ROSMARIN, «Revising article 2: Consumer Protections Needed in Sales of Goods», *ClearingHouse Review*, vol.28, n°10, February 1995, p.1176.

88 M. E. GROTTENHALER, «Consumer Protection and Product Liability», *in Doing Business in Canada*, Matthew Bender & Co., Inc., pp.25-12

89 See H. SPRANGERS, «Elektronisch geld», *Tele-pc*, n°4, August-September 1995, pp.13-16.

90 See *http://www.firstvirtual.com/pubdocs/fineprint-selle*, Q6.1.

91 *Idem*, Q5.2.1.

92 For example, Encyclopaedia Britannica, DigiCash store or Big Mac's Monthy Python Archive Shop.

93 S. LEVY, «Emoney (That's What I Want)», *http://www.hotwired.com/wired/2.12/features/emoney.html*

94 «Electronic Money», *http://www.amex.cox.smu.edu/class/mis4350h/ people/Haninga/Concept/*, 1; W. KENNEDY and J. DIETSCH, «Securing the net», *http://www.hotwired.com/wired/2.12/features/emoney.html*

95 J.-P. LEDRU, «Les cartes bancaires en France», *Banque*, n°563, Oct. 1995, p.22.

96 First Virtual contract, *op. cit.*, Q11.

97 Mark Twain contract, *op. cit.*, point 17.

98 Mark Twain contract, *op. cit.*, point 2.

99 First Virtual contract, *op. cit.*, Q1.2 and Q13.

100 15 *USC* 1693-1693r (1988).

101 Mark Twain contract, *op. cit.*, point 6.

102 First Virtual contract, *op. cit.*, Q8.

103 Mark Twain contract, *op. cit.*, point 9 and 10.

104 First Virtual contract, *op. cit.*, Q8.2 and Q14.2.

105 J. V. VERGARI and V. V. SHUE, Checks, Payements and Electronic Banking, Practising Law Institute, New-York, 1986, p.548.

106 *http://www.firstvirtual.com/pubdocs/fineprint-buye*

107 *http://www.marktwain.com/legal.html*

108 E. F. SCOLES and P. HAY, *Conflict of Laws*, 2nd ed., St Paul, West Publishing Co., 1988, p.669.

109 Directive of April 5 1993 on abusive clauses in contracts concluded with consumers.

110 Point 2, *Conditions and provisions* of the Mark Twain contract, *op. cit.*

111 Point 2, *Conditions and provisions* of the Mark Twain contract, *op. cit.*

112 Q8.2.2.1 and Q11, *Buyer's Agreement with First Virtual Holdings Incorporated*, *op. cit.*

113 L. J. CAMP, M. SIRBU and J. D. TYGAR, «Token and Notational Money in Electronic Commerce», *http://www.cgi.cs.edu.edu/es.cmu.edu/ uses/jeanc/www/usenix.html*, pp.3-4 and 11-12.

114 *Idem.*
115 12 *USC* Sec. 1829, *Bank Secrecy Act.*
116 12 *USC* 1829, *Money Laundering Act.*
117 «Les transfers d'argent sur Internet: un risque de change calculé?», *Online Strategies*, July-August 1994, vol.1, n°4, p.4.
118 S. LEVY, *op. cit.*, p.4.
119 See B. WRIGHT, *The Law of Electronic Commerce, EDI, Email and Internet: Technology, Proof and Liability*, 2nd ed, Boston, Little, Brown & Cie, 1995.

Chapter seven

«Cryptography»

1   D SYX, «Vers de nouvelles formes de signature?», *Droit de l'informatique*, 1986/3, pp.133 ff.
2   «Introduction to Cryptography», *http://www.verisign.com/docs/pk-intro.html*; «RSA's Frequently Asked Questions About Today's Cryptography», *http://www. rsa.com/rsalabs/faq/faq-gurl.html*
3   *Ibidem.*
4   S., LEVY, Crypto rebels, www@wined.com
5   Dorothy. E. DENNING, «Resolving the Encryption Dilemma: the Case for Clipper», *http://web.mit.edu/afs/athena/org/t/techreview/www/articles/july95/denning.html*
6   «OTA Report Summary: Information Security and Privacy in Network Environments», September 1994, *F.T.P.://F.T.P..eff.org/pub/EFF/Policy/Crypto/ota-priv-sec.report*, p.8.
7   D. WISEBROD, «Controlling the Uncontrollable: Regulating the Internet», 4 *M.C.L.R.* 331, 344.
8   «OTA Report Summary», *op cit.*, note 6, p.3.
9   I. JACKSON, iwj10@thor.cam.ac.nk.
10 *International Traffic Arms Regulations*, 22 C.F.R., arts.120-130.
11 «Pretty Good Privacy-Legal Issues», *http://www.mantis.co.uk/pgp/pgp-Legal.html*, 1; M. P. JOHNSON, «Data Encryption and Technical Data Controls in the United States of America», *http://www.eff. org/pub/Privacy/us_crypto_policy.faq*, 2.
12 *International Traffic Arms Regulations*, supra, note 10, art. 120.17.
13 J. C. YATES, Esq., «Bombs and Bytes», 17 October 1994, Morris and Manning Home Page, 2.
14 *Ibidem.*
15 A. SYLVAIN, «Data encryption and the Law(s) - Results», Posted on Talk Politics. Crypto, 15th Dec 1994.
16 B.-J. KOOPS, *Crypto Law Survey, http:www.com.batnet. html*, 3.
17 (EC) Council Regulation n°3381/94 of 19 December 1994, O.J.E.C., 31 December 1994, n°L.367/1 ff.
18 5A002 of the annex.
20 S. ROZENFELD, «Nouvelle réglementation sur la cryptologie», *Expertises*, March 1994, p.86; E. MEILLAN, «Le contrôle juridique de la cryptographie», *Droit de l'informatique et des télécoms*, 1993/1, pp.78-82.
21 J. DUMORTIER, «Stille invoering van cryptografiecontrole in België», *Computerrecht*, 1995/2, p.79; Law of 21 December 1994, *Belgian Official Journal*, 23 December 1994.
22 R. VAN DEN HOVEN VAN GENDEREN, «Het voorlopig voorontwerp tot verbod van cryptografie De horror vacuï van de ondoorbreekbare beveiliging», *Computerrecht*, 1994/4, pp.157 ff.; *http://www/xs4all.nl/-db.nl/english/Legal.html*
23 Bombt Deutschland, *Der Spiegel*, 2/1996, 8 January 1996, pp.106 ff, *http://www.thur.de/ulf/krypto/verbot.html*
24 Article 28, Law 90-1170 of 29.12.1990 on the regulation of telecommunications, O.J., 30.12.1990, amended by Law 91-648 of 11.07.1991.
25 Memorandum presenting the French regulation on cryptology, Interministerial delegation responsible for the security of information systems (DISSI), Issue of 20 June 1995.
26 J. THOREL, <thorel@cnam.fr>, newsgroups:alt.security, talk.politics.crypto
27 J. DUMORTIER, *op.cit.*

Chapter eight

«Crime»

1 See «Pointer to sex info on the net, 3.6», *Archives - name: alt-sex/pointers*
2 M. RIMM, «Marketing Pornography on the Information Superhighway: A. Survey of 917,410 Images, Descriptions, Short Stories, and Animations Downloaded 8.5 Million Times by Consumers in Over 2000 Cities in Forty Countries, Provinces and Territories», *http://trfn.pgh.pa.us/-guest/mrstudy.html*, 7 november 1995.
3 On this question see, among others, C. DURHAM, «Les structures émergentes du droit criminel de l'information: tracer les contours d'un nouveau paradigme», *International Review of Penal Law*, Vol. 63, pp.1371 ff.
4 R. L. DUNNE, «Deterring Unauthorized Access to Computers: Controlling Behaviour in Cyberspace through a Contract Paradigm», 19 May 1994, *http://www.cs.yale.edu/pub/Dunne/jurimetrics/HTML/subsections3_2_3.html*, 1.
5 See G. D. BACKER, «Trespassers will be prosecuted: computer crime in the 1990s», *Computer Law Journal*, 1993, vol.12, pp.61 ff.
6 For a detailed overview of the question, see F. THOMAS, *De internationale rechtshulp in strafzaken*, 1996, forthcoming.
7 Regarding United Nations initiatives, see X , «International review of criminal policy - United Nations Manual on the prevention and control of computer-related crime», *http://www.ifs.univie.ac.at/pr2gq1/rev4344.html#crime*; regarding the European Union, see the Council decision of March 31 1992 on the security of information systems, 92/242/EEC, O.J., 8 May 1992, L 123/19; see also M. MÖHRENSCHLAGER, «Antipiratique européenne : une politique concertée de répression de la criminalité informatique qui prend en compte les nouvelles techniques, les nouveaux comportements et les nouveaux délinquants», *Expertises*, 1990, pp.177 ff. As regards the work of the Council of Europe, see also, among others, B. SPRUYT, «Information Technology Misuse: the Belgian State of Art», *International Yearbook of Law Computers and Technology*, vol.9, 1995, pp.17 ff.
8 See: L. F. YOUNG, «United States Computer Crime Laws, Criminals and Deterrence» (1995) 9 *International Yearbook of Law, Computers and Technology* 1; Edward M. WISE, «Computer Crimes against Information Technology in the United States» (1993) 64 *Revue Internationale de Droit Pénal* 647; W. C. DURHAM, R. C. SKOUSEN, «The Law of Computer-Related Crime in the United States» (1990) 38 *American Journal of Comparative Law* 565.
9 18 U.S.C. §1030.
10 See B. S. DAVIS, «It's Virus Season Again, Has Your Computer Been Vaccinated? A Survey of Computer Crime Legislation as a Response to Malevolent Software» (1994) 72 *Washington University Law Quarterly* 411; Anne W. BRANSCOMB, «Rogue Computer Programs And Computer Rogues : Tailoring the Punishment to Fit the Crime» (1990) 16 *Rutgers Computer Technology Law Journal* 1.
11 *United States* v. *Morris*, 728 F. Supp. 95 (NDNY, 1989).
12 18 *U.S.C.*, s. 2510 (1988).
13 See Donald K PIRAGOFF, «Computer Crimes and Other Crimes against Information Technology in Canada» (1993) 64 *Revue Internationale de Droit Pénal* 201; Anne-Marie BOISVERT, «Communicatique et responsabilité pénale : criminalité informatique et «vol» d'information» in COLLECTIF, *Le droit de la communicatique: Actes du colloque conjoint de l'Université de Poitiers et de l'Université de Montréal, September 1990*, Montreal-Paris, CRDP, Éditions Thémis, LITEC, 1991, p.93; P. ROBERT, «La criminalisation des abus informatiques en droit pénal canadien», in ASSOCIATION CANADIENNE DE DROIT COMPARÉ, *Droit contemporain: rapports canadiens au congrès international de droit comparé, Montréal, 1990*, Cowansville, Éditions Yvon Blais, 1992, p. 680.
14 Art. 342.1 *Cr.C.*.
15 Art. 430 (1) *Cr.C.*
16 See Chapter 4 on the protection of privacy.
17 The recommendation of the Council of Europe on this matter introduces the principle of the subsidiarity of criminal penalties to all other forms of penalty: civil, disciplinary, etc., which means that only the most serious conduct will be subject to criminal penalties. For further details, see M. MÖHRENCHLAGER, *op.cit.*, p.179.

18 Law n°88-19 of January 5 1988 on computer crime; H. CROZE, «L'apport du droit pénal à la théorie générale du droit de l'informatique» (regarding law n°88-19 ofJanuary 5 1988 on computer fraud), *J.C.P.,* 1988, ed. G., Doc., n°3333.

19 J. FRANCILLON, «Les crimes informatiques et d'autres crimes dans le domaine de la technologie informatique en France», *Revue Internationale de Droit Pénal,* vol. 64, pp.291 ff.

20 F. CHAMOUX, «La loi sur la fraude informatique : de nouvelles incriminations», *J.C.P.,* 1988, ed. G., I, 3321.

21 See the Computer Misuse Act 1990 of 29 August 1990.

22 *Computer Misuse Act,* S 17.

23 See the *Interception of Communications Act* 1985, *Encyclopaedia of Information Technology Law,* Sweet & Maxwell, 1994, E1.11.

Chapter nine

«Liability on the Internet»

1 See law of July 29 1881, *DP,* 1881, 4, 65 in respect of the press and communication and more specifically, audiovisual communcation, law n°82-625 of July 29 1982 repealed by the law of December 30 1986 retaining the former section 6 of law n°82-625 in the new section 110.2°; T.G.I. Paris, April 24 1984, *Fiduciaire de France et autres* v. *Galande, D.* 1985, IR, p.47, obs. H. MAISL; *Rev. trim. dr. civ.* 1984, p.517, Obs. J. HUET; T.G.I. Paris, (Référé), 24 April 1984, *Expertises,* 1984, n°62, p.143.

2 See T.G.I. Paris, January 19 1994 and C.A. Paris, May 24 1994, *D.,* 1995, p.271, note C. BIGOT.

3 According to section 1384, paragraph 4 of the French civil code, principals are liable for damage caused by their employees in the positions in which they are employed.

4 Under American law, *Second Restatement of Agency,* § 220(1)) when the latter is carrying out his duties (W. P. KEETON and al, *Prosser and Keeton on the Law of Torts,* 5th ed., St. Paul, West Publishing Co., 1984, pp.501-502). It should be noted that also under American law, the fact that the act committed by an employee has been expressly forbidden by the employer does not neces-sarily relieve the employer of his or her liability: See *Garretzen* v. *Duenckel,* 1872, 50 Mo. 104; *Mautino* v. *Piercedale Supply Co.,* 1940, 338 Pa. 435, 13 A.2d 51; *Riviello* v. *Waldron,* 1979, 47 N.Y.2d 297, 418 N.Y.S.2d 300, 391 N.E.2d 1278; *Marbury Management Inc.* v. *Kohn,* 2d Cir. 1980, 629 F.2d 705, certiorari refused 449 U.S. 1011, 101 S.Ct. 566, 66 L.Ed.2d 469; *Thompson* v. *United States,* D.S.C. 1980, 504 F.Supp. 1087; *Ohio Farmers Insurance Co.* v. *Norman,* App.1979, 122 Ariz. 330, 594 P.2d 1026; *Dickerson* v. *Reeves,* Tex.Civ.App. 1979, 588 S.W.2d 854; Second Restatement of Agency, §230; W. P. KEETON and al, *op. cit.,* p.503. The employer cannot neces-sarily evade his or her liability for gross negligence on the part of an employee. American jurispru-dence states that the employer may be liable even for *torts* committed deliberately by an employee, if this was done in the exercising of the latter's duties: see *Limpus* v. *London General Omnibus Co.,* 1862, 1 H.&C. 526, 158 Eng.Rep. 993; *Cohen* v. *Dry Dock E.B.&B.R. Co.,* 1877, 69 N.Y. 170; *Howe* v. *Newmarch,* 1866, 94 Mass. (12 Allen) 49; *Osipoff* v. *City of New York,* 1941, 286 N.Y. 422, 36 N.E.2d 646; *Sage Club* v. *Hunt,* Wyo.1981, 638 P.2d 161; W. P. KEETON and al, *op. cit.,* p.505. A fortiori, it may therefore be deduced that the employer may also be liable for gross negligence on the part of an employee.

5 See *Stratton Oakmonth, Inc.* v. *Prodigy, gopher://insight.mcmaster.ca: 70/ORO-21250-/org/efc/law/us/ prodigy-24 May 95,* p.6-7.

6 STREET, *Torts,* 7th ed, London, Butterworths, 1983, pp.415-432; W. V. H. ROGERS, «Winfield & Jolowicz», 14th ed, London, Sweat & Maxwell, 1994, pp.205-223.

7 The producer uses his or her own server.

8 Cass. Com., 25 June 1980, *Bull. Civ.,* 1980, IV, p.222; Cass. Com., 27 May 1983, *Bull. Civ.,* 1983, IV, p.135.

9 Restrictive clauses are admitted under the freedom to contract, see *O'Callaghan* v. *Waller & Beckwith Reality Co.,* 15 Ill.2d 436, 155 N.E. 2d 545 (S.Ct. Ill, 1958); E. A. FARNSWORTH, F. WILLIAM, *Contracts: Cases and Materials,* 5th ed., Westbury, The Foundation Press Inc., 1995, pp.388-389.

10 Clauses restricting liability are admitted when they constitute a reasonable means of defining an accord agreed by the parties who freely consent, and whose positions are more or less equal in terms of bargaining power, C. BOYLE and D. R. PERCY, *Contracts : Cases and Commentaries,* 5th ed., Scarborough, Carswell, 1994, p.455.

11 P. S. JAMES, *Introduction to English Law*, 11th ed., London, ed. Butterworths, 1985, pp.295 ff.

12 L. ELIAS, J. GERARD and GIEN KUO WANG, «Le droit des obligations face aux échanges de données informatisées», in *Cahier du CRID*, Namur, ed. Story Scientia, 1992, n°8, p.81. Under Canadian law, there will be doubts as to the validity of a clause restricting liability if this is included in an adhesion contract or when it removes part of the obligation which is the very purpose of the understanding (*Karsales (Harrow) Ltd.* v. *Wallis* [1956] 1 W.L.R. 936, [1956] 2 All E.R. 866 (C.A.); S. M. WADDAMS, *The Law of Contracts*, 3rd ed, Toronto, Canada Law Book Inc., 1993, pp.316-317; C. BOYLE, D. R. PERCY, *op. cit.*, p.455.

   Under American law, when an understanding has the effect of absolving a party from his liability for his own negligence, the courts tend to refuse to implement this clause. The court will consider in particular the public interest involved in the relation between the parties (for example, there is public interest in the relation between a passenger and a public transport operator), and the dominant position of one of the parties compared with the other (an adhesion contract, for example, in which one of the parties has very little bargaining power). See *Chicago and Northwestern Railways Co.* v. *Chapman*, 133 Ill. 96, 24 N.E. 417, 8 L.R.A. 508; *Tyler, Ullman & Co.* v. *Western Union Telegraph Co.*, 60 Ill. 421; *Campbell* v. *Chicago, Rock Island and Pacific Railwway Co.*, 243 Ill. 620, 90 N.E. 1106; E. A. FARNSWORTH, W. F. YOUNG, *op. cit.*, p.389.

13 Under American law, defamation is governed by the *common law* of each of the American states. Under Canadian law, there are specific civil liability systems which generally stay fairly close to the principles of *common law*; D. L. APPLEMAN, «The Law and the Internet», *http://inet.nttam.com*, 12 May 1995, p.6.; *Code criminel*, L.R.C., 1985, c. C-46, ss. 300 and 301.

14 Under English law, generally speaking it would be the author of the defamation who would be held liable if he or she published or authorized publication of the defamatory item. A statement is considered to have been published when it has been communicated or made accessible to a person other than the victim.

15 *Libel* is written defamation and therefore has a permanent form, unlike *slander*, which covers gestural or verbal insults which are only temporary. Defamatory acts on the Internet fall into one or the other of these categories, depending on whether they are temporary and transient (such as a message in a Newgroup which is only stored for a short time) or whether the information is stored for a certain period of time (long-term storage in a Newsgroup server or a Web server); D. LOUNDY, «E-Law 2.0: Computer Information Systems Law and Operator Liability Revisited», *http://www.eff.org/pub/Legal/e-law.paper*, p.19.

16 D. R. JOHNSON and al., «Computer Viruses: Legal and Policy Issues Facing Colleges and Universities», 54 *Educ. L. Rep.* (West) 761, 766; M. GODWIN, «The Law of the Net: Problems and Prospects», *Internet World*, Sept/Oct 1993, *http://eff.org/pub/Legal/law_of_the_net.article*, p.2.

17 See above the chapters on crime and privacy.

18 See above the chapter on privacy. Under American and Canadian law, privacy is protected by constitutional laws and by *common law*. Under English law, the situation is a little more complex as there is no rule on the protection of privacy (see W.V.H. ROGERS, *Winfield & Jolowicz on Tort*, 14th ed, London, Sweet & Maxwell, 1994, p.586). The *European Convention on Human Rights* is applicable in England, and individuals whose privacy has been infringed on the Internet and who have not obtained redress from English judges will systematically win their cases before the European Court of Human Rights. Under French law, see s. 9 of the French Civil Code.

19 See above the Chapter on crime.

20 Invoking this liability presupposes, first of all, that the rights of the author have been infringed on the Internet. In this respect, the reader should refer to the survey of author's rights and their limits: users rights. See the chapter dealing with copyrights on the Internet.

21 See under American law, the *Copyright Act* of 1947, 17 *U.S.C.* s 506.

22 See the *Copyright Act*, R.S.C. 1985, ch. C-42, section 3.

23 See *Copyright, Designs and Patents Act* 1988; *Alfred Bell & Co* v. *Catalda Fine Arts Inc.*, 191 F.ed 99 at 102 (2nd Cir., 1951); *Sega Enterprise Ltd* v. *Richards* (No2) (1983) FSR 73; *British Leyland Motor Corpn Ltd* v. *Armstrong Patents Co Ltd,* (1986) AC 577.

24 French law has penalised such forgery more harshly since a law of 1994; L. DE GAULLE and D. REDON, «la nouvelle législation relative à la répression de la contrefaçon», *J.C.P. - Cahiers de droit de l'entreprise*, n°30, supplement n°3, 1994, p.33.

25 See the UEJF case which broke in France in March 1996.

26 It is difficult to envisage how access providers could be considered liable under French law for private mail which they distribute (and which could, for example, contain incitements to illegal activities).

27 In the case of *New-York Times* v. *Sullivan* (*New-York Times* v. *Sullivan*, 376 U.S. 254 (1964)) and in subsequent cases (*Curtis Publishing Co.* v. *Butts*, 388 US 130 (1967), aff. 351 F.2d 702 (5th CIR. 1965), reh'g denied, 389 US 889 (1967); *Associated Press* v. *Walker*, 388 US 130 (1967), rev'g 393 S.W.2d 671 (Tex.Civ.App.1965), reh'g denied, 389 US 889 (1967); *Geertz* v. *Robert Welsh Inc.*, 418

US 323, 342 (1974)), the American Supreme Court decided that publishers should only be held liable for defamation if the plaintiff was able to prove that they had committed a fault.

28 D. LOUNDY, *op. cit.*, p.31.

29 P. D. KENNEDY, «Publishing on the Internet: Some Legal Protections and Pitfalls», *http://www.eff.org/-pub/legal/inet-publishing-legal.article*, pp.2-4.

30 *Ibidem*, pp.4-5. See the Chapter on advertising and marketing.

31 *Stratton Oakmonth, Inc.* v. *Prodigy, gopher://insight.mcmaster.ca: 70/ORO-21250-/org/efc/law/us/ prodigy-24may95*, pp.2-3.

32 *Seton* v. *American News Co., op.cit.*, 593; D. LOUNDY, *op.cit.*, p.32.

33 See on this criterion for determining the size of the computing system: E. SCHLACTER, «Cyberspace, the Free Market and the Free Marketplace of Ideas: Recognizing Legal Differences in Computer Bulletin Board Functions», *http://www.eff.org/pub/legal/cyberlaw-bbs-freemarket.article*, p.10.

34 *Cubby Inc.* v. *Compuserve*, 776 F.Supp., 135; see also: *Smith* v. *California*, 361 U.S. 950 (1960); *Seton* v. *American News Co.*, 133 F.Supp. 591 (N.D. Fla. 1955); See the discussion of these aspects of the decision in T. HARDY, «The Proper Legal Regime for Cyberspace», (1993) 55 *University of Pittsburgh Law Review* 993, 1001.

35 Law of July 29 1881, *D.P.*, 1881, 4, 65; law of July 3 1985, n°85-660, O.J. 4 July 1985, *J.C.P.*, 1985, ed. G III, 57400 and 57934.

36 For the application of this principle on Minitel, see C.A. Amiens, July 30 1991, *Cahier Lamy*, Sept. 1991, p.12; Cass. Crim., Nov. 17 1992, n° 91/84.848.

37 Section 23 of the law of 1881 categorizes as indictable acts incitements to crimes and offences, via written or printed texts, drawings, engravings, paintings, emblems, images or any other written, spoken or visual medium, or (...) by any means of audiovisual communication. Sections 26 and 27 deal with offences against the State, more precisely offences against the President of the Republic and the counterfeiting of money. Section 29 of the same law defines defamation as «*any allegation or imputation of a fact which injures the honour or consideration of the person or body to whom the fact is imputed*» and insults as «*any offensive expression, terms of contempt or invective which is not based on any fact*». Section 36 concerns the undermining of foreign heads of state and diplomatic officials. Finally, section 38 prohibits the publication of bills of indictment and any other writs pertaining to criminal proceedings or to minor offence proceedings before these have been read out at a public hearing.

38 T.G.I. Paris, May 28 1986, Wild carrots/hemlock case, Soc. Fernand Nathan, *D.*, 1986, Flash, n°25, *Rev. Trim. Dr. Civ.* 1987, 552, obs. J. HUET; *D.*, 1986, I.R., p.319. A publisher marketed a work on edible fruit and plants and a young reader was poisoned after having confused hemlock and wild carrots on the word of the book. The court held that the publisher should ensure that readers could trust the work and considered the publisher to be at fault under the terms of section 1383 of the civil code which states that «*Everyone is liable for the damage he causes, not only through his actions, but also through his negligence or imprudence*». The judge felt in this case that the publisher had created a dangerous situation by irresponsibly disseminating a work of popular appeal which had shortcomings. Admittedly, this solution falls within the field of the written press, but could be extended to cover the Internet.

39 C. TAPPER, *Computer Law*, 4th edition, London, Longman, 1989, p.258.

40 G. ROBERTSON and A. C. L. NICOL, *Media Law*, p.61.

41 G. ROBERTSON and A. C. L. NICOL, *op. cit.*, pp.31-32, 56.

42 G. ROBERTSON and A.C.L. NICOL, *op. cit.*, pp.61-64.

43 3C. TAPPER, *op. cit.*, p.259

44 D. CALOW, *op cit*, p.199.

45 Encyclopedia of Information Technology law, *op.cit.*, p.7062, n°7.213.

46 D. CALOW, «Defamation on the Internet», *The Computer Law and Security Report*, July/August, 95, vol.11, p.200; «Liability for Electronic Dissemination Of Information», *Encyclopedia I.T.L., R .12*, December 1994, pp.7057-7060.

47 ROGERS, *op cit*, p.337. See in this respect *Emmens* v. *Pottle* (1885) 16 QBD 354, CA., *Vizetelly* v *Mudie's Select Library* (1900),2 QB 17O, and *Sun Life Insurance Co. of Canada* v. *W.H. Smith & Co Ltd* (1933) 150 LY 211.

Chapter ten

«Evidence»

1 On the concept of civil law, see below.
2 A fact is defined as any event likely to have effects in law independently of the intention of the author; see L. HENRI, and MAZEAUD, *Leçons de droit civil, les Biens*, tome 2, vol.2, Paris, ed. Montchrestien, 1976, n°1534.
3 A juridical act is an expression of intention which will have effects in law, such as the intention to create, modify, transmit or annul obligations, *Idem*.
4 A contract is an agreement whereby one or several persons accept, one or more other persons, obligations to give, to do or not to do, *Idem*.
5 On the concept of commercial law, see below.
6 In civil law, see s.1348 of the *Civil Code* and P. LECLERCQ, «Faut-il réformer le droit de la preuve?», (1991) 1 *Droit de l'informatique et des télécoms* 5. p.7; in commercial law, see s.109 of the *Commercial Code*; on unrestricted evidence in commercial law, see A. JAUFFRET and J. MESTRE, Droit commercial, Paris, *L.G.D.J.*, 1995, 22nd ed.
7 See under Montpellier, 9 April 1987, J.C.P., 1988, ed. G., II, 20984, note L. BOIZARD; Revue trimestrielle de droit civil, 1988, p.758, ob. P. MESTRE.
8 The trader can usually be defined as the person who repeatedly and habitually purchases goods for resale or offers professional services as a professional activity.
9 The scope of application of these exceptions is so broad that proving a contract on the Internet does not present any real problems, except as regards contracts of significant value, although such contracts are usually concluded further to prior negotiations, which usually resulted in a writing, or in the context of a course of business which has already involved the signing of a written master agreement.
10 Article 1341, al.1 of the French *Civil Code*.
11 Cass. civ., 4 December 1984, *J.C.P.*, 1985, IV, p.60; Bordeaux 16 February 1988, *D.S.*, 1990, p.141; Cass. civ., 28 June 1989, *Journ. not. av.*, 1990, art.60111, p.1157.
12 Trib. civil de Dijon, 16 November 1954, *Jurisclasseur Périodique*, ed. Générale, 1955, II, p.8550.
13 Cass. com., judgment of 7 February 1995, *Lexilaser*, judgment n°315; Cass. 10 January 1995, *Lexilaser*, judgment n°82; L. HENRI, and MAZEAUD , *Leçons de droit civil, les Biens*, tome 2, vol.2, Paris, ed. Montchrestien, 1976, n°1534; A. MYNARD, «Télématique et preuve en droit civil québécois et français: une antinomie?», *Droit de l'informatique et des télécoms*, 1992, p.20.
14 P. LECLERCQ, *op. cit.*, p.10.
15 Cass. civ., 17 March 1982, *Bull. Cass. fr.*, 1982, I, n°114; Cass. civ. 15 April 1980, *Bull. Cass. fr.*, 1980, I, n°113; Poitiers, (Ch. civile), 25 November 1992, *D.*, 1993, IR, p.117.
16 P. LECLERCQ, *op. cit.*, p.7.
17 Cass. civ., 27 January 1971, *Bull. civ.*, I, n°34.
18 Montpellier, 1ère ch., Section D, 9 April 1987, *J.C.P.*, ed Générale, 1988, II, 20984, note M. BOIZARD.
19 BAUDRY-LACANTINERIE, *Des obligations*, t.IV, n°2272; Cass. soc., 2 November 1951, *Bull. Cass. fr.*, 1951, III, p.718.
20 See s.1348 of the French *Civil Code* and X. MALENGREAU, «Le droit de la preuve et la modernisation des techniques de rédaction, de reproduction et de conservation des documents», *ann. Dr.* 1981, p.121.
21 See Versailles, 25 September 1989, *D.*, 1989, I.R., p.293.
22 P. LECLERCQ, *op. cit.*, p.14.
23 See s.109 of the *Commercial Code*.
24 Com. 21 June 1988, *J.C.P.*, 1989, II, 21170, note P. DELEBECQUE.
25 Cass. (ch. comm.), December 8 1980, *Jurisdata*, n°0452.
26 Decree of November 29 1983 (n°83/1020, *J.O.*, December 1 1983), in application of the law of April 30 1983 on the harmonization of the accounting obligations of traders and certain companies (Law n°83/353, *O.J.*, 3 May 1983).
27 *Evidence act* of 1995, Halsbury's statutes of England, 1995.
28 On these two rules, see in particular C. TAPPER, *Computer Law*, 4th ed., London, New York, Longman, 1989, pp. 372 et 377; A., KEANE, *The Modern Law of Evidence* , 3rd ed., Butterworths, London, Dublin, Edinburgh, 1994, p.193 ff. and 19 ff.;M. HIRST, «Computers and the English Law of Evidence», *Law, Computers & Artificial Intelligence*, vol.1, n°3, 1992, p.368 ff and 377 ff; Sweet & Maxwell, *Encyclopedia of Information* Technology Law, ch.11.13 and 11.12.

29 The application of the *Civil Evidence Act* 1995 to documents produced by computer is established in view of the very broad definitions of the terms *document* and *copy* : see. Section 13 of the *Civil Evidence Act*1995 and C. TAPPER, «Reform of the Law of Evidence in Relation to the Output from Computers», p.83; Sweet & Maxwell, *Encyclopedia of Information Technology Law,* ch.11.23, update: 4 December 1994.

30 However, it should be noted that *Rules of court* still have to be worked out to define the specific nature of this new system.

31 Section 13 of the *Civil Evidence Act: document means anything in which information of any description is recorded.*

32 See. C. TAPPER, «Reform of the Law of Evidence in Relation to the Output from Computers», *International Journal of Law and Information Technology,* vol.3, n°1, p.82; C. TAPPER, «Evanescent Evidence», *International Journal of Law and Information Technology,* vol.1, n°1, 1993, p.44.

33 See. C. TAPPER, *Computer Law,* 4th ed., London and New-York, Longman, 1989, p.369.

34 This is the *standard of proof.*

35 See M. SILVERBAF, «Evidence», in C. REED, *Computer Law,* Blackstone Press, London, 1989, p.184; A. KEANE, *The Modern Law of Evidence , op. cit.,* p.73.

36 *The maker of the original statement* is the person who has personal and first hand knowledge of the fact in question, see the *Civil Evidence Act* 1995, s. 4(2)(a).

37 *Fed.R.Evid,* s. 40; B.WRIGHT, *The Law of Electronic Commerce; EDI, E-mail, and Internet: Technology, Proof, and Liability,* 2nd ed., Little, Brown and Company, Boston, 1995, p.7-4; J. SOPINKA, S. LEDERMAN, A. W. BRYANT, *The Law of Evidence in Canada,* Toronto, Butterworth's, 1992, p.21; V. DEL BUONO, Ministry of Justice, «Admissibilité en preuve des documents informatiques», 1990, 1.

38 *Fed, R. Evid.,* s. 901(a); B. WRIGHT, *op. cit.,* p.8-1.

39 *R.* v. *Morris,* [1983] 2 S.C.R. 190, 7 C.C.C. (3d) 97, 36 C.R. (3d) 1, 48 N.R. 341, 1 D.L.R. (4th) 385, per Lamer J., at 201, S.C.R.; *in* J. SOPINKA et al., *op. cit.,* note 35, p.21.

40 B. WRIGHT, *op. cit.,* p.8-2.

41 *IDEM,* p.8-3.

42 *IDEM.,* p.8-2.

43 *Kohlmeyer & Co.* c. *Bowen,* 126 Ga. App. 700, 192 S.E.2d 400 (1972); RESTATEMENT (SECOND) of Contracts §134 comment a (1981), dans B. WRIGHT, *Id.,* p.16:8.

44 RESTATEMENT (SECOND) of Contracts §134 comment a (1981), *in* B. WRIGHT, *Id.,* p.16:8.

45 *Hessenthaler* v. *Farzin,* 388 Pa. Super. 37, 564 A.2d 990 (1989), *in* B. WRIGHT, *Id.,* p.16-17.

46 American Bar Association (ABA) Report at 1688 n.177, *in* B. WRIGHT, *Ibid.*

47 *Id.,* p.16-2.

48 «Susceptible of evidentiary connection to the signatory», *In re Carlstrom,* 3 U.C.C. Rep. Serv. 766 (Callaghan) (D. Me., Bankr. 1966), in B. WRIGHT, *Id.,* p.16-18.

49 B. WRIGHT, *Id.,* p.16:19.

50 *Digital Signatures Act,* Utah Code Ann. 1953, §46-3-101 and seq.

51 *Id.,* §46-3-401.

52 *Id.,* § 46-3-402.

53 *Civil Code of Québec,* s. 2827; P. TRUDEL, *La preuve et la signature électronique dans l'échange de documents informatisés au Québec,* p.83.

54 B. WRIGHT, *op. cit.,* p.10-2; *R.* v. *Elworthy* (1967), 10 Cox C.C. 579, L.R. 1 C.C.R. 103 (C.A.); *Pelrine* v. *Arron* (1969), 3 D.L.R. (3d) 713 (N.S.C.A.), at 724 , in J. SOPINKA et al, *op. cit.,* p.931.

55 As regards the best evidence rule: B. WRIGHT, *Ibid;* Fed. Rules Evid., s. 1002; M. M. MARTIN, *Basic Problems of Evidence,* 6th ed., American Law Institute-American Bar Association, Philadelphia, 1988, p.448;*R.* v. *Elworthy* (1967), 10 Cox C.C. 579, L.R. 1 C.C.R. 103 (C.A.); *Pelrine* v. *Arron* (1969), 3 D.L.R. (3d) 713 (N.S.C.A.), at 724 , quoted in J., SOPINKA et al, *op. cit.,* p.931; P. TRUDEL, *op. cit.,* p.46; V., DEL BUONO, *op. cit.,* 6-7. As regards the hearsay rule: *Fed. R. Evid.,* ss. 801, 802; *Code de la preuve,* s. 27(2)a), Commission de réforme de droit, rapport sur la preuve, ministère des Approvisionnements et Services, Canada, 1977; P. TRUDEL, *op. cit.,* pp.44, 49; V. DEL BUONO, *Id.,* 4; J. SOPINKA et al, *Id.,* p.156; J.-C. ROYER, *La preuve civile,* Cowansville, Les Éditions Yvon Blais Inc., 1987 n°671 p.244, and n°639, p.232.

56 *Fed. R. Evid.,* s.1002; M. M. MARTIN, *Basic Problems of Evidence, op. cit.,* p.448; P. TRUDEL, *op. cit.,* p.46; V. DEL BUONO, *op. cit.,* pp.6-7.

57 J.-C. ROYER, *op. cit.,* n°671 p.244, P. TRUDEL, *Id.,* p.44.

58 P. TRUDEL, *Id.,* p.47.

59 *Fed. R. Evid.,* s. 1001(1); P. TRUDEL, *Id.,* p.48.

60 *Fed. R. Evid.,* s. 1001(3).

61 B. WRIGHT, *op. cit.,* p.10-3.

62 *Transport Indemnity Co.* c. *Seib,* 178 Neb. 253.

63 *Fed. R. Evid.*, s. 803(6); M. M. MARTIN, *op. cit.*, p.387.
64 See*United States* v. *Vela*, 673 F.2d 86, reh'g denied, 677 F.2d 113 (5th Cir. 1982).
65 B. WRIGHT, *op. cit.*, pp.9-8,9-9.
66 *UCC*, s. 2-105.
67 *UCC*, s. 8-102.
68 UCC, s. 1-201 (46).
69 *Clason* v. *Bailey*, 14 Johns. 484 (N.Y. 1817); UCC 2-201 Official Comment 1; B. WRIGHT, *op.cit.*, p.16-9.
70 *Wigmore on Evidence*, Toronto, Little, Brown and Co., 1983, vol.1 par. 7a; P. TRUDEL, *op. cit.*, p.99.
71 Wigmore on evidence, *Ibid.*
72 French law recognises that the provisions on evidence do not involve public order (Cass. soc. 19 June 1947, *Gaz. Pal.*, 1947, 2, p.284; Cass. 29 October 1918, *S.*, 1920, I, p.158; Cass., 8 November 1989, *Droit de l'informatique*, 1990-2, p.44, note J. VASSEUR; See also X. LINANT de BELLE-FONDS & A. HOLLANDE, *Droit de l'informatique et de la télématique*, 2nd ed, Paris, Delmas et Cie, 1990, p.1-11; Civ., 8 Nov.1989, *D.*, 1990, p.369, note GAVALDA) and therefore allows the parties to define in a contract the way of proving the content of the obligations (for example by setting aside the pre-eminence of the written document) and to apply their own probative system by mutual agreement (PLANIOL et RIPERT, par ESMEIN, *Droit Civil des obligations*, T. VII, n°1428; Cass. soc. 24 March 1965, *J.C.P.*, 1965, II, 14415; Fr. GALLOUEDEC-GENUYS, *Nouvelles technologies de l'information et droit de la preuve*, 1990, La Documentation Française, Paris; C. LUCAS DE LEYSSAC, «Les conventions sur la preuve en matière informatique», *Travaux de l'AFDI*, «Informatique et droit de la preuve», ed. des Parques, 1987, pp.151 and 154; I. De LAM-BERTERIE , «La valeur probatoire des documents informatiques dans les pays de la CEE», *RIDC*, 1992, n°3, p.678 ff; Paris, October 17 1984, *D.*, 1985, *I.R.*, p.343, Obs. M. VASSEUR; Paris, March 29 1985, *D.* 1986, *I.R.*, p.326).
73 B. WRIGHT, «Alternatives for signing electronic documents»,*The computer law and security report,* May-June, (1995) 11 CLSR, pp.136-139.
74 Y. POULET, «Probate law : From Liberty to Responsibility», *EDI Law Review,* n°2, 1994, p.83-100.

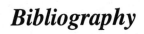

Bibliography

Chapter one

«Your first steps on the Internet and the law»

References

BARNETT, B. S., «Law of International Communications in the United States», *Law and Economics of International Telecommunications*, Baden-Baden, Auflage, vol.4, 1988.

HANK, I., «Traffic rules on Canada's information highway: the regulatory framework for new cable and telephone services», *Developping Multimedia Products*, Toronto, 1994.

Articles

CRABIT, E. and BERGEVIN, J., «Le cadre réglementaire des services de la société de l'information: laboratoire pour un nouveau droit du marché intérieur», *Revue du Marché Unique Européen*, 1995, 1, pp.54 ff.

Chapter two

«Copyright on the Internet»

References

DOMMERING, E., J., HUGENHOLTZ, P. B., GINSBURG, J. C., KARNELL, G. W. G., KOOPMANS, T. and VIVANT, M., *Protecting Works of Fact, Copyright, Freedom of Expression and Information Law*, Boston, Deventer, Kluwer Law and Taxation Publishers, 1991.

EPSTEIN, S. and JONES, J. M., *Intellectual property at a crossroads: Global Pyracy and International Competitiveness*, Congressional Economic Leadership Institute, 1990.

POULLET, Y., *Advices and Topics of Law and Information and Technology*, Prof. G.P.V. Vandenberghe (ed), Hollande, Kluwer, 1988.

STROWEL, A., *Droits d'auteur et Copyright-Divergences et convergences - Etude de droit comparé*, Bruxelles, Bruylant, 1993.

WILEY, J. and SONS, L., *World Wide Web marketing: integrating the Internet into your Marketing Strategy*, New-York, 1995.

Articles

ABELSON, H. and FISCHER, M., «6.095/STS095: Readings on Intellectual Property Restrictions on Software», *http://www.swiss.ai.mit.edu/6095/readings-2.html*, mars 1995.

ADDY, G., «Notes for remarks to the advisory council on the Information Highway», *http://info.in.go.ca/-info-highway/documents/addy.06-15-94.e.text*

A Guide to Canada's Export controls, «Crypto-expert controly», *gopher://insight.memaster:ca:10/ORO-6329-/org/etc/events/crypto/expert-controls-apr.txt*

ANDERSEN, M. B., «The UNCITRAL Draft model law on E.D.I. - its history and its fate», *http://www.diat.una-treal.ca/CRDP.*

AUSTIN, D., «Software Licencing», 1994, *http://spirit.com.au/«dan/law/swguide/licencing.html#chap4.0.*

BAIR, R., «Electronic Commerce of Component Information (ECCI) Program», *http://www.sandia.gov/-ecci/white-paper.html*

BARLOW, J. P., «Jackboots on the Infobahn: Clipping the Wings of Freedom», 1993, *http://www.eff.org/pub/-Privacy/infobahn-jackboots-barlaw-eff.article*

BENNAHUM, D. S., «The trouble with E-cash», *http://www.reach.com/matrix/troublewithcash.html*

BENYEKHLEF, K., «Réflexions sur le droit de la protection des données personnelles à la lumière des propositions de la Commission des Communautés Européennes», *Media &Communications Law Review*, 1991-1992, pp.149-206.

BENYEKHLEF, K. and GAUTRAIS, V., «Echange de documents informatisés-contrat type commenté», *http://www.droit.umontreal-ca/Nouveautés/contrat-type.html*

BENYEKHLEF, K., «Les transactions dématérialisées sur les voies électroniques: panorama des questions juridiques», *http://www.droit.umontreal.ca/CRDP/Conferences/AE/Benyekhlef.html*

BORENSTEIN, N. S., and al., «Perils and Pitfalls of Practical CyberCommerce», *http://www.fv.com/pubdocs/-fv~austin~txt*

BRINDSON, D. J., RADCLIFFE, M. F., «Intellectual Property Law Primer for Multimedia developers», *http://www.eff.org/CAF/law/ip-primer*

CARRIERE, L., «OMC-Propriété intellectuelle - Canada: L' adhésion du Canada à l'Accord instituant l'organisation mondiale du commerce et les modifications conséquentes aux lois canadiennes de propriété intellectuelle», *Cah. P.I.*, vol.7, n°3, may 1995, pp.439-445.

CARROLL, T., «Frequently asked questions about copyright», *http://www.cis.ohio-statc-edu/hypertext/fag/usenet/-Copyright-FAQ/part3/faq.html*

CARROLL, T., *http://www.cis.ohio-statc-edu/hypertext/fag/usenet/Copyright-FAQ/part2/faq.html*

CAVOUKIAN, A., «Preserving Privacy on the Information Highway: fact or fiction?», *Presented at a special symposium at the University of Waterloo*, November 26 1994.

CHAIRMAN, J. D. Dingell, «Federal trade commission deception policy statement», Washington, *http://www.web.com/-~lewrose/deceptionpol.html*, October 14 1983.

CHAUM, D., «Prepaid Smart Card Techniques: A brief Introduction and Comparison», *http://www.digicash.com/-publish/cardcom.html*

«CICN and Acceptable Use Policy», *<NIC.MERIT.EDU>/nsfnet/acceptable.use.policies/cicnet.txt*, december 1991.

CLARKE, R. A., «A normative regulatory framework for computer matching», *The John Marshall Journal of Computer & Information Law*, vol.XIII, 1995, n°4, pp.585-633.

«Copyright Basics», *gopher://manuel.loc.gov/00/copyright/circs/circ01*

Corporation for Research and Educational Networking, «Acceptable Use Policy», *<nic.merit.edu>/-acceptable.use.policies/cren.txt*

COULTER, J. D., «Computers, Copyright and Substantial Similarity: the Test Reconsidered», *The John Marshall Journal of Computer and Information Law*, 1995, vol.XIV, n°1.

«Data Protection, Privacy & the Freedom of Information», *the Legal Environment of computing*, pp.191-209.

DINNISSEN, P., «DigiCash announces cost breakthrough in secure chip technology for smart cards», *http://www.digicash.com/publish/blue-press.html*

ELKIN-KORENT, N., «Copyright law and social dialogue on the information superhighway: the case against copyright liability of bulletin board operators», *Cardozo Arts & Entertainment Law Journal*, 1995, vol.13, *http://yu1.yu.edu/csl/journals/aelj/articles/13-2/elkin.html*

FARRELL, P. and ALLEN, C., «Visa Etablishes International Consortium for Electronic Purse Specifiations, *http://ganges.cs.tcd.ie/mepierce/Projet/pro/visa-html*

FRANKEL, S. D., «The Impact of the Charter on Electronic Surveillance», *The Advocate*, 1993, vol.51, pp.45-50.

GAGNE, S., «La protection juridique de la réalité virtuelle ou l'imbroglio juridique dans l'univers de l'électrobohême», *les cahiers de propriété intellectuelle*, janv. 1995, vol.7, n°2, pp.181 ff.

GINSBURG, J. C., «Global Use Territorial Rights: Private International Law Questions on the Global Information Infrastructure», *Copyright Society of the U.S.A. Journal*, summer 1995, pp.318 ff.

GODWIN, M., «Crimes and criminal procedure», *http://www.eff.org/pub/legal/ecpa.law*

GOLDBERG and al., «Judicial Developments», *Copyright Society of the U.S.A. Journal*, 1995, pp.353 ff.

GREENBERG, T. R., «E-mail and voice mail: employee privacy and federal wiretap statute», *The American University law Review*, October 1994, vol.44, n°1, pp.219-253.

GREGURAS, F., « Copyright clearances and moral rights», 30 nov. 1995, Palo Alto (Californie), *http://www.bat-net.com/oikoumene/mmcpyrt-doubts.html*

HARDY, I. T., «Contracts, Copyright and Preemtion in a Digital World», *University of Richmond Journal of Law & Technology*, april. 1995, vol.2, n°1, *http://www.urich.edu/«jolt/vlil/hardy.html*

HERNANDEZ, R. T., «Computer Electronic Mail and privacy», 11 janvier 1987, Chula vista, (California), *http://www.eff.org/pub/CAF/law/privavy.email*

http://www.leepfrog.com/E-Law/E-Law/Part_IV.html

http://www.leepfrog.com/E-Law/E-Law/Part_V.html

http://www.leepfrog.com/E-Law/E-Law/Part_VI.html

Info Hi Adv. Council Copyright & the Info Hi. Prel. Report of the Copyright Subcom., *http://info.ic.gc.ca/info-highway/ih.html*

JOHNSON, M., «Crypto Policy in the USA», *http://www.eff.org/pub/Privacy/us-crypto-policy.faq*

KADIE, C., «Intentional infliction of emotional harm», *http://www.eff.org/pub/CAF/law/privacy-invasion*

KARP, I., «The Herbert Tenzer Memorial Conference: Copyright in the Twenty-First Century, Formalities and the Future: The Fate of Sections 411 and 412, A Future Without Formalities», *Cardozo Arts & Entertainment Law Journal*, 1995, vol.13, pp.521 ff., *http://yu1.yu.edu/csl/journals/aelj/articles/13-2/karp.html*

KARP, I., «A Future without Formalities», *Cardozo Arts & Entertainment Law Journal*, 1995, vol. 13, *http://yu1.yu.edu/csl/journals/aelj/articles/13-2/karp.html*

KIM, S. H. M., «In re alappat: a strict statutory interpretation determining patentable subject matter relating to computer software?», *Journal of computer & information law*, 1995, vol. XIII, pp.637 ff.

KLEIN, A. P., «Reinventing the examination process for patent applications covering software-related inventions», *Journal of Computer & Information Law*, 1995, vol.13, pp.231 ff.

KOEGEL, J. B., «Bamboozlement: the repeal of copyright registration incentives», *Cardozo Arts & Entertainment Law Journal*, 1995, vol. 13, *http://yu1.yu.edu/csl/journals/aelj/articles/13-2/koegel.html*

LADAS et PARKY, «Intellectal Property Provisions of GATT», *http://www.ladas.com/gatt.html*

LEMLEY, M. A., «Rights of attribution and integrety in online communications (article 2)», 1995, *http://www.law.cornell.edu/"jol/lemley.html*

LEVY, S., «E-Money (that's what I want)», *http://www.hotwired.com/wired/2.12/features/emoney.html*

LOUNDY, D. L., «Revising the copyright law for electronic publishing», *http://www.leepfrog.com/E-Law/Revising-HyperT.ht*

LOUNDY, D. L., «Revising the copyright law for electronic publishing», *The John Marshall Journal of Computer and Information Law*, 1995, vol.XIV, n°1.

LOUNDY, D. L., «Constitution Protects All Modes of Speech», *http://www.leepfrog.com/E-Law/CDLB/-Terrorism.html*

LUPO, Anthony, V., «Potential Liability for On-Line Service Providers», *http://www.web.com/-~lewrose/article/online.html*

METALITZ, S., «The Herbert Tenzer Memorial Conference: Copyright in the Twenty-First Century, Information Superhighway: The Challenge of Multimedia Technology, The National Information Infrastructure», *Cardozo Arts & Ent. L. J.*, 1995, vol.13, pp. 465 ff., *http://yu1.yu.edu/csl/journals/aelj/article/13-2/metalitz.html*

METALITZ, S., «The national information infrastructure», *Cardozo Arts & Entertainment Law Journal*, 1995, vol.13, *http://yu1.yu.edu/csl/journals/aelj/articles/13-2/metalitz.html*

MILOSEVIC, Z., «Electronic Commerce on the Internet: What is still missing?», *http://inet.nttam.com.*

MORGAN, M. F., «Trash talking: the protection of intellectual property rights in computer software», *Ottawa Law Review*, 1994, vol.26, n°2.

NATT GANTT, L. O., «An affront to human dignity: electronic mail monitoring in the private sector workplace», *Harvard Journal of Law & Technology*, 1995, vol.8, n°2, p.345.

«Northwestnet Acceptable Use Policy», <*nic.merit.edu*>/*nsfnet/acceptable.use.policies/northwestnet.txt*, may 1988.

«OTA Report Summary-Information Security and Privacy in Netword environments», *ftp://ftp.eff.org/-pub/EFF/Polray/Crypto/dta-pri-soc.report*

PERLMUTTER, S., «Freeing copyright from formality», *Cardozo Arts & Entertainment Law Journal*, 1995, vol. 13, *http://yu1.yu.edu/csl/journals/aelj/articles/13-2/perlmutt.html*

PERTSCHUK, M., and al., «Federal Trade Commission Unfairness Policy Statement», *http://www.web.com/~lewrose/unfairpol.html*

RACICOT, M., «La protection des logiciels en droit canadien», in *Développements récents en droit de la Propriété Intellectuelle*, Canarvsville, Yvon Blais, 1991.

RIDDLE, M., «Sysop Liability for Enroute (and/or Encrypted) Mail», *http://www.eff.org/pub/Privacy/Crypto-mail-liability-article*

ROUART, N., «Déclin ou renouvellement de la Convention de Berne», *Cahiers de propriété intellectuelle*, 1995, vol. 7, n°2, pp. 277-286.

ROSE, L., «Cyberspace and the Legal Matrix: Laws or Confusion?», *http://www.eff.org/pub/legal/-cyberspace-legal-matrix.article*

ROSEN, H. M., «Telecommunications Fraud and the Criminal Law», *Media &Communications Law Review*, 993-1995, n°4.

ROZENFELD, S., «Reverse Engineering de logiciels- Des pratiques à double tranchant», *Expertises*, pp.7-8.

SAEZ, C., «Enforcing copyrights in the age of multimedia», *Rutgers Computer & Technology Law Journal*, 1995, vol.21, pp.351 ff.

SCHLACHTER, E., «Intellectual property protection regimes in the age of Internet», *schlachtere@cooley.com*

SCHLACHTER, E., «Cyberspace, the Free Market and the Free Marketplace of Ideas: Recognizing Legal Differences in Computer Bulletin Board Functions», *http://www.eff.org/pub/legal/cyberlaw-bbs-free-market-article*

SCOTT, M. D., «Frontier issues: pitffalls in developping and marketing multimedia products», *Cardozo Arts & Entertainment Law Journal*, 1995, vol.13, pp.413 ff; *http://yu1.yu.edu/csl/journals/aelj/articles/13-2/scott.html*

SIEBER, U., «The Emergence of Criminal Information Law», In *Amongot Friends*, pp.117-129.

SIM, P., «Electronic Libel: Responsability of BBS Operators», *http://www.mbnet.mb.ca/~psim/libel.html*

SIM, P., «Privacy on the Information Highway», *http://www.mbnet.mb.ca/~psim/secure.html*

SIM, P., «The New Electronic Document: A Challenge for the Legal System», *http://www.mbnet.mb.ca/~psim/comp_doc.html*

SIM, P., «Security, Privacy and Electronic Commerce», *http://www.mbnet.mb.ca/~psim/secure.html*

SIM, P., «Legal Problems of Electronic Data Interchange», *http://www.mbnet.mb.ca/~psim/edi.html*

SOPINKA, J., «Freedom of speech and privacy in the information Age», University of Waterloo, *gopher://insight.memaster.ca:10/ORO-51356-/org/efc/doc/slsp/sopinka.txt*

SORKIN, B. R., «The Herbert Tenzer Memorial Conference: Copyright in the Twenty-First Century, Formalities and the Future: The Fate of Sections 411 and 412, The Futility of a Future Without Formalities», *Cardozo Arts & Ent. L. J.*, 1995, vol.13, pp.589 ff., *http://yu1.yn.edu/csl/journals/aelj/articles/13-2/sorkin,html*

SORKIN, B. R., «The futility of a future without formalities», *Cardozo Arts & Entertainment Law Journal*, 1995, vol. 13, *http://yu1.yu.edu/csl/journals/aelj/articles/13-2/sorkin.html*

STAMETS, R. A., «Ain't Nothin' like the Real Thing, Baby: The Right of Publicity and the Singing Voice», *http://www.law.indiana.edu/fclj/v46/no2/stamets.html*

TEMPLETON, B., «Copyright Myths FAQ», *The Copyright Website, http://www.benedict.com/temple.html#temple*

TRUDEL, P., «La protection des droits et des valeurs dans la gestion des réseaux ouverts», Centre de recherche en Droit public de l'Université de Montréal, *http://www.droit.umontreal.ca/CRDP/conferences/AE/TrudelGerinLajoie*

WADE, H., «Court 705 (1973)», *Suprême Court Reporter*, pp.705-738.*www.web.com/~lewrose/unfairpol.html*

ZIMMERMANN, Ph., «Pretty Good Privacy - Legal Issues», *http://www.mantis.co.uk/pgp/pgp-legal.html*

http://ganges.cs.ted.ie/mepierce/Project/Pro

http://www.digicash.com/products/cafe.html

http://www.cs.yale.edu/pub/dunne/jurimetrics/html

Chapter three

«Freedom of expression»

References

NOWAK, J. E., ROTUNDA, R. D., and YOUNG, J. N., *Constitutional Law*, 2nd ed., St. Paul, West Publishing, 1991.

RIGAUX, F., *La protection de la vie privée et des autres biens de la personnalité*, Brussels - Paris, Bruylant - L.G.D.J., 1990.

Articles

ABELSON, H. and FISCHER, M., «Readings on Computers, Academic Freedom, and Free Spech», *http://www.swiss.ai.mit.edu/6095/readings-4.html, june 1995.*

APPLEMAN, D. L., «The Law and the Internet», *http://inet.nttam.com, 12 may 1995.*

BROOKS, Th. D., «Catching Jellyfish in the Internet: The Public-Figure Doctrine and Defamation on Computer Bulletin Boards», *Rutgers Computer & Law Technology Journal*, vol.21, n°2, 1995, pp.461-471.

BRYANT, M. J., «Section 2(b) and libel law: Defamatory Statements about Public Officials», Media & Communications Law Review, 1991-1992, pp.336-343.

GOLDWIN, M., «Virtual community standards», *http://www.eff.org/pub/legal/virtcom-standards.article.*, January 30 1995.

HUELSTER, P. A., «Cybersex and community standards», *Boston University law review*, may 1995, vol.75, n°3, pp.865 ff.

«Lawyers in Cyberspace», *http://www.kbs.citri.edu.au/law/node4.htm/#SECTION*

LOUNDY, D., «E-Law 2.0: Computer Information Systems Law and Operator Liablity Revisited», *http://www.eff.org/pub/Legal/e-law.paper*

IDEM, «E-Law 3.01: Computer Information Systems Law and System Operator Liability in 1995», *http://www.leepfrong.com/E-Law/E-Law/Part_VI.htm*

IDEM, «Whose standards? Whose Community?», Chicago Daily Law Bulletin, *http://www.leepfrog.com/E-Law/CDLB/AABBS.html*, 1er août 1994, p.5.

MITCHELL, M., «Electronic misbehavior», Inside Illinois, *http://www.swiss.ai.mit.edu/6095/assorted-short-pieces/electronic-misbehaviour.txt*, November 4 1994.

RIGAUX, F., «La liberté d'expression et ses limites», *Rev. Trim. Dr. H.*, 1995, p.401.

ROSE, L., «Cyberspace and the Legal Matrix: Laws or Confusion?», *http://www.eff.org/pub/Legal/cyberspace-legal-matrix.article*, p.1.

ROSENBERG, R. S., «Free speech, Pornography, Sexual Harassment, and Electronic Networks: An Update and Extension», in *The Electronic Superhighway*, pp.127 ff.

SHINER, R. A., «Advertising and freedom of expression», *University of Toronto law journal*, 1995, vol. 45, pp.179 ff.

VOORHOOF, D., «Defamation and libel laws in Europe - the framework of Article 10 of the European Convention on Human Rights (ECHR)», *Media Law and Practice*, 1992, p.250.

Electronic Frontier Foundation Statement on 1996 Telecommunicatons Regulation Bill», *http://www.eff.org/pub/Alerts/Cda_020296_eff.statement*

Chapter four

«Protection of privacy on the Internet»

References

BENYEKHLEF, K., *La protection de la vie privée dans les échanges internationaux d'informations*, Montréal, Thémis, 1992.

ENSOUSSAN, A., *Les fichiers des personnes et le droit*, Paris, Hermès, 1991.

Conseil de l'Europe, *Les nouvelles technologies: un défi pour la protection de la vie privée?*, Strasbourg, 1989.

Encyclopedia of information and technology law, UK, Sweet and Maxwell, 1994.

GILCART, S., *Douze constitutions pour une Europe...*, Diegem, Kluwer, 1994.

MATSCHER, F. and PETZOLD, H., «Protection des droits de l'homme: la dimension européenne.» *Mélanges en l'honneur de Gérard J. Wiarda*, Köln, Carl Heymans Verlag, 1988.

RIGAUX, F., *La protection de la vie privée et des autres biens de la personnalité*, Brussels - Paris, Bruylant - L.G.D.J, 1990.

Articles

ALKEMA, E. A., «The third-party applicability or «Drittwirkung» of the European Convention on Human Rights», in MATSCHER, F. and PETZOLD, H., Protection des droits de l'homme: la dimension européenne. *Mélanges en l'honneur de Gérard J. Wiarda*, Köln, Carl Heymans Verlag, 1988, pp. 33-45.

BENYEKHLEF, K., «Les transactions dématérialisées sur les voies électroniques: panorama des questions juridiques», Centre de recherche en droit public, Université de Montréal, *http://www.droit.umontreal.ca/CRDP/ Conferences/AE/Benyekhlef.html*, 9.

BERKVENS, J. M. A., «Gemeenschappelijk standpunt privacy-richtlijn», *Computerrecht*, 1995, p.103.

COHEN JONATHAN, G., «Les écoutes téléphoniques», in MATSCHER, F. and PETZOLD, H. (ed.), Protection des droits de l'homme: la dimension européenne. *Mélanges en l'honneur de Gérard J. Wiarda*, Köln, Carl Heymans Verlag, 1988, pp.97-105.

GANTT, L. O. N., «An Affront to Human Dignity: Electronic Monitoring in the Private Sector Workplace», *Harvard Journal of Law and Technology*, 1995, vol.2, p.360.

GREENBERG, Th. R., «E-mail and Voice Mail: Employee Privacy and the Federal Wiretap Statute (Comment)», *The American University Law Review*, 1994, vol.44, n°1, p.248.

LOUNDY, D., «E-Law 2.0: Computer Information Systems Law and Operator Liability Revisited», *http://www.eff.org/pub/Legal/e-law.paper, p.22.*

RIDDLE, M., «Sysop Liability for Enroute (and/or Encrypted) Mail», FIDO NEWS, November 7 1993, vol.10, n°45, *http://www.eff.org/pub/Privacy/ Crypto_mail_liability.article*, p.3.

SEDALLIAN, V. and LANGLOIS, Ph., «Le grand secret...le plus partagé du monde», *Planète Internet*, 1996, pp.28-29.

SOPINKA, J., «Freedom of Speech and Privacy in the Information Age», Symposium on Free Speech and Privacy in the Information Age, University of Waterloo, 26 *novembre 1994, gopher://insight.mcmaster.ca:70/ORO-51356-/org/efc/doc/sfsp/sopinka.txt*

Chapter five

«The Internet and commercial communication»

References

CARROLL, J. and BROADHEAD, R., *Canadian Internet Handbook*, Scarborough, Prentice Hall, 1995.

LAFFINEUR, J. and GOYENS, M., *La Télématique grand public en Belgique*, Bruxelles, ed. Story Scientia, 1989.

MAXEINER, J.R. and SCHOTTHÖFER, P., *Advertising Law in Europe and North America*, Boston, Kluwer Law and Taxation Publisher, 1992.

NELSON, H. L. and al., *Law of Mass Communications: Freedom and Control of Print and Broadcast Media*, 6ième ed., Westbury, The Foundation Press Inc., 1989.

POTVIN, L., *La personne et la protection de son image étude comparée des droits québecois, français et de la common law anglaise*, Cowansville, Yvon Blais, 1991.

RESNICK, R. and TAYLOR, D., *The Internet Business Guide*, Indianapolis, Sams Publishing, 1994.

RIGAUX, F., *La protection de la vie privée et des autres biens de la personnalité*, Brussels-Paris, Bruylant-L.G.D.J., 1990.

ROSE, D., *Minding your Cybermanners on the Internet*, Indianapolis, Alpha Books, 1994.

TRIBE, L.H., *American Constitutional Law*, 2nd ed., Mineola, Foundation Press, 1988.

YOUNG, D. M. and FRASER, B. R., *Canadian Advertising and Marketing Law*, vol.1, Rel. n°4, Scarborough, Carswell, 1995.

Articles

«Federal Trade Commission Deception Policy Statement», *http://www.web.com/~lewrose/deception-pol.html*, October 14 1983, pp.4-13.

GANTT, L.O., «An Affront to Human Dignity: Electronic Monitoring in the Private Sector Workplace», *Harvard Journal of Law and Technology*, n°2, Printemps 1995, p.374.

GROIA, E. and LEDERMAN, S., «Advertising Prosecutions: You Can Run But You Can't Hide», in *Absolutely the Best conference You will ever Attend on Advertising Claims*, Insight Press, 1992, pp.4-6.

HOLMES, J., «Meeting your competitor in court», in *Absolutely the Best conference You will ever Attend on Advertising Claims*, Insight Press, 1992, p.5.

MOGG, J., «Communiquer avec les communicateurs», *Communications Commerciales*, Brighton, n°1, juillet 1995, p.1.

TEBOUL, A., «Publicité et Télécommunication», in *Juris PTT* n°25, 1991, p.36.

TRUDEL, P., «La protection de la vie privée et le droit à l'image aux États-Unis», in Liberté de la Presse, Respect de la vie privée et de l'image en droit comparé, *Actes de Colloques de l'I.F.C.*, 22-23 mars 1996.

WATERSCHOOT, P., «Les communications commerciales européennes et la société de l'information», *Communications Commerciales*, p.15.

Chapter six

«Electronic commerce»

References

AUDIT, B., *Droit international privé*, Paris, ed. Économica, 1991.

IDEM, La vente internationale des marchandises, Paris, L.J.D.J., 1990.

BATTIFOL, H. and LAGARDE, P., *Droit international privé*, t.1, 8th ed. and t.2, 7th ed, Paris, L.G.D.J., 1993.

CALAMARI, J. and PERILLO, J., *The Law of Contracts*, 3rd ed., St Paul, West Publishing Co, 1987.

CHESHIRE, FIFOOT and FURMSTON, *Law of contract*, 11th ed., London, Butterworths, 1986.

DAVID, R. and PUGSLEY, D., *Les contrats en Droit anglais*,. Paris, L.J.D.J., 1989.

DIENER, P., *Le silence et le droit*, Thése Bordeaux, 1975.

ELIAS, L., GERARD, J. and GIEN KUO WANG, *Le droit des obligations face aux échanges de données informatisées*, Namur - Brussels, C.R.I.D - Story scientia, 1992.

Encyclopaedia Britannica, DigiCash store or Big Mac's Monthy Python Archive Shop.

FARNSWORTH, E. A. and YOUNG, W. F., *Contracts: case and Materials*, 5th ed., Westbury, The Foundation Press Inc., 1995.

GHESTIN, J., *Traité de droit civil. Les obligations: le contrat*, 2nd ed., Paris, L.G.D.J., 1980.

GRILLIOT, J. and SCHUBERT, F. A., *Introduction to Law and the Legal System*, 4th ed., Boston, Houghton Mifflin Company, 1989.

GRUA, F., *Contrats bancaires*, t.1, Paris, Économica, 1990.

GUEST, A. G., *Chitty on contracts* , London, Sweet & Maxwell, 1983.

JONES, S. A., *The law relating to credit cards*, Oxford, BSP Professional Books, 1989.

LAFFINEUR, J. and GOYENS, M., *La télématique grand public en Belgique*, Brussels, éd. Story Scientia,1989.

LINANT de BELLEFONDS, X. and HOLLANDE, A., *Contrats informatiques et télématiques*, 3e ed., Paris, J. Delmas and Cie, 1992.

IDEM, Droit de l'informatique et de la télématique, 2nd ed. Paris, J. Delmas and Cie, 1990.

PINEAU, J. and BURMAN, D., *Théorie des Obligations*, 2nd ed., Montréal, Thémis, 1988.

PLANIOL, RIPERT and ESMEIN, *Traité pratique de droit civil français*, 2nd ed., t.VI, «Obligations», First part, Paris, L.G.D.J.

SCOLES, E. F. and HAY, P., *Conflict of Laws*, 2ⁿᵈ ed., St Paul, West Publishing Co., 1988.

SMITH, J. C., *The law of the contract*, London, Sweet & Maxwell, 1993.

STERME, J. and al., *World wideweb marketing: Integrating the Internet into your Marketing Strategy*, New York, John and Sons Inc, 1995.

THUNIS, X. and SCHAUSS, M., *Aspects juridiques du paiement par carte*, Namur -Brussels, C.R.I.D - Story-Scientia, 1988.

TREITLE, G. H., *The law of the contracts*, London, Stevens & Sons, 1987.

WADDAMS, S.M., *The Law of Contracts*, 3rd ed., Toronto, Law Book Inc., 1993.

WITZ, Cl., *Les premières applications jurisprudentielles du droit uniforme de la vente internationale*, Paris, L.J.D.J., 1995.

WRIGHT, B., *The Law of Electronic Commerce, E.D.I., Email and Internet: Technology, Proof and Liability*, 2nd ed., Boston, Little Brown & Cie, 1995.

Articles

ADDY, G.-N., «Notes for remarks to the advisory council on the information highway», Ottawa, *http://info.ic.gc.ca/info-highway/documents/addy. 06-15-94.e.text*, 15 june 1994.

ALLIX, J., «Consommateurs et paiements électroniques transfrontières», *Banque*, n°536, mars-april 1993.

ARIRA, G., «Banques et commerce électronique», *Banque*, n°560, june 1995.

«Background on related products/projects»,

http://www.digicash.com/

BORENSTEIN, N. S., FERGUSON, J., and al. «Perils and Pitfalls of Pratical CyberCommerce - The Lessons of the First Virtual's First Year», to be presented at: Frontiers in Electronic Commerce», Austin, Texas, *http://www.fv.com/pubdocs/fv-austin.txt,* October 1995.

BUDNITZ, M. E., «Federal Regulation of Consumer Disputes in Computer Banking Translations», *Harvard Journal on Legislation,* 1983, pp.31-98.

CAMP, L. J., SIRBU, M. and TYGAR, J. D., «Token and Notational Money in Electronic Commerce», *http://www.cgi.cs.edu.edu/es.cmu.edu/ uses/jeanc/www/usenix.html,* October, 1995, pp 3-4 and 11-12.

CHAUM, D., «Online Cash, Checks»,*http://www.digicash.com/publish/online.html*

«Digital Cash & Ecash», *http://www.digicash.com/digicash/company.html*

«Electronic Commerce and the NII», *http://www.droit.umontreal.ca/CRDP/*

«Electronic Money», *http://www.amex.cox.smu.edu/class/mis4350h/ people/Haninga/Concept/* 1

«FBOI», Announcement, *http://ganges.cs.tcd.ic/mepierce/project/Press/fboi.html*

«First Virtual», *http://www.fv.com./info.intro.html*

GALLAND, M. W., «Legal Aspects of a Paperless Letter of Credit - Implications for the Transportation Industry and the Advancement of Electronic Data Interchange on Internet», *http://www.usfca.cdn/usf/-gallma10/EDI.html#RTFToC1£*

GAUDEMET-TALLON, H., «Convention de Rome du 19 june 1980 sur la loi applicable aux obligations contractuelles», *R.T.D. eur.,* jul.-sept. 1992.

GHESTIN, J. et MARCHESSAUX-VAN MELLE, I., «L'application en France de la directive visant à éliminer les clauses abusives après l'adoption de la loi n°95-96 du 1er february 1995», *J.C.P.,* ed. G, I, 1995, n°3854.

GOLDWIN, M.,«Crimes and Criminal Procedure», *http://www.eff.org/pub/legal/ecpa.law/fair-use-and-copyright-excerp/*

GREDOT, F., «Le contrat porteur et la loi», *Banque,* n°563, oct. 1995, pp.36 ff.

GREGURAS, F. M., GOLOBIC, T. A., MESA, R. A., and DUNCAN, R., «Electronic Commerce: On-line Contract Issues», *http://www.batnet.com?oikoumene?ec-contraqcts.html,* p.2 ff.

GRIFFITHS, M. and McINTYRE, B., « 'And free with...' the law relating to free offers», *Journal of Media Law and Practice,* vol.14, n°3, 1993, pp.109-112.

GROTTENHALER, M. E., «Consumer Protection and Product Liability», *in Doing Business in Canada,* Matthew Bender & Co., Inc., pp.25-12.

http://www.firstvirtual.com/pubdocs/fineprint-buye

http://www.firstvirtual.com/pubdocs/fineprint-selle Q6.1

http://www.marktwain.com/legal.html

Information Highway Advisory Council, «Canadians must act to build on opportunities: Information highway advisory Council report», *http://info.ic.gc.ca/info-highway/documents/09-27-95.e.* September 27, 1995.

KENNEDY, W. and DIETSCH, J., «Securing the net», *http://www.hotwired.com/wired/2.12/features/-emoney.html*

LANINGA, T., «Electronic Money», *http://amcx.cox.smv.edn/class/mis4350h/people/Haninga/concept/*

LEDRU, J.-P., «Les cartes bancaires en France», *Banque,* n°563, oct. 1995, p.22 ff.

LEVY, S., «E-money (That's What I Want)», *http://www.hotwired.com/wired/2.12/features/emoney.html*

LLOYD, I., «Shopping in Cyberspace», *International Journal of Law and Information Technology,* vol.1, n°3, pp.335-348.

LINEHAN, M., and TSUDIK, G., «Internet Keyed Payments Protocol», July, 19955, *http://www.zurich.ibl.com:80/Technology/Security/extern/ecommerce/spec*

MATONIS, J. W., «Digital Cash & Monetary Freedom», *http://www.isoc.org/in95prc/HMP/PAPER/136/html/paper.html,* April, 1995.

MARKOFF, J., «A Credit Card for On-Line Sprees», *http://www.fv.com/gabletxt/ny-times.html*

MILOSEVIC, Z. and BOND, A., «Electronic Commerce on the Internet: What is still Missing?», http://inet.nttam.com., April 28 1995.

NIGGL, J., «The emegence of EDI standars and electronic markets», *http://www-iwi.unisg.ch/events/rpabs4.html*

NILL, Ned C. and FERGUSON, Daniel M., «Electronic Data Interchange: A Definition and Perspective», *http://www.premcnos.com/Resources/periodicals/edi-forum/article.html*

ROSMARIN, Y. W., «Revising article 2: Consumer Protections Needed in Sales of Goods», *ClearingHouse Review,* vol.28, n°10, February 1995, pp.1176 ff.

SAXBY, S., «A Jurisprudence for Information Technology Law», *International Journal of Law and Information Technology*, vol.2, n°1, pp.1-31.

SPRANGERS, H., «Elektronisch geld», *Tele-pc*, n°4, août-septembre 1995, pp.13 ff.

SZABO, N., «Smat Contacts», *http://www.digicash.com/~/smart-contracts.html*

WebTech, Inc., «Internet banking and security», 1995, *http://www.sfnb.com/wpaper.html*, may 17.

ZAKI, A. S., «Regulation of electronic funds transfer: impact and legal issues», *Communications of the ACM*, fevrier 1983, vol.26, n°2, pp.112 ff.

Chapter seven

«Cryptography»

Articles

ABELSON, H. and FISCHER, M., «6.095/STS095: Readings on Encryption, and National Security», *http://www.swiss.ai.mit.edu/6095/readings-3.html*

CHAUM, D., «Security without Identification: Card Computers to make Big Brother Obsolete», (Publications from DigiCash), *http://www.digicash.com/publish/bigbro.html/*

DEMBERGER, J., «Votpcryp public domain cryptographic software», *http://www.eff.org/pub/legal/cases/demberger-v-odtc-crypto-export.letters.*, april. 1995.

DENNING, D. E., «Resolving the Encryptions Dilemma: The Case for Clipper», *http://web.mit.edu/afs/-athena/org/t/techreview/www/articles/july95/denning.html*

DUMORTIER, J., «Stille invoering van cryptografiecontrole in België», *Computerrecht*, 1995, 2, p.79.

«First Fully Authenticated Digital Video Survillance System Features Advanced RSA Technology», *http://www.rsa-com/rsa/pr/Gemini-system.html*

http://www/xs4all.nl/-db.nl/english/Legal.html

«Introduction to Cryptography», *http://www.verisign.com/docs/pk_intro.html*

JACKSON, I., *iwj10@thor.cam.ac.nk*

JOHNSON, M. P., «Data Encryption and Technical Data Controls in the United States of America», *http://www.eff. org/pub/Privacy/us_crypto_policy.faq*, p.2.

LEVY, S., «Crypto rebels», *www@wined.com*

IDEM «Crypto Rebels», *http://www.hotwired.com/wired/1.2/features/crypto.rebels.html.*, oct. 1995.

LITTERIO, F., «Why are One-Time Pads Perfectly Secure?», *http://world.std.com/~franl/crypto/one-time-pad-html*

LOUNDY, D., «Try decoding the latest in munitions-wear», *Chicago Daily Law Bulletin*, *http://www./ecpfrog.com/E-Law/CDLB/Encryption.htlm/.*, 14 sept. 1995, pp.6 ff.

MEILLAN, E., «Le contrôle juridique de la cryptographie», *Droit de l'informatique et des télécoms*, 1993, 1, pp.78-82.

«Motorola to Apply RSA Technology to Family of Information Security Products for Worldwide Communication of Sensitive Data», *http://www.rsa.com/rsa/pr/Motorola-signet.html/*

Notice de présentation de la réglementation française sur la cryptologie, Délégation intermin-istérielle pour la sécurité des systèmes d'information (DISSI), Edition of 20 june 1995.

«OTA Report Summary: Information Security and Privacy in Network Environments,» *ftp://ftp.eff.org/pub/EFF/Policy/Crypto/ota-priv-sec.report*, September 1994, p.8.

«Pretty Good Privacy-Legal Issues», *http://www.mantis.co.uk/pgp/pgp-Legal.html*, 1.

«Questions & Answers Regarding the Paul Kocher Timing Attack on Public Key Cryptosystems», An RSA Press Brief, RSA Data Security, Inc., *http://www.rsa.com/rsaqa.htlm.*, 11 december 1995.

ROGERS, P., «Encryption with *Pretty Good Privacy*», *http://www.ozemail.comm.au/~paulr/pgptxt.html*, mars 1995.

ROZENFELD, S., «Nouvelle réglementation sur la cryptographie», *Expertises*, mars 1994, p.86.

«RSA & Intuit To Offer Internet Banking Connection», *http://www.rsa.com/pr/rsa-intu.html*

«RSA Laboratories», (a Division of RSA Data Security, Inc.), «RSA's Frequently Asked Questions About Today's Cryptography»,, *http://www.rsa.com/rsalabs/faq/faq-rsa.html*, may 1995.

«RSA's Frequently Asked Questions About Today's Cryptography»,
http://www.rsa.com/rsalabs/faq/faq-des.html, may 1995.

«RSA's Frequently Asked Questions About Today's Cryptography»,
http://www.rsa.com/rsalabs/faq/faq-gov.html, may 1995.

«RSA's Frequently Asked Questions About Today's Cryptography»,
http://www.rsa.com/rsalabs/faq/faq-misc-html, may 1995.

«RSA's Frequently Asked Questions About Today's Cryptography»,
http://www.rsa.com/rsalabs/faq/faq-gnrl.html, may 1995.

«RSA's Frequently Asked Questions About Today's Cryptography»,
http://www.rsa.com/rsalabs/faq/faq-ccd.html, may 1995.

«RSA's Frequently Asked Questions About Today's Cryptography»,
http://www.rsa.com/rsalabs/faq/faq-km.html, may 1995.

«RSA's Frequently Asked Questions About Today's Cryptography»,
http://www.rsa.com/rsalabs/faq/faq-gurl.html

SYLVAIN, A., «Data encrytion and the Law(s) - Results», Posted on *Talk Politics. Crypto,* december 15 1994.

SYX, D., «Vers de nouvelles formes de signature?», *Droit de l'informatique,* 1986, 4, pp.133 ff.

THOREL, J., *<thorel@cnam.fr>,* alt.security.talk.politics.crypto

TOEDT, D. C., «Encryption: An inexpensive Alternative to Escrow?», *The Computer Lawyer,* vol.11, nov.1994, pp.19 ff.

«Trip Report - USENIX Summer 1994 technical Conference», *http://www.oldkingcole.com/trip-report.html*

VAN DEN HOVEN VAN GENDEREN, R., «Het voorlopig voorontwerp tot verbod van cryptografie De horror vacuï van de ondoorbreekbare beveiliging», *Computerrecht,* 1994, 4, pp.157 ff.

WISEBROD, D., «Controlling the Uncontrollable: Regulating the Internet», 4, *M.C.L.R.,* pp.331-344.

X, «Bombt Deutschland», *Der Spiegel, http://www.thur.de/ulf/krypto/verbot.html,* january 8 1996, pp.106 ff.

YATES, J.C., Esq., «Bombs and Bytes», october 17 1994, Morris and Manning Home Page, p.2.

ZIMMERMANN, Ph., «Pretty Good Privacy, Public Key Encryption for the Masses»,
http://camelot.reckefeller.edu/pgp.info/, july. 1993.

Chapter eight

«Crime»

References
THOMAS, F., *De internationale rechtshulp in strafzaken,* 1996, to be published.

Articles
BACKER, G. D., «Trespassers will be prosecuted: computer crime in the 1990s», *Computer Law Journal,* 1993, vol.12, pp.61 ff.

BOISVERT, A. M., «Communicatique et responsabilité pénale: criminalité informatique et «vol» d'information», *in Le droit de la communicatique: Actes du colloque conjoint de l'Université de Poitiers et de l'Université de Montréal, septembre 1990,* Montréal-Paris, CRDP, ed. Thémis, LITEC, 1991, p.93.

BRANSCOMB, A. W., «Rogue Computer Programs And Computer Rogues: Tailoring the Punishment to Fit the Crime» *Rutgers Computer Technology Law Journal,* 1, n°16, 1990.

CHAMOUX, F., «La loi sur la fraude informatique: de nouvelles incriminations», *J.C.P.,* 1988, ed. G., I, n°3321.

CROZE, H., «L' apport du droit pénal à la théorie générale du droit de l' informatique (à propos de la loi n° 88-19 du 5 janvier 1988 relative à la fraude informatique)», *J.C.P.,* 1988, ed. G., Doc., n°3333.

DAVIS, S. B., «It's Virus Season Again, Has Your Computer Been Vaccinated? A Survey of Computer Crime Legislation As A Response to Malevolent Software», Washington University Law Quarterly, 1994, vol.72, p.411.

DUNNE, R. L., «Deterring Unauthorized Access to Computers: Controlling Behaviour in Cyberspace through a Contract Paradigm», 19 mai 1994, *http://www.cs.yale.edu/pub/Dunne/jurimetrics/HTML/-subsections3_2_3.html, 1.*

DURHAM, C., «Les structures émergentes du droit criminel de l'information: tracer les contours d'un nouveau paradigme», *International Review of Penal Law,* vol.63, pp.1371 ff.

DURHAM, W. C. and SKOUSEN, R. C., «The Law of Computer-Related Crime in the United States», *American Journal of Comparative Law,* 1990, vol.38, p.565.

FRANCILLON, J., «Les crimes informatiques et d'autres crimes dans le domaine de la technologie informatique en France», *Revue Internationale de Droit Pénal,* vol.64, pp.291 ff.

MÖHRENSCHLAGER, M., «Antipiratique européenne: une politique concertée de répression de la criminalité informatique qui prend en compte les nouvelles techniques, les nouveaux comportements et les nouveaux délinquants», *Expertises,* 1990, pp.177 ff.

PIRAGOFF, D. K., «Computer Crimes and Other Crimes against Information Technology in Canada», *Revue Internationale de Droit Pénal,* vol.64, p.201.

RIMM, M., «Marketing Pornography on the Information Superhighway: A Survey of 917, 410 Images, Descriptions, Short Stories, and Animations Downloaded 8.5 Million Times by Consumers in Over 2000 Cities in Forty Countries, Provinces, and Territories», *http://trfn.pgh.pa.us/guest/mrstudy.html,* 7 novembre 1995.

ROBERT, P., «La criminalisation des abus informatiques en droit pénal canadien», in *Association canadienne de droit comparé, Droit contemporain: rapports canadiens au congrès international de droit comparé, Montréal, 1990,* Cowansville, Yvon Blais, 1992, p.680.

SPRUYT, B., «Information Technology Misuse: the Belgian State of Art, *International Yearbook of Law Computers and Technology,* vol.9, 1995, pp.17 ff.

WISE, E. M., «Computer Crimes against Information Technology in the United States», *Revue Internationale de Droit Pénal,* vol. 64, p.647.

X, «International review of criminal policy - United Nations Manual on the prevention and control of computer related crime», *http://www.ifs.univie.ac.at/pr2gq1/rev4344.html#crime*

YOUNG, L. F., «United States Computer Crime Laws, Criminals and Deterrence», *International Yearbook of Law, Computers and Technology,* 1995, vol.9, p.1.

Chapter nine

«Liability on the Internet»

References

BERTRAND, A., «La responsabilité du fait des banques de données en France», in *Liability for on-line data bank services,* ed. U. SIEBER, 1991.

CHOISY, M. G., «La responsabilité des parties dans les contrats conclus entre serveurs et utilisateurs de banques de données», *Télématique,* t. I, ed. Story-Scientia, 1984.

ELIAS, L., GERARD, J. and GIEN KUO WANG, «*Le droit des obligations face aux échanges de données informatisées»,* Namur, ed. Story Scientia, 1992, n°8.

Encyclopedia ITL, R.12, december 1994, n°7.

HOGG, P. W., *Constitutional Law of Canada,* 3rd ed., Scarborough, Carswell, 1992.

LINANT de BELLEFONDS, X. and HOLLANDE, A., *Contrats informatiques et télématiques,* 3rd ed., Paris, ed. Delmas, 1992.

LINANT de BELLEFONDS, X. and HOLLANDE, A., *Droit de l'informatique et de la télématique,* 2nd ed., Paris, ed. Delmas, 1990.

RESNICK, R. and TAYLOR, D., *The Internet Business Book,* Indianapolis, Sams Publishing, 1994.

Articles

APPLEMAN, D. L., «The Law and the Internet», *http://inet.nttam.com,* 12 may 1995.

CALOW, D., «Defamation on the Internet», *The Computer Law and security report,* vol.11, july-august 1995, pp.199-200.

HAMOUX, F., «La loi sur la fraude informatique: de nouvelles incriminations», *J.C.P.,* ed. G, I, 1988, p.3321.

CROZE, H., «L'apport du droit pénal à la théorie générale du droit de l'informatique (à propos de la loi n°88-19 du 5 janvier 1988 relative à la fraude informatique)», *J.C.P.*, ed. G, I, 1988, p.3333.

DE GAULLE, L. and REDON, D., «la nouvelle législation relative à la répression de la contrefaçon», *J.C.P.-Cahiers de droit de l'entreprise*, 1994, n°30, supplément n°3, p.33.

DEVÈZE, J., «Le vol de biens informatiques», *J.C.P.*, 1985, I, p.3210.

DUNNE, R., «Deterring Unauthorized Access to Computers: Controlling Behaviour in Cyberspace through a Contract Paradigm», *http://www.cs.yale.edu/pub/Dunne/jurimetrics/HTML/subsection 3_3_1*, may 19 1994.

GODWIN, M., «The Law of the Net: Problems and Prospects», Internet World, *http://eff.org/pub/Legal/law_of_the_net.article*, sept-oct 1993.

GUILLAUME, E., «La réforme des postes et télécommunications: le passage du statut d'usager d'un service administratif à celui de client d'un service public industriel et commercial», *Rev. fr. droit adm.*, 1991, 2, p.239.

HARDY, T., «The Proper Legal Regime for Cyberspace», *University of Pittsburgh Law Review*, 1993, vol.55, pp.993-1001.

http://www.eff.org/pub/Legal/Cyberspace_leggal_matrix.article

HUET, J., «Droit de l'informatique: le régime juridique de la télématique interactive», *J.C.P.*, I, 1984, p.3147.

JOHNSON, D.R. et al., «Computer Viruses: Legal and Policy Issues Facing Colleges and Universities», *Educ. L. Rep.* (West), vol.54, pp.761-766.

KEETON, W. P. et al., *Prosser and Keeton on the Law of Torts*, 5ᵗʰ ed., 1984, pp.30-164.

KENNEDY, P., «Publishing on the Internet: Some Legal Protections and Pitfalls», *http://www.eff.org/pub/legal/inet-publishing-legal.article*

LOUNDY, D., «E-Law 2.0: Computer Information Systems Law and Operator Liability Revisited», *http://www.eff.org/pub/Legal/e-law.paper*

MAISL, H., «Communications mobiles, secret des correspondances et protection des données personnelles», *D.I.T.*, 1995, 2, pp.13 ff.

RIDDLE, M., «Sysop Liability for Enroute (and/or Encrypted) Mail», *FIDO NEWS*, vol.10, n°45, *http://www.eff.org/pub/Privacy/Crypto_mail_liability.article*, november 7 1993.

SCHLACTER, E., «Cyberspace, the Free Market and the Free Marketplace of Ideas: Recognizing Legal Differences in Computer Bulletin Board Functions», *http://www.eff.org/pub/legal/cyberlaw-bbs-freemarket.article*

SIM, P., «Copyright and Electronic Media Part 2: The Challenge of the New Media», *http://www.mbnet.ca/~psim/copyrt.html*

TRIALLE, J.-P., «Responsabilité du fait des produits: logiciels, banques de données et informations», *D.I.T.*, 1991, 1.

VIVANT, M. and LUCAS, A., «Droit de l'informatique», *J.C.P.*, 1993, ed. E, n°18.

Chapter ten

«Evidence»

References

AMORY, B. and THUNIS, X., «Dématérialisation, authentification et responsabilité, le Droit continental», *Les transactions internationales assistées par ordinateur*, Paris, Litec, 1987.

BAKER, R. W., *The Hearsay Rule*, London, Pitman, 1950.

BERTRAND, A. and al., *Informatique et droit de la preuve*, Paris, ed. des Parques, 1987.

CROSS, R. and TAPPER, C., *Cross on Evidence*, 7th ed., London, Butterworth's, 1990.

ELIAS, L., GERARD, J. and KUO WANG, G., *Le Droit des obligations face aux échanges de données informatisées*, Namur - Bruxelles, CRID - Story Scientia, 1992.

GALLOUEDEC-GENUYS, F. and al., *Une société sans papier? Nouvelles technologies de l'information et droit de la preuve*, Paris, La Documentation Française, 1990.

HENRI and MAZEAUD, *Leçons de droit civil, les Biens*, t.2, vol.2, Paris, ed. Montchrestien, 1976.

JAUFFRET, A. and MESTRE, J., Droit commercial, 22rd ed., Paris, *L.G.D.J.*, 1995.

KEANE, A., *The Modern Law of Evidence*, 3ʳᵈed., London, Dublin, Edinbourgh, Butterworth's, 1994.

LINANT de BELLEFONDS, X. and HOLLANDE, A., *Droit de l'informatique et de la télématique*, 2nd ed., Paris, Delmas and Cie, 1990.

MARTIN, M.-M., *Basic Problems of Evidence*, 6th ed., Philadelphia, American Law Institute-American Bar Association, 1988.

POULET, Y., WILLEMS, V. and LOBET-MARIS, C., *Vers une société de l'information*, Bruxelles, éd. Story scientia, 1995.

REED, C., *Computer Law*, london, éd. Blackstone press limited, 1989.

ROYER, J.-C., *La preuve civile*, Cowansville, Les Editions Yvon Blais Inc., 1987.

SOPINKA, J., LEDERMAN, S. N. and BRYANT, A.W., *The Law of Evidence in Canada*, Toronto, Butterworth's, 1992.

Sweet et Maxwell, *Encyclopedia of Information Technology Law*, December 1994.

TAPPER, C., *Computer Law*, 4ᵗʰ ed., London, New-York, Longman, 1989.

TREGARTHERN, J.B.C., *The Law of Hearsay Evidence*, London, Stevens & Sons Ltd., 1915.

TRUDEL, P., LEVEBVRE, G. and PARISIEN, S., *La preuve et la signature électroniques dans l'échange de documents informatisés au Québec*, Québec, Les publications du Québec, 1993.

THUNIS, X. and SCHAUSS, M., *Aspects juridiques du paiement par carte*, Brussels, ed. Story Scientia, 1988.

WALDER, J., *E.D.I. and the Law*, London, ed. Bleinheim Online, 1989.

WRIGHT, B., *The Law of Electronic Commerce; E.D.I., E-mail, and Internet: Technology, Proof, and Liability*, 2nd ed., Boston, Little, Brown and Company, 1995.

Articles

AMORY, B. and POULLET, Y., «Le Droit de la preuve face à l'informatique et à la télématique», *R.I.D.C.*, 1985, 2, pp.331-352.

BENSOUSSAN, A., «Contribution théorique au droit de la preuve dans le domaine informatique», *Expertises*, 1990, pp.425-430.

IDEM, «La convention de preuve dans les accords d'interchange», *Cahier Lamy du Droit de l'Informatique*, juillet 1993, suppl. au n°50.

CAPRIOLI, E., «Les limites des accords d'E.D.I.: la solution des Editerms», *Cahiers Lamy du Droit de l'Informatique*, juillet 1993, suppl. au n°50.

IDEM, «Contribution à la définition d'un régime juridique pour la conservation des documents: du papier au message électronique», *D.I.T.*, 1993, 3, pp.5-17.

CNUDCI: échanges de données informatisées, *D.I.T.*, 1992, 1, pp.71-78.

COSTES, L., «Vers un Droit du commerce international sans papier?», *RDAI/IBLJ*, 1994, n°6, pp.735-752.

DE LAMBERTERIE, I., «La valeur probatoire des documents informatiques dans les pays de la C.E.E.», *R.I.D.C.*, 1992, 3, pp.641-685.

DOM, J.-P., «L'informatique, le notaire et le contrat», *D.I.T.*, 1992, 4, pp.6-14.

GOBIN, P., «Les questions soulevées par l'E.D.I.», *Journal de réflexion sur l'informatique*, n°22, 1992, pp.32-35; «Aspects techniques de l'E.D.I.», *Journal de réflexion sur l'informatique*, 1992, n°22, pp.5-14.

HIRST, M., «Computers and the English Law of Evidence», *Law Computers & Artificial Intelligence*, 1992, vol. 1, n°3, pp.368 et s.

HUET, J., «Formalisme et preuve en informatique et télématique, éléments de solution en matière de relations d'affaire continues ou de rapports contractuels occasionnels», *J.C.P.*, ed. G, 1989, I, n°3406.

HUET, J., «Aspects juridiques du télépaiement», *J.C.P.*, ed. G, 1991, I, n°3524.

IDEM, «Aspects juridiques de l'E.D.I., échanges de Données Informatisées (Electronic Data Interchange), *D*, 1991, Chr. XXXVII, pp.181-190.

IDEM, «La valeur juridique de la télécopie (ou fax), comparée au télex», *D*, 1992, Chr. VII, pp.34-36.

JABUREK, W.J., «E.D.I. Law in Austria - Waiting for the EC?», *The E.D.I. Law Review 2*, 1995, pp.1-8.

LECLERCQ, P., «Faut-il réformer le Droit de la preuve?», *Droit de l'informatique et des télécoms*, 1991, 1, pp.5-15.

LUCAS DE LEYSSAC, C., «Les conventions sur la preuve en matière informatique», *Travaux de l'AFDI*, «Informatique et droit de la preuve», 1987, pp.151-154.

MALENGREAU, X., «le droit de la preuve et la modernisation des techniques de rédaction, de reproduction et de conservation des documents», *ann. Dr.*, 1981, p.121.

MCKEON, Jr., «Electronic Data Interchange: Uses and Legal Aspects in the Commercial Arena», *John Marshall Journal of Computer & Information Law, 12*, p.511.

MYNART, A., «Télématique et preuve en Droit civil québécois et français: une antinomie?», *D.I.T.*, 1992, 4, pp.15-25.

IDEM, «Un nouveau dispositif de preuve pour l'EDI basé sur la sécurité», *Expertises*, mai 1994, pp.187-191.

PIETTE-COUDOL, T., «La facture électronique», *Expertises*, n°136, february. 1991, pp.9-12.

POULET, Y., «Probate law: From Liberty to Responsability», *E.D.I. Law Review,* 1994, n°2, pp.83-100.

REED, C., «Computer Records as Evidence-Back to the Beginning», *J.B.L.,* 1993, p.505.

IDEM, *Computer Law,* Blackstone Press, London, 1989, p.184.

ROZENFELD, S., «Incertitude sur la valeur probante», *Expertise*, 1991, pp.384-387.

TAPPER, C., «Evanescent Evidence», *International Journal of Law and Information Technology,* 1993, vol.1, n°1.

IDEM, «The Law Commission's Report on the Reform of the Hearsay Rule» *Computer Law and Security Report»*, 1994, 10(2), p.86.

IDEM, «Reform of the Law of Evidence in Relation to the Output from Computers», *International Jurnal f Law and Information Techoology*, 1995, vol.3, n°1, p.82.

TEDIS programm: «the european model E.D.I. agreement», Final draft, july 1991.

WRIGHT, B., «Alternatives for signing electronique documents», *The computer law and security report*, Mai-juin 1995, 11 CLSR.

XUEREF, C. and BROUSSE, P., «E.D.I.: des «Editerms» pour traiter les problèmes juridiques de l'échange de Données Informatisées: propositions pour l'avenir», *D.I.T.*, 1992, 3, pp.1 ff.

Abbreviations

Arr. . . . . Arrêté.

Bull. cass. civ. . . . . *Bulletin des chambres civiles Cour de cassation française.*

Bull. cass. comm. . . . *Bulletin des chambres commerciales Cour de cassation française.*

Bull. cass. crim. . . . . . . *Bulletin des chambres criminelles Cour de cassation française.*

C. . . . . Communication.

C.A. . . . . Cour d'appel.

Cah.Dr.Inf. . . . . Cahier de Droit de l'Informatique (Lamy).

Cass. civ. . . . . Cour de cassation française, chambre civile.

Cass. comm. . . . . Cour de cassation française, chambre commerciale.

Cass. crim.. . . . . Cour de cassation française, chambre criminelle.

C.civ. . . . . French Civil Code.

C.comm. . . . . French Commercial Code.

CcQ.. . . . . Code civil Québecquois.

Chr.. . . . . Chronique.

C.J.E.C. . . . . Court of Justice of European Community.

C.N.U.D.C.I. Commission des Nations Unies pour le Droit du

. . . . Commerce International.

Chap. . . . . Chapter.

Circ.. . . . . Circulaire.

C.L.D.I. . . . . *Cahiers Lamy du Droit de l'informatique.*

C.N.I.L. . . . . Commission nationale Informatique et Liberté.

D.. . . . . Recueil *Dalloz.*

D. and I. . . . . *Law and informatic.*

D.I.R. . . . . *Dalloz,* Informations rapides.

D.I.T.. . . . . Revue *Droit de l'informatique et des télécommunications.*

D.I.. . . . . Revue *Droit de l'informatique.*

D.S. . . . . Recueil *Dalloz Sirey.*

E.C.P.A. . . . . Électronic Communications Privacy Act 1987.

E.D.I. . . . . Électronic Data Interchange.

EDIFACT . . . . Électronic Data Interchange for Administration, Commerce

. . . . and Transport.

ed. . . . . Edition.

Exp.. . . . . *Expertises.*

idem. . . . . The same author.

J.-cl. . . . . *Jurisclasseur.*

J.C.P. (G). . . . . *Semaine juridique,* Edition generale.

J.C.P. (E) . . . . *Semaine juridique,* Édition entreprise.

J.O.C.E.. . . . . *Journal officiel du Conseil d'Etat.*

O.J.E.C. . . . . Journal official of European Community .

J.T. . . . . Journal des tribunaux.

Jurisdata ou JD . . . . Banque de données juridiques Juridial/Jurisdata.

L. . . . . Legislation.

Le Monde Inf. . . . . *Le Monde informatique.*

Lexis . . . . Banque de données juridiques Lexis.

LRC . . . . Lois révisées du Canada.

L.R.Q. . . . . Lois refondues du Québec.

n° . . . . Number.

N.C.P. . . . . Nouveau Code pénal.

obs. . . . . Observation.

P.G.P. . . . . Pretty Good Privacy.

p. ou pp. . . . . Page ou Pages.

Q.B. . . . . Queen's Bench.

Q.B.D. . . . . Queen's Bench Division.

R.C.S. . . . . Recueil des arrêts de la cour suprême du Canada.

Rev. int. dr. comp. . . . . *Revue internationale de droit comparé.*

Rev. trim. dr. civ. . . . . *Revue trimestrielle de droit civil.*

RSA. . . . . Rivest, Shamir et Adleman.

S.W.I.F.T. . . . . Society for Worldwide Interbank Financial.

t. . . . . Tome.

TED. . . . . Transfert Électronique de Données.

TEDIS . . . . Trade Electronique Data Interchange Système.

TEF . . . . Transfert Électtronique de Fonds.

Trib. civ. . . . . Tribunal civil.

Trib. comm. . . . . Tribunal de commerce.

Trib. corr. . . . . Tribunal correctionnel.

T.G.I. . . . . Tribunal de grande instance.

Trib. inst. . . . . Tribunal d'instance.

UCC . . . . Uniform Commercial Code.

U.N.C.D.I. . . . . Uniform Rules of Conduct for Interchange of Trade by
. . . . Telecommunication.

U.S.C. . . . . United States Code.

vol. . . . . Volume.

S. . . . . See.

WLR . . . . Weekly Law Review.

Contents

Preface 11
Foreword 19
Acknowledgments 25

General introduction 31

Part One:
The Internet in practice and in business 37

Introduction 39
A. Where does the Internet come from? 40
B. Some technical details 41
C. Internet in practice:
   eight communications applications 42
   1. Electronic mail or e-mail 42
   2. The World Wide Web (WWW or Web) 43
   3. Telnet 43
   4. F.T.P. (File Transfer Protocol) 44
   5. Gopher 44
   6. Mailing lists 44
   7. Discussion groups 45
   8. The chat function or IRC (Internet Relay Chat) 46

D. The Internet and business 46
   1. The Internet for commercial transactions 46
      a. The Internet for advertising and marketing 46
      b. The Internet for commerce 47
      c. The Internet for making and receiving payments 48
   2. The Internet for communications (internal and external 49
   3. Internet for research, development, and the exchange of
      professional information 49
   4. The Internet for personnel management and recruitment . 50

Part Two:
The law on the Internet 53

Introduction 55

Chapter 1 - Your first steps on the Internet
and the law 61

Why ask questions? 63

What questions? 64
I. Users 65
II. Service providers 66
A. Licensing regimes 66
  1. Internet access providers (IAPs) 66
    a. The regime applicable in Europe 66
      a.1. National regimes..................................... 66
      a.2. The attempt at European harmonization............ 68
      a.3. The European Telecommunications Office (ETO). 68
    b. The system applicable in North America 69
  2. Servers 70
B. Free provision of services and the Internet.................... 71
  1. The free provision of services within the European Union.... 71
  2. The free provision of services within the *NAFTA*......... 74

To summarize... 75

Chapter 2 - Copyright on the Internet 77

Why ask questions? 79
What questions? 79

Introduction.. 81
I. Which works are protected on the Internet?............... 82
A. The general conditions governing the protection of a work. 82
B. The different types of protected work on the Internet....... 83
  1. Written works 83
  2. Musical or audiovisual works............................. 84
  3. Images.. 84
  4. Software... 84
  5. Databases 85
    a. The principles of protection 85
    b. Web pages 86

**II. The rights of the author and of the user regarding
protected works in circulation on the Internet** 87
A. The author's rights... 87
  1. Who owns copyrights on the Internet? 87
  2. The different types of rights 87
    a. The author's moral rights............................... 88
    b. The author's patrimonial rights......................... 88
      b.1. Right of reproduction 89

Contents

b.2. Right of transformation 89
b.3. Right of distribution 89
b.4. Right of public communication 90
B. The legal limits (exceptions) to copyrights: the user's rights 90
1. The user's rights in general 90
2. The user's rights as regards software 92
3. The user's rights on the Internet 93
   a. The user and electronic mail (e-mail) 93
     a.1. Can a user send a protected work via e-mail? 93
     a.2. Can the addressee of an e-mail copy it and: 93
       1- return it to the original author? 93
       2- send it to a newsgroup or to a mailing list? 93
       3- send it to a specified third party?(forward) 94
   b. The user and file transfers (F.T.P.) 94
     b.1. Server 94
     b.2. User 94
   c. The user and surfing on the Web 95
     c.1. Consulting Web pages 95
     c.2. Downloading tiles from Web pages 96
C. The contractual limits to copyrights: contracts concluded
between the author and the user 96
1. Explicit authorization 96
2. Implicit authorization 97

III. Penalties 98

To summarize... 99

Chapter 3 - Freedom of expression 100

Why ask questions? 103
What questions? 103

Introduction 104
**I. Internet and freedom of expression in the United States
and in Canada** 105
A. The affirmation of freedom of expression 105
B. The limits of freedom of expression 105
1. Defamation 105
   a. Criteria of defamation 105
   b. How can liability for defamation be avoided? 107
2. Other restrictions on freedom of expression 108

II. Internet and freedom of expression in Europe 109
A. The affirmation of freedom of expression 109
B. The limits of freedom of expression 109

To summarize.... 112

Chapter 4 - Protection of privacy on the Internet 113

Why ask questions? 115
What questions? 115

Introduction 117

**I. Protection of the confidentiality of files, mail
  and communications circulating on the Internet** 118
A. Confidentiality and government authorities.............. 119
  1. Under American and Canadian law..................... 119
  2. Under European law 121
B. Confidentiality between private parties.................. 121
  1. Under American and Canadian law 124
  2. Under European law 124
  3. Netiquette, current practices and the use of technology
    to maintain confidentiality 126

**II. The Internet and regulations regarding computerized
  processing of personal data** 127
A. Under American and Canadian law 128
B. In Europe 129
C. International transfers of personal data on the Internet.. 131

To summarize... 132

Chapter 5 - The Internet and commercial communication 135

Why ask questions? 136
What questions? 136

Introduction 136
**I. The Internet and the regulation of advertising
  in North America and in Europe** 137
A. Applying the general rules................................. 137
  1. Regulations related to the nature of the product....... 137
    a. Tobacco.. 138

b. Alcohol.. 138
2. Regulations related to the advertising audience 139
3. Regulations related to the methods used:
misleading and comparative advertising............... 139
a. Misleading advertising.................................. 139
b. Comparative advertising 140
B. Advertising restrictions applicable to the Internet 141

II. Telemarketing on the Internet 142
A. Internet and advertising telecanvassing.................. 142
1. Solicitation via electronic mail........................ 142
2. Intrusion into newsgroups............................. 143
B. Internet and offers related to commercial telecanvassing. 145

To summarize....... 146

Chapter 6 - Electronic commerce........................... 147

Why ask questions?.. 149
What questions?.. 149

Introduction 150

I. Concluding contracts via the Internet..................... 151
A. General rules applicable to all contracts................. 151
1. The conclusion of contract on the Internet via e-mail
and via the Web.. 151
a. General rules governing the conclusion of contracts
(on the Internet)....................................... 151
b. The application of these rules to electronic commerce
via e-mail 153
c. The application of the rules to electronic commerce
via the Web 154
2. The time and place of contract formation.................. 154
a. *Upon expedition of the acceptor's consent*
(expedition theory) 155
b. *Upon the sending of the acceptor's acceptance*
(transmission theory).................................. 155
c. *Upon reception of acceptance by the offeror*
(reception theory)..................................... 155
d. *Upon the offeror's knowledge of the acceptation*
(information theory) 155

3. The validity of contracts concluded via the Internet .. 156
    a. Consent.......... 156
    b. Legal capacity.......... 157
    c. The object of the contract.......... 158
4. A master contract to facilitate concluding contracts
    via the Internet?.......... 158
    a. The master contract and its advantages.......... 158
      1) The time and place of formation of future
        contracts concluded on the Internet 159
      2) The law applicable to the contract 159
      3) Methods of interpreting or fulfilling
        the agreement in the event of a dispute 159
      4) The admissibility and probative value of certain
        computer documents 159
      5) The jurisdiction having competence to settle
        disputes according to its own rules 159
      6) Provisions which are contrary to to rules
        of public order 159
    b. A simplified form of the master contract:
      the electronic trading letter 160
5. Contracts concluded via the Internet and consumer
    protection law 161
B. Rules specific to certain contracts or to certain categories
of contracts.......... 162
    1. Adhesion contracts 162
    2. Internet and international sales.......... 163
    3. EDI agreements on the Internet?.......... 164

II. Payment via the Internet.......... 165
A. Payment by ordinary credit card.......... 166
    1. The moment of payment 166
    2. Using credit cards without a code number-dangerous,
      yes, but for whom?.......... 166
    a. Contractual solutions.......... 167
    b. Legislative solutions 167
B. The new electronic intermediaries and virtual money ... 169
    1. *First Virtual Holdings Incorporated* or the new
      electronic intermediaries 169
    2. *DigiCash* or *E-money*.......... 170
    3. The legal issues raised by the new electronic
      intermediaries and virtual money.......... 171
    a. Contracts and consumer protection.......... 171

a.1. The competent court and applicable law 171
a.2. Consumer protection 171
1- Under American law 171
2- Under European law 173
  b. Beyond contracts 173

To summarize... 175

Chapter 7 - Cryptography 177

Why ask questions? 179
What questions? 179

Introduction 180
I. Existing cryptography technologies 181

**II. *Pretty Good Privacy*, the *Clipper Chip* and
*Trusted Third Parties*** 182

III. Is the use and export of cryptography and PGP legal? .. 183
A. In North America 183
B. In Europe 184

To summarize... 186

Chapter 8 - Crime 187

Why ask questions? 189
What questions? 189

Introduction 190
I. American law 192

II. Canadian law 193

III. European national legal systems 194

To summarize... 196

Chapter 9 - Liability on the Internet 197

Why ask questions? 199
What questions? 199

Introduction 200
I. The framework of liability on the Internet 201
  A. The various actors of Internet liability 201
  B. Contractual liability 202
    1. The various contractual relations between Internet actors 202
      a. The various contractual relations between
      Internet actors 202
        *a.1. Contractual relations between an access
        provider and subscribers* 202
        *a.2. Contractual relations between a server and
        the access provider who disseminates
        or provides it with permanent access* 203
        *a.3. Contractual relations between a producer,
        particularly a professional producer, and
        the server who disseminates its products* 203
        *a.4. Contractual relations between certain servers
        or professional producers and their users* 204
        *a.5. Contractual relations between authors
        and producers* 204
        a.6. Contractual relations between users 205
        *a.7. The employer's liability employee conduct
        on the Internet* 205
      b. Contractual relations in the field of the provision of
      professional information, publishing and production .. 206
      b.1. The provision of professional information 206
      *b.2. The fields of publishing and production on
      the Internet* 207
    2. Liability clauses 208

II. Invoking the liability of the various actors 208
  A. The user's liability 209
    1. Liability invoked by another user 209
      a. Liability for defamation 209
      b. Liability for invasion of privacy 209
    2. Liability invoked by the access provider or the server. 210
    3. Liability invoked by the copyright holder 210
  B. Liability of the server and the access provider 211
    1. Liability invoked by the user 211

a. «Editorial» liability 211
   a.1. «Editorial» liability under American and
      Canadian law 211
   1- Liability as a «primary» publisher 212
   2- Liability as a distributor or «secondary publisher».. 212
   a.2. «Editorial» liability under French law 213
   a.3. «Editorial» liability under English law 214
   1- Liability for defamation 215
     - Liability as a publisher. 215
     - Liability as a distributor 216
   2- Liability for disseminating false information 216
  b. Recourse which do not fall within the regime
  of editorial liability. 217
   b.1. Under North American law 217
     1- Liability for invasion of privacy 217
     2- Liability for incorrectly labeled files 217
     3- Liability for viruses and malicious software .. 218
   b.2. Under French law 218
     1- Liability for invasion of privacy 219
     2- Liability for the dissemination of malicious
       software 219
     3- Liability for incorrectly labeled files 219
     4- Civil liability for the content of information
       (apart from editorial liability). 219
   b.3. Under English law. 220
     1- Liability for invasion of privacy 220
     2- Liability for the dissemination of viruses,
      damage caused by hackers and incorrectly
      labeled files. 220
  2. Liability invoked by the author 220
  C. Author's liability. 221
  D. The liability of telecommunications operators 222

To summarize... 223

Chapter 10 - Evidence 225

Why ask questions?. 227
What questions?. 227

Introduction 228
I. In Europe. 229

A. French law... 229
1. Proof of facts... 229
2. Proof of contracts.. 229
   a. Proof of civil contracts concluded via the Internet. 230
     a.1. Contracts which need not be proven by a writing,
        and which facilitate use of the Internet 230
        1- Contracts worth less than 5,000FRF 230
        2- A party produces a «commencement of proof
        in writing»... 231
        3- Certain common practices which preclude
        the drafting of a writing......................... 231
        4.- Admission.. 232
     a.2. Contracts which must be proven by a writing-
        Internet and the signed and original writing
        requirement... 232
        1- A signed writing?................................. 232
        2- An original?.. 233
   b. Proving commercial contracts concluded on
     the Internet... 235
B. England (and Wales)..................................... 235
1. The admissibility of Internet computer documents ... 236
2. The authentication of computer documents:
   business and public authority or not? 236
   a. Business and public authority 236
   b. What about Internet users who cannot be described
     as businessmen or public authorities?............... 237
   c. The probative value of Internet computer documents . 237

II. In North America 238
A. The Internet computer document must be authenticated 239
B. Does an Internet computer document constitute both an
   exception to the *hearsay rule* and to the *best evidence rule*? 241
   1. The *best evidence rule* and the *hearsay rule*.......... 241
   2. Exceptions to the *best evidence rule* which allow
     the admission of computer documents................. 243
   3. Exceptions to the *hearsay rule* which allow
     the admission of computer documents................. 243
C. Specific legal regimes 244

III. Caution is essential 245
    A. The evidence agreement: yes, but........................ 245
    B. Use reliable techniques, as well as durable and
       preferably inalterable media............................. 246

To summarize.... 247

Part Three: Twenty business contracts for the Internet 251

  1. Internet access provider agreement.......................... 254
  2. Internet system operator agreement......................... 257
  3. Supply of information agreement............................ 259
  4. Internet publishing agreement.............................. 262
  5. Online space «rental» and related services agreement...... 265
  6. Online advertising agreement 269
  7. Online brokerage agreement................................. 272
  8. Agreement for the «rental» of online advertising space 275
  9. Online multimedia product development agreement 278
  10. Online market survey agreement........................... 281
  11. Online distribution agreement 284
  12. Web page development and maintenance agreement 288
  13. Online research agreement 291
  14. Online lobbying and marketing agreement................. 293
  15. Online forum participant agreement........................ 295
  16. Agreement for online database access..................... 297
  17. Master retail sales agreement 299
  18. Electronic commerce agreement between professionals ... 301
  19. Certifying authority agreement............................ 304
  20. Acceptable use policy 306

Outlook 309
References 313
Bibliography... 339
Abbreviations 355
Contents 359

As the cover of this book has been written on the publisher's sole initiative, the author wants to specify that "lecturer" should read "former visiting researcher" and that the term "international" as well as all references to his clients should be removed, those mentions being incompatible with his code of professional ethics.